Sarah Barrow is Professor of Film and Media Studies at the University of East Anglia, UK. She has had numerous studies of Hispanic film published, including in special issues of the *Transnational Cinemas* and *New Cinemas* journals. She co-edited *The Routledge Encyclopaedia of Films* (2015), a major collection of 200 essays on films from all over the world.

'By examining key films that tackle issues of contemporary violence, Sarah Barrow provides an excellent study of Peruvian cinema's responses to the Shining Path era of the 1990s and 2000s, bringing together sharp cinematic analysis and trauma studies.'

– Jeffrey Middents, American University; author of *Writing National Cinema: Film Journals and Film Culture in Peru* (2009)

'*Contemporary Peruvian Cinema* is an essential addition to the field of Latin American cinema. Meticulously researched, deeply knowledgeable and accessible, this comprehensive study provides incisive readings of landmark films and draws attention to undeservedly neglected ones.'

– Deborah Shaw, University of Portsmouth

TAURIS WORLD CINEMA SERIES

Series Editors:
Lúcia Nagib, *Professor of Film at the University of Reading*
Julian Ross, *Research Fellow at the University of Westminster*

Advisory Board: Laura Mulvey (UK), Robert Stam (USA), Ismail Xavier (Brazil), Dudley Andrew (USA)

The *Tauris World Cinema Series* aims to reveal and celebrate the richness and complexity of film art across the globe, exploring a wide variety of cinemas set within their own cultures and as they interconnect in a global context. The books in the series will represent innovative scholarship, in tune with the multicultural character of contemporary audiences. Drawing upon an international authorship, they will challenge outdated conceptions of world cinema, and provide new ways of understanding a field at the centre of film studies in an era of transnational networks.

Published and forthcoming in the World Cinema series:

Allegory in Iranian Cinema: The Aesthetics of Poetry and Resistance
By Michelle Langford

Animation in the Middle East: Practice and Aesthetics from Baghdad to Casablanca
Edited by Stefanie Van de Peer

Basque Cinema: A Cultural and Political History
By Rob Stone and María Pilar Rodriguez

The Battle Lines of Beauty: The Politics, Aesthetics and Erotics of West African Cinema
By James Stuart Williams

Brazil on Screen: Cinema Novo, New Cinema, Utopia
By Lúcia Nagib

The Cinema of Jia Zhangke: Realism and Memory in Chinese Film
By Cecília Mello

The Cinema of Sri Lanka: South Asian Film in Texts and Contexts
By Ian Conrich and Vilasnee Tampoe-Hautin

Contemporary New Zealand Cinema: From New Wave to Blockbuster
Edited by Ian Conrich and Stuart Murray

Contemporary Portuguese Cinema: Globalising the Nation
Edited by Mariana Liz

Cosmopolitan Cinema: Cross-cultural Encounters in East Asian Film
By Felicia Chan

Documentary Cinema: Contemporary Non-fiction Film and Video Worldwide
By Keith Beattie

Documentary Cinema of Chile: Confronting History, Memory, Trauma
By Antonio Traverso

East Asian Cinemas: Exploring Transnational Connections on Film
Edited by Leon Hunt and Leung Wing-Fai

East Asian Film Noir: Transnational Encounters and Intercultural Dialogue
Edited by Chi-Yun Shin and Mark Gallagher

Film Genres and African Cinema: Postcolonial Encounters
By Rachael Langford

Impure Cinema: Intermedial and Intercultural Approaches to Film
Edited by Lúcia Nagib and Anne Jerslev

Latin American Women Filmmakers: Production, Politics, Poetics
Edited by Deborah Martin and Deborah Shaw

Lebanese Cinema: Imagining the Civil War and Beyond
By Lina Khatib

New Argentine Cinema
By Jens Andermann

New Directions in German Cinema
Edited by Paul Cooke and Chris Homewood

New Turkish Cinema: Belonging, Identity and Memory
By Asuman Suner

On Cinema
By Glauber Rocha
Edited by Ismail Xavier

Palestinian Filmmaking in Israel: Narratives of Place and Identity
By Yael Freidman

Performing Authorship: Self-inscription and Corporeality in the Cinema
By Cecilia Sayad

Queer Masculinities in Latin American Cinema: Male Bodies and Narrative Representations
By Gustavo Subero

Realism in Greek Cinema: From the Post-war Period to the Present
By Vrasidas Karalis

Realism of the Senses in World Cinema: The Experience of Physical Reality
By Tiago de Luca

The Spanish Fantastic: Contemporary Filmmaking in Horror, Fantasy and Sci-fi
By Shelagh-Rowan Legg

Stars in World Cinema: Screen Icons and Star Systems Across Cultures
Edited by Andrea Bandhauer and Michelle Royer

Thai Cinema: The Complete Guide
Edited by Mary J. Ainslie and Katarzyna Ancuta

Theorizing World Cinema
Edited by Lúcia Nagib, Chris Perriam and Rajinder Dudrah

Viewing Film
By Donald Richie

Queries, ideas and submissions to:

Series Editor: Professor Lúcia Nagib – l.nagib@reading.ac.uk

Series Editor: Dr. Julian Ross – rossj@westminster.ac.uk

Cinema Editor at I.B.Tauris, Maddy Hamey-Thomas – mhamey-thomas@ibtauris.com

Contemporary Peruvian Cinema

History, Identity and Violence on Screen

SARAH BARROW

I.B. TAURIS
LONDON · NEW YORK

For David

Published in 2018 by
I.B.Tauris & Co. Ltd
London • New York
www.ibtauris.com

Copyright © 2018 Sarah Barrow

The right of Sarah Barrow to be identified as the author of this work has been asserted by the author in accordance with the Copyright, Designs and Patents Act 1988.

All rights reserved. Except for brief quotations in a review, this book, or any part thereof, may not be reproduced, stored in or introduced into a retrieval system, or transmitted, in any form or by any means, electronic, mechanical, photocopying, recording or otherwise, without the prior written permission of the publisher.

Every attempt has been made to gain permission for the use of the images in this book. Any omissions will be rectified in future editions.

References to websites were correct at the time of writing.

Tauris World Cinema Series

ISBN: 978 1 78453 821 7
eISBN: 978 1 78672 335 2
ePDF: 978 1 78673 335 1

A full CIP record for this book is available from the British Library
A full CIP record is available from the Library of Congress

Library of Congress Catalog Card Number: available

Printed and bound by CPI Group (UK) Ltd, Croydon, CR0 4YY

Contents

List of Plates	ix
Acknowledgements	xiii
Introduction: Peruvian Cinema and Culture	1
Histories of Violence	4
Diversity in Context	5
Contemporary Peruvian Fiction Cinema	9
In Focus: Writing on Peru and Peruvian Cinemas	11
1 Cinema, State and National Identity	17
Crisis and Legislation of the 1970s	23
Neoliberal Reforms of the 1990s	26
Cinema After Fujimori: Impact of Political Turmoil	28
2 Cinema, Transition and Turmoil	33
Conflicting Identities and National Crisis: *La boca del lobo* (Francisco Lombardi, 1988)	35
The Hybridisation of National Identity: *Ni con dios ni con el diablo* (Nilo Pereira del Mar, 1990)	59
Identity, Violence and Social Responsibility: *Alias la gringa* (Alberto 'Chicho' Durant, 1991)	79
3 Cinema, Oppression and Ideology, 1992–2000	93
Female interventions: *La vida es una sola* (Marianne Eyde, 1993)	95
Identity, Agency and Social Development: *Anda, corre, vuela …/Run, Walk, Fly …* (Augusto Tamayo, 1995)	109
Creating an Icon: *Coraje/Courage* (Alberto Durant, 1998)	123

Contents

4	**Cinema, Memory and Truth, 2000–2004**	137
	Shaping Memories of National Trauma: *Paloma de papel/Paper Dove* (Fabrizio Aguilar, 2003)	139
	Stasis, Dislocation and Open Wounds: *Días de Santiago/Days of Santiago* (Josué Méndez, 2004)	154
5	**New Generations and Open Wounds, 2005–2016**	173
	Seeking Closure	173
	Fractured Continuities	176
	Conclusion	184

Notes	189
Bibliography	215
Filmography	228
Index	230

List of Plates

1. *El candidato* (Álvaro Velarde, 2016, Velarde Producciones) – President Fujimoto rages from his prison cell
2. *La hora final* (Eduardo Mendoza de Echave, 2017, La Soga Producciones) – Filming on location in Lima, with the actor Pietro Sibille
3. *La boca del lobo* (Francisco Lombardi, 1988, Incan Film/Tornasol Films) – Lieutenant Roca looks on at the bodies of traitors on the steps of the church
4. *La boca del lobo* (Francisco Lombardi, 1988, Incan Film/Tornasol Films) – Sergeant Vitín Luna is locked up for having defied orders from his lieutenant
5. *Ni con dios ni con el diablo* (Nilo Pereira del Mar, 1990, Urpi Producciones) – publicity poster
6. *Ni con dios ni con el diablo* (Nilo Pereira del Mar, 1990, Urpi Producciones) – Jeremías joins the miners in his search for work
7. *Alias la Gringa* (Alberto Durant, 1991, ICAIC/TVE) – 'La Gringa' takes up arms
8. *Alias la Gringa* (Alberto Durant, 1991, ICAIC/TVE) – an inmate is stabbed during a game of basketball
9. *La vida es una sola* (Marianne Eyde, 1993, Kusi Films) – Shining Path rebel Comrade Meche leads her group into action
10. *La vida es una sola* (Marianne Eyde, 1993, Kusi Films) – villagers are threatened with death by Shining Path rebels
11. *La vida es una sola* (Marianne Eyde, 1993, Kusi Films) – villagers are forced to become killers and mourn their dead

List of Plates

12. *Anda, corre, vuela* (Augusto Tamayo, 1995, Casablanca Films) – publicity poster showing Gregorio and Juliana running away from danger
13. *Coraje* (Alberto Durant, 1998, Agua Dulce Films) – María Elena Moyano galvanises her community of women into protest again Shining Path intimidation
14. *Coraje* (Alberto Durant, 1998, Agua Dulce Films) – publicity poster
15. *Paloma de papel* (Fabrizio Aguilar, 2003, Luna Llena Films) – young Juan is forced to take up arms
16. *Días de Santiago* (Josué Méndez, 2004, Chullachaki Producciones) – Santiago
17. *Días de Santiago* (Josué Méndez, 2004, Chullachaki Producciones) – Santiago and his former comrades
18. *Las malas intenciones* (Rosario García-Montero, 2011, Barry Films/Garmont Films) – Cayetana watches the world go by from her family's summer balcony, apparently distanced from real life and events
19. *Las malas intenciones* (Rosario García-Montero, 2011, Barry Films/Garmont Films) – Cayetana waits for her driver to arrive to take her home from school, protecting her from everyday life
20. *NN* (Héctor Gálvez, 2014, Piedra Alada Producciones/Séptima Films/Autentika Films/MPM Film) – Fidel searches for clues as to the identity of a victim of violence
21. *Magallanes* (Salvador del Solar, 2015, CEPA Audiovisual/Nephilim Producciones/Proyectil/Péndulo Films/Tondero Producciones) – Magallanes the taxi driver is confronted with the consequences of his past
22. *La última tarde* (Joel Calero, 2016, Factoria Sur/BF) – Ramón and Laura wander through the streets of Barranco as they wait for their divorce papers to be signed

List of Plates

23. *La última tarde* (Joel Calero, 2016, Factoria Sur/BF) – Laura

24. *La última tarde* (Joel Calero, 2016, Factoria Sur/BF) – Ramón

All images appear with the permission of their directors and/or have been provided by the Filmoteca de Lima.

Images 16 and 17 appear with the permission of ©trigon-film.org

Acknowledgements

The completion of this book owes much to many people, in particular those who share a love of cinema, Latin America and Peru. Most of all, I would like to express my deepest gratitude to those Peruvian contacts and comrades who have assisted me in many different ways since my first visit to their country in 1997, foremost of whom is the indomitable and wonderfully generous Norma Rivero, guardian of the Filmoteca de Lima. They also include Álvaro Velarde, Jorge Zavaleta, Marianne Eyde, Josué Méndez, Natalia Ames, Fabrizio Aguilar, Stefan Kaspar, Ricardo Bedoya, Isaac León Frías, Chicho Durant, Rosario García-Montero and Enid 'Pinky' Campos. These determined filmmakers, critics and cinephiles are amongst those who have generously shared their time and ideas generously over the last two decades, and several have also kindly provided many of the images for this book.

I owe a great big thank you to David Wood at Sheffield for his patience as I worked on an earlier version of this project and for always asking when this book would be ready!

Thanks also to the wonderfully warm network of Latino/a colegas who have patiently listened to countless papers on Peruvian cinema, probed with their insightful comments and joined in numerous collaborations: Deborah Shaw, Stephanie Dennison, Nuria Triana-Toribio, Jeffrey Middents, Clara Garavelli, Beatriz Tadeo Fuica, Tamara Falicov, David Wood (Mexico City), Niamh Thornton, Carolina Rueda, Leslie Marsh – amongst many others committed to the study and enjoyment of Latin American cinemas and cultures.

I will always also remember and be thankful for the support of Anglia Ruskin University friends Tanya Horeck, Tina Kendall, Joss Hands, Neal Curtis, Jussi Parikka, Milla Tiainen and John White for inspiration and solidarity; and for the kindness of University of Lincoln comrades Krista Cowman, Harriet Gross, Karen Savage, Mark O'Thomas, Mary Stuart. Thank you to both institutions, to the British Academy and to Santander

Acknowledgements

for the grants that have enabled me to return to visit Peru year after year in an attempt to deepen my understanding of the ways culture, politics and society interlock and interrelate.

I am exceedingly grateful to the reviewers of the draft manuscript for their care, attention and thoughtful comments, as well as to Maddy Hamey-Thomas and David Campbell at I.B.Tauris for their dedication throughout the editorial and production processes.

And a final special thank you to my family for their support, encouragement, love and patience throughout this project.

Introduction: Peruvian Cinema and Culture

> Cinema is, first and foremost, the projection of a cultural identity which comes to life on the screen. It mirrors, or should mirror, this identity. But that is not all. It should also 'dream' it. Or make it flesh and blood, with all its contradictions. Unlike Europe, we are societies in which the question of identity has not yet crystallised. It is perhaps for this reason that we have such a need for cinema, so that we can see ourselves in the many conflicting mirrors that reflect us.[1]

The role of cinema in shaping, reflecting and contesting perceptions of national identity is the central interest of this study of contemporary Peruvian cinema. The formation of Peruvian national identity has long been in transition as different cultural groups vie for agency and visibility, and the challenges of integration are brought to bear. Meanwhile, the development of cinema production in Peru has been slow and the relationship of filmmakers with the Peruvian state has often been fractious. Yet their desire and capacity to capture, portray, draw attention to and probe landmark events, figures and debates of national concern have been as strong as elsewhere in Latin America, where cinema has become a key instrument of political endeavour and a popular form of creative expression.

This book examines the relationship between cinema, state and identity in Peru, through the lens of several key cinematic interpretations of the political violence between the military and insurgent group Sendero Luminoso (Shining Path) that began in 1980. It explores representations of that violence in some of the most critically and commercially successful Peruvian feature films of recent times, and looks in particular at portrayals of landmark events, characters and consequences of the bloody conflict between the state and Shining Path that threatened to destabilise the nation entirely. It considers these representations in the context of a time of great change for Peruvian society as well as of transition for Peruvian national cinema, and addresses the relationship between developments in film policy and the reflection and shaping of Peruvian national identity in cinema. As such, it draws on and develops the wider debates about the nature and function of national cinemas, as well as on discussions between artists, cultural theorists and sociologists about the evolution of *Peruanidad* (Peruvian-ness) since the declaration of independence from Spain in the nineteenth century.

The project has been motivated by a desire to interrogate the relationship between culture and society through exploring the role of cinema as a response to intense national political crisis that coincides with a time of crisis for the national filmmaking industry itself. The main part of this study consists of close analyses of feature films that were produced in response to the political crisis of the Shining Path conflict between 1988 and 2004, and understands them as different ways of articulating those crises. It explores the extent to which these films provoked debate about the major civil conflict and its aftermath, and examines broader questions pertaining to the relationship between national identity, violence, memory and culture. It also looks at how these films were made despite the acutely difficult circumstances for cultural production generally. In no way intended as an all-inclusive list of every Peruvian film that has ever featured an aspect of the Shining Path crisis, instead it has adopted the approach of interweaving close textual analysis of films that offer a range of cinematic styles with contextual study of national political events and developments in cultural policy. In so doing, I hope that this project sheds some light on the complex relationship of national cinema to ideology and culture in Peru.

Since 2009, there has been a flurry of new feature films dealing in various ways with reflections on the impact on collective and individual memory and identity as a result of the Shining Path violence and several of these are discussed in the final chapter. The rationale for focusing in greater detail in this study on films from 1988–2004 is that these appear to set the tone and approach that all since then adopt. They were made during the period when the state was struggling to work out what its relationship with cinema should be, allowing for a detailed discussion about that relationship that still resonates today.[2] In summary, the corpus of films taken together provokes debate about 'national' identity formation through officially sanctioned cultural products, and reflections on their wider circulation via the global festival circuit. Most importantly, the socio-political context remains highly pertinent: in 2011, lawyers for Shining Path submitted 360,000 signatures to register a new political party, Movadef. Although the electoral authority denied the registration on the grounds that the organisation advocated terrorism, Movadef remains active with its campaigning. Indeed, on 1 May 2017 there were demonstrations in front of Parliament in Lima by members of the group which provoked widespread press attention, while in July 2017, rumours of a presidential pardon for President Fujimori – jailed for 25 years in 2009 after having been found guilty of crimes against humanity by seven different trials. Moreover I argue that the themes and concerns of the films analysed in detail carry forward to today and the references made to some of the more recent films that continue to explore this key period of modern Peruvian history demonstrate the ongoing relevance of this topic. Indeed, while putting the final touches to this project, several more Peruvian films that fit the topic of this book are making their mark. Álvaro Velarde's *El candidato/The Candidate*, for example, was released in 2016 and continues to circulate via the festival circuit with awards that include one for best script at the prestigious Figueira Film Art event in Portugal (September 2017). Also released in September 2017 was Eduardo Mendoza's feature *La hora final/ The Final Hour*, based on the operation that led to the capture of Shining Path leader Abimael Guzmán, exactly twenty five years after that highly significant event. (See Plates 1 and 2)

Histories of Violence

The various histories of Peru are marked by episodes of intense conflict between and within cultural groups, from exotic accounts of the brutal rituals and battles of pre-Columbian Chavín, Moche and Incan cultures, to reports of harsh subordination of the indigenous peoples by Spanish conquistadors, and more recent border conflicts with Ecuador. Throughout the 1980s and the early 1990s, reports of massacres and executions committed by the Shining Path insurgency group dominated national and international news about Peru.[3] Meanwhile, the Western media seems to have been mainly interested either in reports of archaeological discoveries that offer further apparent evidence of the brutality of the nation's quasi-mythical past, or in the brutality of the nation's contemporary leaders and the inevitability of further sets of national crises.[4] It is perhaps inevitable therefore that Peru's national filmmakers, with an eye to both domestic and international markets, have chosen repeatedly to use violence as a thematic device in their works. They do so by drawing, for example, on myths and characters from Peru's pre-Hispanic past, as well as on the more everyday crime stories that frequently appear in the domestic mass media and increasingly on social media platforms.[5] Indeed, an analysis of the most prominent themes in Peruvian cinema during its centenary highlighted the dominance of such violence-related topics as prison, crime, delinquents, the military, death and terrorism.[6]

Several questions frame this analysis of the relationship between an important period for the Peruvian nation and its cinema. Above all, it has been relevant to examine the effect of the conflict with Shining Path on both the production context and the thematic content of films made in Peru, and the way the relationship between filmmakers and the state that developed during the 1990s continues to have resonance today. This has led to an investigation of the ways in which issues of Peruvian national identity have been framed and contested on the cinema screen. The extent to which such films have succeeded in challenging hegemonic constructions of nation dictated by state institutions that seek to maintain the political and social status quo is also considered. One of the aims has been to explore the way these films, as cultural products, raise questions about some of the assumptions made about the recent conflict and, more broadly, about the relationship between violence and identity. In this regard, it has proved essential to look at the way these films, despite their mainly realist intentions, go beyond the reflectionist approach regarded by most contemporary film theorists as 'primitive'.[7] At the same time, it is important to acknowledge that they also resist the more overtly political practices and approaches of other Latin American filmmakers, including some of their predecessors from the Escuela de Cine de Cusco (the Cusco Film School) of the 1950s and 1960s. Instead, it is argued, they embed political statements within classically structured narratives and utilise the systems of signs that have become integral to the distinctive symbolic language of cinema in order to offer provocative versions of recent events.[8] Special emphasis is placed on the development of characters who cross boundaries and defy expectations, and who take on broader symbolic significance as representative of national concerns. As such, these films also seem to contribute to the construction and redefinition of more complex notions of national identity that challenge essentialist stereotypes of race, class and gender in Peru. This study thus seeks to affirm the importance of cinema at a time of national crisis, by exploring the ways in which a small number of thematically interlinked feature films offer diverse ways of understanding an important period of modern national history, while at the same time provoking debate about the nature of Peruvian identity. As shown by the references in the final chapter to more recent films on this topic, from *Tarata* (2009) by Fabrizio Aguilar to *La última tarde* (2016) by Joel Calero, these debates about violence, about identity, about the relationship between cinema and state are still important to an understanding of the contemporary cultural, social and political landscape of Peru.

Diversity in Context

Although the concept of the nation-state is a relatively modern one and subject to constant debate as to its relevance, 'nevertheless, most people these days expect our membership of the nation to bind us together'.[9] Many film theorists acknowledge that national cinema has played an important role in the creation of nations as 'imagined political communit[ies]',[10] helping to shape 'a shared culture, shared memories of a constructed past'.[11]

Moreover, while Andrew Higson has suggested that a national cinema might be defined in terms of its potential to reflect and express 'pre-existing [notions of] national identity, consciousness, or culture', he is also clear that it is capable of shaping new ideas that contribute to the evolution of such concepts.[12] He further points out that although 'national films will draw on identities and representations already in circulation – and often they will naturalize those identities … [they might] also produce new representations of the nation'.[13] Since the mid-1990s, there has been increasing and more overt acknowledgement of the need to understand national cinema's more active role in the formation of identities and the resistance to dominant ideologies. Meanwhile, many of the same theorists now draw attention to the need to understand the uncertain and shifting relationship between national cinemas and national cultures. Moreover, the general desire for a national culture to reflect and respond to the diversity of experiences that exists within any single nation has become clear. Higson, for example, has admitted that until recently he was himself 'perhaps at times rather too ready to find … films presenting an image of a coherent, unified, consensual nation'.[14] With these debates in mind, the films selected for this study are examined in terms of their various political and aesthetic approaches to representing the conflict with Shining Path – indicative of a range of perspectives – and the effect of that conflict on the evolution of perceptions of cultural and national identity in modern Peru. The extent to which these films go beyond an apparently straightforward process of recounting events and instead encourage viewers to look for different ways of understanding those events and the people involved is also addressed.

Higson, like many others working in this area, has turned his attention to 'those perspectives that call attention to cultural diversity'[15] and, with that call in mind, this project takes account of diversity in several ways. It explores the ways in which the plurality and instability of Peruvian national identity are dealt with on screen and considers the diversity of formal and ideological approaches to such representations. It also reflects critically on the different directors who have created the films and considers the extent to which disenfranchised minority communities have participated in the cinematic writing of Peruvian history. It draws particular inspiration from Susan Hayward's conceptual work on national cinemas, in which she refutes the idea of nations as enduring, unchanging entities. She reminds us that such concepts as nation and national identity have been 'forged and sustained by certain networks of power [and that] nationalist discourses around culture work to forge the link ... between nation and state'.[16] Echoing the work of French cultural theorist Paul Virilio on the relationship between war and cinema, she suggests we should 'reterritorialise the nation ... not as bounded, demarcated and distinctive but as one within which boundaries constantly criss-cross both haphazardly and *unhaphazardly*'.[17] She also points to the increasing interest in sites of difference within a nation since the 1960s. In Latin America, the desire to embrace difference was marked, for example, by the emergence of Third Cinema after the Cuban Revolution, both of which which were committed to social and cultural emancipation. Indeed, Third Cinema set out to intervene 'in the process of creating new people, new societies, new histories, new art and new cinemas'.[18] The idea of national cinema therefore offers a complicating paradox in that 'it will always – in its forming – go against the underlying principles of nationalism and be at cross-purposes with the originating idea of the *nation* as a unified identity'.[19] This contention is examined in the context of the development of the Peruvian nation, national identity and national cinema, and by addressing the complex relationship between them at a time of intense political and cultural crisis via a close analysis of the selected film texts.

The perspective of diversity seems especially pertinent when exploring the cinematic representation of a nation that remains as culturally differentiated as Peru, and which continues to struggle to reconcile the deep schisms between its constituent geographic, political and social elements. Whereas some countries have had to confront the realities of diversity only very latterly, the Peruvian nation has grappled with it for several hundred years and continues to do so. Peru has a complex history that has seen national borders shift constantly, and a range of different peoples (from pre-Inca civilisations and the Inca empire to Spanish conquistadors and, more latterly, migrant workers from Japan and China) take part in the often violent evolution of a fragile nation-state. This does not mean, however, that with diversity comes equality of opportunity or visibility, since within Peru there are 'enormous hierarchies of race, gender, class, etc.'.[20] Moreover, like so many subjects of postcolonial nations, Peruvians are generally identified, problematically, as belonging to one of three distinct social groups: 'the white colonials, the indigenous colonized, and the African and Asian immigrant-workers'.[21] Meanwhile, the complex concept of *mestizaje*, while arguably the key to understanding and negotiating contemporary Peruvian identity, remains a problematic area for most.[22] To complicate matters further, the problem of racism, and of inequality more generally, is rarely discussed in any public arena in Peru. As Peruvian philosopher and sociologist Gisele Velarde laments, 'here, no-one speaks openly about uncomfortable topics such as racism or poverty'.[23] Such difficulties with dealing with these issues crops up time and time again in the films presented in this study, from Lombardi's landmark work *La boca del lobo* (1998) in which failures to communicate across cultures leads to devastating consequences for all, to Aguilar's second feature *Tarata* (2009) in which a middle-class creole family in Lima is shown struggling to understand each other's pain as well as to appreciate the even more difficult circumstances faced by their indigenous housekeeper, in the aftermath of one of the deadliest explosions in Lima.

Indeed, the development and definition of Peruvian national identity since achieving independence from Spain have been viewed as a conundrum by a range of prominent national writers and politicians, many of whose work has informed this study. For example, José Carlos Mariátegui, Víctor Andrés Belaúnde, José María Arguedas and Antonio Cornejo Polar have all, as Martha Ojeda points out, 'studied, analyzed and theorized about the hybrid and heterogeneous nature of Peruvian culture', mainly emphasising the tensions and encounters between the indigenous and European groups.[24] From the early part of the twentieth century, debates around the place of indigenous culture within concepts of the nation became increasingly important, if irritating for the political elite, since 'indigenismo sought above all to question the hegemonic concept of national identity based on creole Lima'.[25] Since then, racial and ethnic identities in Peru have been more widely acknowledged as 'shifting, decentred, relational constructions, subject to a politics of identity, culture and difference that encompasses gender, sexuality, religion and other cultural expressions'.[26] For, as Wood notes, culture is neither fixed nor homogeneous and 'Peruvian culture in particular is characterised by diversity and by a dynamic relationship – at times problematic – between various cultural spheres and their processes and products'.[27]

Contemporary Peruvian Fiction Cinema

Part of what makes the set of films chosen for this study so distinctive is that they all, in different ways, draw attention to the divisions and rifts between state and society, and contribute to dispelling the myth of a coherent and unified national identity. They reveal and examine the complexities of a society that is shown as *still* struggling to come to terms with the realities of its multicultural identity. Perhaps even more pertinent is the knowledge that these films were all at least part-funded by state resources and as such form part of the official national cinema framework, despite the challenges they pose to an understanding of the conflict with Shining Path, and hence to issues of contemporary national and cultural identity more generally. Most of the films were circulated via a range of screening conditions to different parts of the country, and several have also been critically acclaimed on the international film festival circuit. This is not however an exhaustive list of titles; it is a selection of some of those that allow for the deepest discussion. Moreover, there are undoubtedly more films to come on this topic as the issues provoked by the Shining Path violence continue to resonate throughout Peruvian society and culture. Indeed I suggest that they form part of the scars that Hodgin and Thakkar refer to as representative of ongoing trauma.[28]

Investigating the cinematic representation of political violence in chronological order, this project takes as its point of departure Francisco Lombardi's powerful and influential account of the state response to the Shining Path insurgency in his award-winning feature, *La boca del lobo/The Lion's Den* (1988). Most of the films selected for close discussion draw upon events, people, images and stories that were already in circulation throughout the national and international public spheres. Some are dramatic reconstructions of specific real events, while others create fictional accounts that help (re)shape memories of a significant period in national history. Most were released after the conflict officially ended with the capture of the group's leader Abimael Guzmán in 1992, and continue to raise uncomfortable questions about the complicity of civil society in the suffering of many impoverished Peruvian citizens. As such, they have been largely associated with a socialist political vision that was largely discredited through its own uncertain response to the violence, to be replaced by contemporary regimes of technocracy and neo-liberalism. The choice of a set of films that have refused to comply with a broader reluctance to speak about a difficult period of national history, including a final chapter that demonstrates how this continues to be an important topic for contemporary Peruvian cinema and society has led to the need for this project to address the wider issues of the role of national cinema as a forum for testimony and debate. The persistent return to representation of a controversial topic that many might have preferred to forget prompts a further set of questions on the purpose of collective memory. Moreover, the final two sections of this study consider the re-emergence and, hence, persistent remembering of this important era, first via a discussion of two very different films released shortly after President Alberto Fujimori's political demise, *Paloma de papel/Paper Dove* (Fabrizio Aguilar, 2003) and *Días de Santiago/Days of Santiago* (Josué Méndez, 2004), and finally by acknowledging the range of award-winning films that have embedded memories of the conflict in their narratives in different ways over the last 10 years.

Most of the films selected for close study were made and released during a time of great crisis for Peruvian national cinema itself, when the problematic but supportive protectionist cinema policy that had been introduced in 1972 was abolished, and new legislation that philosophically was more in keeping with the prevailing emphasis on neoliberal free market practices was introduced in its place in the mid-1990s. Despite the promise of regular funding competitions, a lack of resources and diminished technical infrastructure led to a difficult period for Peru's national filmmakers. Increasing restrictions on freedom of expression throughout the 1990s due to anti-terrorist legislation that was maintained even after the main insurgent threat had been eliminated affected the extent to which productions could explore issues of social and national concern in explicit terms. Meanwhile, the exhibition infrastructure and demography of cinema-goers changed completely as locally-owned, city-centre premises closed or divided their large screens into several smaller, more profitable ones, and US-style multiplexes opened in suburban shopping malls.[29]

Nevertheless, there emerged several important films that dared to explore aspects of the Shining Path conflict and its social consequences in ways that drew attention not only to flaws in the counter-insurgency strategies of the various regimes involved, but also to entrenched institutional and social prejudices. This resonated with an important and recurrent feature of Peruvian cinema that insisted on exploring the nation's social reality as a way of connecting with domestic audiences and offering an alternative to more commercial domestic and international productions. As Peru's most well-known filmmaker, Francisco Lombardi, has remarked, when he began to make films in the late 1970s it was 'at a time when Peruvian cinema was making its first faltering steps in relation to its environment'.[30] Christian Wiener, cultural commentator and former Director General of the Arts and Creative Industries in the Ministry of Culture of Peru, has also reflected on this impulse by national filmmakers to tackle issues of immediate social concern: 'somehow, most of our filmmakers learnt their craft at the same time as getting to know their country and its social and cultural inequalities'.[31] Moreover, given the tradition of cultural production being part of counter-hegemonic discourse since the early twentieth century in Peru, it is perhaps not surprising to note that several national filmmakers have sought ways to bring aspects of the Shining Path conflict to the cinema screen. Such source material has offered plenty of scope for visual spectacle and also allowed for the development of memorable stories based on issues of social and political concern. In turn, these stories have given rise to the development of a body of films with emphasis on exploring the links between political violence and national identity, and have in effect resulted in a revitalisation of Peruvian national cinema itself.

In Focus: Writing on Peru and Peruvian Cinemas

Until recently there has been very little work published on Peruvian cinema that is written in English; nevertheless, a significant body of work produced by Peruvian writers, often in collaboration with the main festivals there, has developed since the launch of the important film journal *Hablemos de cine* in 1965 by a group of students who were passionate about cinema and encouraged by the work of the likes of the editors of *Cahier du cinema* in France: Isaac León Frías, Federico de Cárdenas, Juan M. Bullitta and Carlos Rodríguez Larraín, later joined by Ricardo Bedoya.[32] The primary book-length works on Peruvian cinema up to 1972, the year of the introduction of protective cinema legislation, include Giancarlo Carbone's two edited volumes of eyewitness accounts from critics and filmmakers of the time, and Violeta Núñez Gorritti's critical study of the so-called 'golden age' of Peruvian cinema, 1936–1950.[33] These comprehensive projects have helped to inform the historical cinematic framework for this study, alongside John King's history of Latin American cinema, *Magical Reels*, which in its overview of the cinemas of the Andes makes a brief but important address to the Peruvian context and some key developments up to 2000.[34] Most of the monographic studies of contemporary Peruvian cinema have been developed by Ricardo Bedoya, an academic film historian and critic. These include a critical history of Peruvian cinema up to 1995, a detailed analysis of the work of Francisco Lombardi, Peru's most productive and internationally acclaimed filmmaker, a comprehensive illustrated dictionary of Peruvian films, incorporating edited reviews of each entry, and an annotated book of stills, all of which were published as part of the celebrations of the centenary of Peruvian cinema in 1995.[35] These texts offer insightful analyses of the form and context of the work of most of Peru's filmmakers, while also documenting the development of cinema legislation in Peru since 1972. Two of his chapters, on individual films and their portrayals of violence, have appeared in edited collections in English, and a recent text provided thematic analyses of most of the films released in Peru from 2000 until 2015, including several under discussion here.[36] Also very influential in terms of generating a heightened and sophisticated film culture in Peru has been Bedoya's blog, 'Paginas del diario de satan/Pages from Satan's diary', which comments on all aspects of cinema activity across Peru.[37] Meanwhile, over the last decade, essays on Peruvian cinema have featured in several edited collections and journals published in English, French and Spanish, most of which emphasise aspects of cultural diversity and violence.[38]

Also vital to this project has been the work by Jeffrey Middents on film culture in Peru. In his *Writing National Cinema* (2009), Middents acknowledges that although published academic work on Peruvian cinema remains reasonably scarce, film criticism has been a thriving activity there, as elsewhere in Latin America, since the late 1960s, when, as he notes, filmmakers and writers reacted 'to dominating forces within their cultures with a new sense of politically motivated activism'.[39] Indeed, several Peruvian film journals have proved invaluable to this study, including *Hablemos de Cine* and its many successors such as *La Gran Ilusión* and *Tren de Sombras*, *Butaca Sanmartina* and *Abre los Ojos*. Essays, reviews and interviews published in *La Gran Ilusión* have been particularly relevant as it stands out as the only national cinema journal to have reviewed all the Peruvian films made in the 1990s and documented the rapidly changing legislative framework for cinema in Peru throughout that difficult decade. Moreover, analyses of primary material from the government body for national cinema documenting the changing legislation during the period under scrutiny have also been essential.[40] Finally, but most significantly, the resources of the Peruvian National Film Archive (La Filmoteca), alongside attendance at screenings and events at the annual Lima Film Festival, have provided the most compelling evidence of critical and audience response that helped frame the debate offered here about the cultural role of national cinema within a context of political, economic and social difficulty.

A range of theoretical literature that deals with issues of national identity, both general and pertaining specifically to the Peruvian context, has been drawn upon in developing this project. Contemporary debates that rage between locally based journalists and commentators every year as Independence Day approaches about the complexity and evolution of *Peruanidad* have been particularly enlightening, as have my own discussions with academics, critics and filmmakers who were willing to converse openly on these topics. The themes of memory and trauma began to emerge more strongly during the early period of research, which coincided with public debates resulting from the work of Peru's Truth and Reconciliation Commission, 2001–2003. With this in mind, it has been important also to draw upon psychoanalytical approaches to the understanding of social structures, human relationships, the unconscious and the way such concepts are associated with cinema, referencing the work, for example, of Sigmund Freud, Elizabeth Jelin, Gonzalo Portocarrero, Erich Fromm and Kaja Silverman. This will be seen in particular in Chapter 4, in the analyses of Aguilar's *Paloma de papel*, which traces its protagonist's memory of a traumatic violent event that marked the end of his childhood, and Méndez's *Días de Santiago*, which portrays the collapse of its protagonist's subjectivity as he struggles to cope with brutal events of both past and present.

Chapter 1 offers a historical overview of both early Peruvian cinema and the debates that emerged throughout the twentieth century about Peruvian cultural identity. It sets out the contexts for the cinematic and national crises of the period under scrutiny in this book and addresses some of the specificities of contemporary Peruvian cinema, including its relationship with state institutions and the shift from protectionist to free market approaches to culture at a period when the nation was also dealing with the economic, social and political aftermath of the conflict with the Shining Path.

Chapters 2–4 present the critical analyses of the films outlined above, addressed chronologically and grouped in such a way as to reflect and interrogate the various political and legislative contexts that prevailed between 1988 and 2016. These chapters all focus on examining the diverse approaches taken by these works to providing a cinematic response to the recent period of political conflict and its impact on Peruvian society and identity. As such, close textual analysis is marked by discussion of pertinent issues such as urban migration, *mestizaje*, indigenous rituals and belief systems, and gender positions. Consideration is also given to the domestic and international reception of the films, and the relationship between such films and the Peruvian authorities.

The role of Peruvian national cinema in challenging dominant discourses of identity which appear still to privilege white patriarchal culture, and in shaping new perceptions of the nation, is discussed in the fifth and final chapter with reference to several of the most recent films from Peru that tackle themes provoked by the Shining Path conflict from a range of perspectives that resonate strongly with those chosen for the closer analyses in the earlier chapters. The problematic sense of violence as an inescapable, inevitable and integral element of Peruvian national identity as highlighted by those films which have performed most successfully on the global market is set out, as is the challenge to stereotypes of gender roles offered by several of the films. In all areas, issues of 'intertextual and socio-political and/or socio-cultural coherence [that are] implicitly or explicitly assigned to the nation' are addressed in the context of this specific topic, further highlighting the undeniable complexity of national cinema debates.[41] Finally, the project considers the capacity of Peruvian cinema, still a fragile ecology, to contribute effectively to public debate about issues of national concern, when, as Michael Chanan suggests in his discussion of Latin American filmmakers who lack vigorous and sustained state support, 'everything would seem to be against the idea'.[42]

1

Cinema, State and National Identity

A survey of the major trends in the history of Peruvian cinema suggests that the relationship between the emergence of the moving image as a popular form, changes on the social and political landscape, and the development of national identity formation in Peru have been complex, contradictory and at odds with developments elsewhere. It has been suggested that the advent of cinema at the end of the nineteenth century coincided in most parts of the world with the period when modernity was already 'at full throttle … a watershed moment in which a series of sweeping changes in technology and culture created distinctive new modes of thinking about and experiencing time and space'.[1] However, the reality for the majority of Latin American countries was quite different. As Ana M. López points out, it simply is not possible to link the rise of cinema in this region to 'previous large-scale transformations of daily experience resulting from urbanization, industrialization, rationality and the technological transformation of modern life'.[2] Such transformations were only just starting to take place, so that when cinema, the ultimate expression of cultural modernity, was launched across the world, the positive consequences of modernity in Latin America were 'above all a fantasy and a profound desire'.[3] Accordingly, the specific historical trajectory and circumstances of cinema in Peru and its impact (both as an agent of social change and as a reflection of the nation) need to be taken fully into account when analysing the contemporary films that are relevant to this study. This chapter reviews some of the key developments in the history of Peruvian cinema, highlights landmark films, considers its relationship with the state and society, and interrogates its contribution to building and reflecting a sense of national identity.

According to Bedoya's account based on newspaper reports of the time, the arrival of cinema in Peru was warmly welcomed in Lima, in particular by the capital's social elite, who greeted the new technology as the very incarnation of the modernity to which they aspired. The first public screening in Peru took place in the capital city on 2 January 1897, using the Vitascope equipment developed by the acclaimed North American inventor Thomas Edison. It was attended by President of the Republic Nicolás de Piérola and consisted of two hours of rural and urban views. Electric power had to be specially installed and there was musical accompaniment using a phonograph, also a novelty for Peruvian spectators. When the Lumière brothers' French cinematograph invention arrived one month later, audiences were able to enjoy much improved picture quality, wider screen formats and topics which celebrated movement and technology. For the most part, the early Peruvian film spectator was affluent and belonged to Lima's aristocratic society, itself largely modelled upon the European way of life.[4] Moreover, Piérola was inspired in the reconstruction of his capital city by the images of Paris that he saw on screen. For him, the capital of France was an iconic city of modern sophistication, with its grand spacious boulevards and fashionable inhabitants, that he would attempt to emulate.[5] As for domestic film production, Piérola's regime (1895–1899) privileged and encouraged the newsreel and documentary forms as modes of expression ideally suited to flaunting the efforts made by the so-called Aristocratic Republic to modernise and expand its capital using funds raised from the export of its sugar, cotton, rubber, wool and silver. Furthermore, many of the early moving images made in Peru coincided with the first aviation flights in the country, with images of Lima taken from the air aimed at provoking a sense of communal pride at such overt displays of progress and modernity.

Demographic changes accompanied these technological and economic developments, with the emergence of an urban-industrial society that gave rise to new social groups such as the middle class, the industrial bourgeoisie and the working class. Nevertheless, for some time, the nation continued to be ruled by the aristocratic elite, and participation in political decisions was restricted to the most privileged strata of society. Indeed, by the time that cinema was introduced in Peru, still only 5% of the population had the right to vote. Modernisation and political agency had not yet reached the majority of the Peruvian people. Gradually, however, some of the authoritarian values and principles of colonialism were rejected, and gave way to the more positivist and liberal ideas of twentieth-century Europe. From 1900 onward, the middle classes became an important political force, often by forming strategic alliances with farm and factory workers. The complex issue of indigenous rights became vital as interest was sparked in specific Latin American cultural identities, and more populist, nationalist regimes were established which 'sought to initiate a process of change which … democratized the political structures'.[6]

During the first half of the twentieth century, cinema from the US, Mexico and Europe became increasingly popular with Peruvian audiences, while attempts to create a national film industry were compromised by political tensions and economic constraints. Construction of film exhibition spaces emerged as the first commercial priority, and a small number of companies were established by Peruvian businessmen who were eager to take financial advantage of the opportunities provided by distributing and screening foreign films in Peru. At around the same time, production of documentaries by local filmmakers was regularised, as these were used as 'fillers' to complement screenings of foreign feature films. Most concentrated on celebrating urban Lima society, and several were sponsored by the state to record events such as the grand carnivalesque celebrations held annually in Lima to commemorate Peruvian Independence (1821) and the battles of Junín and Ayacucho (1824). In some of them, President Augusto Leguía (1919–1930) was depicted speaking proudly of the growing grandeur and wealth of his country, sharing his vision of long-lasting prosperity thanks to collaboration with foreign capital and technology. As Bedoya explains, early national cinema in Peru found itself 'firmly attached to official ideology and history'.[7] Such films ignored the realities of hardship and social exclusion that prevailed throughout the country, especially outside Lima, and sidestepped the tensions between nationalism and cosmopolitanism that marked Peruvian culture during the 1920s.[8]

Notwithstanding, these state-sanctioned films served as nation-builders in that they offered uncritical images of people sharing the celebration of a common history and contributed to the imagining of a nation that 'regardless of the actual inequality and exploitation that may prevail … [was] conceived as a deep, horizontal comradeship'.[9] As Larrain points out, 'the power of an entertaining spectacle transmitted through images is very useful to create and maintain traditions that boost national feelings'.[10] But despite strong governmental support for the documentary form, Peruvian cinema generally lagged behind: by the 1920s, as much of the rest of the world embraced the introduction of sound to the moving image medium, Peruvian filmmakers were only just beginning to grapple with the production of the nation's first silent features. Such delay highlighted the profound lack of technological resources, ongoing investment and experienced filmmakers in a country still struggling with the pressures of industrialisation and the complications of social fragmentation. Leguía's approach to modernisation was, it turned out, simply to block any radical change that would benefit the lower social classes, and to open the country to further investment by US companies.[11]

In stark contrast with the relationship between government and cinema in the field of documentary, Peru's first fiction films were quietly critical of the regime's national vision and in particular of the impact of Western-style progress on the social majority. They privileged instead the more traditional life experienced by the indigenous and *mestizo* (mixed race) masses living in provincial towns and rural communities, and thus presented a challenge to the very idea of a coherent, stable and homogeneous national identity that was at the heart of the regime's quest for recognition as a modern state. *Camino de la venganza/The Road to Revenge* (Luis Ugarte and Narciso Rada, 1922), for example, focuses provocatively on the opposition between rural and urban life and values, contrasting the supposed innocence of the former with the apparent corruptive forces of the latter. It tells a simple story of cruelty and revenge, depicting the kidnap of a young innocent girl from a highland community by a villainous military captain, who carries her off to the dangers and temptations of the capital city. The sense of conflict is established between a morally idyllic rural life, where work on the land alternates with collective gatherings for eating and dancing, and the dangers of Lima, a city replete with threat and temptation.[12] In reality, while Lima was regarded by some as a site for dreams and opportunities, in contrast to the impoverished countryside, for others it quickly became a place where poor immigrants from the provinces would be forced to submit to various forms of exploitation and humiliation. This conflict between urban and rural cultural values echoed the political stance of the *indigenista* movement which emerged in Peru during the 1920s, as it did in other Latin American countries with large indigenous communities. This movement, founded on the influential work of political organiser and cultural critic José Carlos Mariátegui, spoke out in favour of a return to indigenous, Andean values and customs, and a rejection of the European cultural heritage that he believed had been imposed violently upon the countries of Latin America.[13] Moreover, the focus on the tension between urban and rural life was thereafter to become a recurrent theme of Peruvian cinema, as in other cultural forms. Indeed, the complexities of cultural encounter between different social groups from different parts of Peru with different relationships to the state are investigated in the corpus of films under discussion in this study.

By the 1930s, governments and political leaders worldwide had become acutely aware of cinema's capacity to influence the thoughts and actions of their citizens as well as to delight the upper classes, and they tried to harness it as the ideal medium through which to convey their aims and aspirations. In Peru, President Luis M. Sánchez Cerro (1930–1933) proposed legislation that supported the creation of a touring cinema school, a sort of 'mobile cinema service with the aim of incorporating the indigenous population into the nation'.[14] Cinema thus became central to the ambitious project of spreading mass education throughout the country and mobilising an overarching sense of national identity formation imposed by the state. The mobile units and their stock of 'instructional' films were to be financed by the taxes received by the censorship board in return for classification of films. However, the project soon collapsed as audiences paid little attention to images sent from Lima that bore little relevance to their own lives. Nevertheless, the strictly instrumental and pedagogic approach to the development of a national cinema in Peru was one that would be taken up again a few decades later with more effective results.

Film activity in Peru virtually ground to a halt during the 1930s as the national economy, largely dependent upon the export of its raw materials, was devastated by the Wall Street crash. Attempts were made to sustain production by a handful of key individuals but even these projects failed in such unstable circumstances. Later that decade, the production company Amauta Films was established. Named after the journal founded by the aforementioned Mariátegui, it continues to hold an important place in the history of Peruvian national cinema and influenced one of the directions this would take in reflecting and shaping a sense of national identity that harked back to a focus on the rural and indigenous way of life. As the government of the time, led by General Benavides (1933–1939), became ever more repressive and intent on aggressive modernisation of the country, Amauta Films made feature-length movies that offered a sentimental view of traditional middle- and working-class life in the *barrios* of Lima, which presented a challenge to the sense of nationhood desired by Benavides. These were popular in some areas since they depicted local issues, but competition from the more glamorous fare offered by the US, Italy and Mexico in particular – countries whose film industries were actively supported by their governments – eventually contributed to the demise of the company at the end of the 1930s.

Apart from a handful of notable exceptions, the few Peruvian films that were made from the 1940s to the 1970s tended to reproduce the conventions of popular European or US movies and were lacking in any distinctive local colour or national sentiment; indigenous communities were almost completely absent from the screen.[15] Films were amateurish and unsophisticated in quality, production was sporadic, and commercial investment was reserved for the distribution and exhibition of foreign films. Many filmmakers left Peru, and their films were lost, so that no infrastructure was left for their successors, who were forced to start again from scratch. As John King confirms, these decades constituted a 'barren period for the development of cinema' in Peru.[16]

Crisis and Legislation of the 1970s

Given its turbulent history, it is difficult to disagree with Bedoya's assessment that for cinema in Peru, 'the instability of crisis has been the normal condition and the natural state in each and every one of the stages in its intermittent existence'.[17] However, one important period appears to have been at odds with this general assessment of events. In the early 1970s, the populist military regime led by General Juan Velasco Alvarado (1968–1975) took a longer-term interest in the capacity of cinema production to support its own modernisation projects. Whereas in the past such support had been singularly self-serving, instrumental and short-lived, legislation passed in 1972 (Law 19327) provided sufficient flexibility and longevity for a range of filmmakers with varying ideological approaches to benefit from the scheme and develop a degree of continuity verging on the creation of a stable national film industry.

Velasco's shock seizure of power in 1968 changed the course of Peru's political and economic development, shifting away from traditional right-wing pro-business policies to a more radical nationalist framework. Velasco promoted himself as defender of the poor; he redistributed land owned by the agricultural elite and re-nationalised private oil and mining companies. His political intervention in the development of national cinema complemented his overarching socialist reform programme. According to observations by cinema lawyer José Perla Anaya, Velasco responded positively to appeals for support from businessmen and filmmakers who had collaborated on drafting amendments to existing legislation.[18] In particular, his regime felt it was time to start using Peruvian images to replace the foreign ones that had dominated national screens since the advent of cinema in Peru. With this in mind, his Minister for Industry, Jiménez de Lucio, urged national producers to create films that 'reflected Peruvian reality and take the humanist message of revolution and solidarity to every corner of the country'.[19]

The 1972 Cinema Law was by no means an isolated piece of legislation; rather, it was part of an ambitious government project to intervene in the arena of mass communications intended to stimulate national media production, and to convert it into an educational tool for consolidating national culture and unity.[20] Furthermore, evidence of a healthy national film industry could be used by the state as official affirmation to potential investors of Peru's technological maturity and modernisation, of its acquisition and mastery of technology on a grand scale.[21] In fact, Bedoya contends that the legislation was established primarily to ensure that national filmmakers would use moving image technology to promote the state's radical nationalist programme of social reform both domestically and overseas.[22] In reality, the potential benefits of a national film industry in supporting Velasco's regime politically and economically were so wide-ranging that the supervision and monitoring of its development were placed at the heart of the government, within the Ministry for Industry. This uncomfortably prominent position threatened to leave little room for filmmakers to challenge Velasco's social reforms via their films. Moreover, it suggested a lack of clarity regarding a national cultural role for cinema and was arguably at the root of much of the subsequent political confusion and artistic stagnation. Nevertheless, many filmmakers took full advantage of the financial and political support with which to pursue their art. As King states:

> Within a brief period, over a hundred and fifty production companies were set up to provide films.... More than seven hundred shorts were produced in a decade and were shown throughout the countryside, the producer recouping his/her investment from box-office receipts. Cineastes could thus gradually afford to invest in equipment and began working in groups. Within a few years, the first features would be made.[23]

To set this all in motion, Cinema Law 19327 created a set of incentives which favoured so-called 'Peruvian cinematic work' (article 4) and placed national identity and ownership at its heart. These incentives included the following points: the film should be made by a national film production company with at least 80% of the capital in the hands of Peruvian investors; the director must be Peruvian or a foreigner resident in Peru; at least 80% of the filming must have been carried out on national territory; the originating text (if an adaptation) and/or the scriptwriter must be Peruvian; and the language used by the actors must be Castellano, Quechua, Aymara or another Peruvian language.[24] A new administrative organisation,

COPROCI (Comisión de promoción cinematográfica/Commission for Cinema Promotion), was established to take responsibility for the bureaucracy and decision-making associated with the new legislation. This government-appointed body had the specific task of granting guaranteed screening rights for approved works. As well as nationality, COPROCI based these all-important decisions on the potentially subjective criteria of artistic or educational value.[25] While their proclaimed aim was to ensure a high degree of objectivity in the certification of Peruvian films, elaborate explanations for controversial decisions were often required. The inevitable subjectivity of any classifying body, especially one that for a long time did not include a representative from the filmmaking community itself, would become the focus of much debate, and ultimately contributed to a loss of confidence in a system that was until 1986 regulated by civil servants unfamiliar with even the basics of cinematic production.[26]

Randal Johnson argues that 'outside of the United States, direct government support of national film industries is the rule rather than the exception'.[27] Protectionist measures in various forms have been a common feature of many so-called 'infant' film industries in Latin America, the general aim of which has been to encourage and boost a field threatened by foreign competition, enabling it to achieve economies of scale before moving to more independent models of operation.[28] However, despite all its supposed benefits, the first Peruvian Cinema Law 19327 gradually lost its claim to legitimacy amongst filmmakers, exhibitors and viewers, the very people it was set up to serve. Directors ceased to trust the decisions made regarding guaranteed screenings, and protest groups challenged the perceived rigid bureaucracy of COPROCI. Exhibitors refused to show many of the poor-quality shorts which came their way, and in any case were simply unable to find slots in which to show them all. Bedoya notes that, at the same time, they were tempted by lucrative offers from the distributors of US blockbusters, who strictly forbade any financial return to the maker of an accompanying locally made short. Meanwhile, audiences grew tired of low-quality domestic fare that simply reminded them of the harshness of their own lives, and most provincial and suburban cinemas, where the appeal of locally made movies had been greatest, went out of business during the 1980s and early '90s, when the country's economic and political crisis was at its worst.[29] Cinema-going in Peru, as elsewhere during this period, became a means to escape as opposed to a means to protest. Moreover, Shining Path violence led to the imposition of curfews and other restrictions on movement, regular power cuts interrupted almost every screening, and with hyperinflation ticket prices spiralled out of the reach of most people.

Neoliberal Reforms of the 1990s

In 1992, the protective legislative framework of Cinema Law 19327 was suspended, and by the end of 1994 the neoliberal regime of President Alberto Fujimori (1990–2000) had introduced a more market-oriented cinema law that forced Peruvian filmmakers to compete directly with their overseas counterparts without the kind of resources and political support that they had previously enjoyed. In the event, by the time the new Cinema Law 26270 was in place, plans for US-financed and US-programmed multiplex cinemas in affluent areas of Lima were under way, audience demographics had shifted almost entirely to the middle and upper classes, and national filmmaking had all but ground to a halt.

A series of new measures was put in place to underpin national cinema in Peru. A new body, CONACINE (Consejo nacional de cinematografía/ National Cinema Council), based within the Ministry of Education, was set up to replace COPROCI as the main administrative body charged with administering national film policy. Duties included the organisation of competitions that would determine the recipients of the annual prize money of 1.5 million US dollars promised by Fujimori. According to the legislation, two competitions for feature proposals and four for short films already made would be held annually. In all, 6 feature projects and 48 shorts were to receive a financial reward from the state each year, and in this way it was hoped that constant film production would be assured. This 'competition' funding model was based loosely on similar experiments set up in Europe and elsewhere in Latin America during the 1980s and '90s.[30] Other ambitious plans included a programme of cinema education, the organisation of film archives and the co-ordination of a national cinema register.

The key objective of the new legislation as compared with its predecessor was that national cinema henceforth should be regarded principally as an important national cultural activity, and secondarily as an industrial activity and overt signifier of the country's progress towards modernisation. The basic premise of the approved law was recognition of the cultural role played by filmmaking and the duty of the state to support and promote it.[31] In the new Constitution of 1993, Fujimori even proclaimed that one of the state's responsibilities was 'to develop and preserve culture with the aim of affirming the cultural identity of the nation, without seeking economic return'.[32] Nevertheless, despite such fine words of support, no more than half a dozen feature films and around 30 shorts were awarded funding between 1994 and 2000, partly because of the government's consistent failure to make available the promised resources, partly because the Ministry of Education required them more urgently for basic education programmes and partly because the necessary matched funds were almost impossible to locate, especially for short films. Moreover, when compared with the annual sum of $40 million promised to Argentinian filmmakers in 1995, the $1.5 million promised by Fujimori in 1994 seemed woefully inadequate.

The outspoken national filmmaker Armando Robles Godoy was emphatic in his criticism of the new system. In a newspaper article he protested at what he perceived to be state indifference towards its national cinema, claiming that lack of financial commitment would lead to its complete abolition, a death throe that began in 1992, with the actions of the Ministry of Finance and what he saw as its sterile dogma of market-oriented policy.[33] In the same article, producer Andrés Malatesta continued in a similar vein, protesting that national cinema was crucial to national identity. He, like several others at the time, pressed for a return to the 'clear quotas and guaranteed exhibition ... [of] the 1972 Cinema Law' in spite of its acknowledged deficiencies.[34]

Despite much fanfare and excitement at the announcement of fresh legislation and economic investment, delays in administration resulted in four barren years for domestic film production.[35] In the end, the majority of the resources promised by the state for this law to be upheld were allocated to more urgent social programmes, with the result that between

1998 and 2001 just 10 Peruvian feature films were released and only five of those received partial funding from the state.[36] Since the 1994 Cinema Law 26270 stated that up to six feature film projects a year could be awarded funding from 1996, up to 36 projects could have been supported by the end of 2001. Hundreds of applications were in fact submitted by hopeful filmmakers. However, CONACINE was given little money to award and administer, and Fujimori's regime collapsed suddenly in 2000 amidst dramatic discoveries of widespread institutional and individual corruption. Without adequate resources, the quality of many projects continued to decline and most of the films that were released failed to engage the interest of the Peruvian public.

Cinema After Fujimori: Impact of Political Turmoil

After Fujimori's abrupt departure from government in 2000 amidst allegations of widespread corruption and abuses of power, the political turmoil and need for broad economic restructuring meant that plans for improved legislation to support national cinema were put on hold. However, as in earlier times of crisis, Peruvian filmmakers continued to make their case and to fight for funds and support to develop what they believe to be an important means of expression of national identity and cultural diversity. Nevertheless, from year to year the situation fluctuated. For example, Isaac León Frías reported in his annual review of film activity that some recognition had been made of the need to support national filmmakers more actively:

> The Peruvian Film Congress stressed the need for a new legal framework to support production within the liberal economic model ... and film-makers [had] begun to put pressure on the new government of President Alejandro Toledo to do more for their industry.[37]

One year later, however, he reported that, yet again:

> The long-awaited new film legislation ... remained in a kind of limbo, while Peruvian legislators [were] preoccupied with more pressing social concerns ... that ma[d]e the plight of the

film industry seem trivial, and ma[d]e it virtually impossible for CONACINE to improve the situation.[38]

Notwithstanding, in the late 1990s, a new generation of filmmakers emerged in Peru, amongst them Fabrizio Aguilar, Alvarao Velarde, Adrián Saba, Palito Ortega Matute, Josué Méndez, Claudia Llosa, Salvador del Solar, Enid Campos and Rosario García-Montero, whose methods of working are in some ways distinguished from those of their predecessors through their more transnational and multimedia approaches. Several of them benefited from education and training opportunities overseas, and most have also gained experience within the domestic television, advertising, music and theatre sectors. They have turned increasingly to sources of funding beyond the national institutional framework, such as awards and grants initiatives from festivals with policies of supporting new filmmakers from around the world, and transatlantic projects such as Ibermedia, which draw together and co-ordinate the distribution of resources from Spain and Latin American countries.[39] As a result, Peruvian film production has gained considerable momentum, with a few titles, including those discussed in Chapters 4 and 5, gaining international recognition via the festival and box office circuits.

All the same, the situation remains precarious for Peruvian cinema as national legislation and state support vie with other social priorities, and competition for external resources becomes increasingly fierce. A principal objective must be to determine the role filmmakers play in a world where, on the one hand, national boundaries are constantly eroded by the pressures of the global marketplace, but where, on the other hand, the desire to belong to a national community and to take part in the shaping of national identity remains strong. Moreover, as Ann Marie Stock has acknowledged, 'despite the multicultural collaboration driving filmmaking in the [Latin American] region, critical discourse continues to privilege cultural authenticity' and production infrastructure tends to exclude those films that ignore the demand to be clearly distinguishable on a national level.[40] Viewed historically within the Peruvian context, we can see that under Velasco's regime in the 1970s, filmmakers were granted a clear, if somewhat functional, nation-building role within the national political agenda, acknowledged via a protectionist legislative system and flexible financial support. Under Fujimori throughout the 1990s, this shifted to the promise of a broader cultural role with competition-based funding support and a more independent administrative body. In the event, however, filmmakers ended up isolated during this period, and the administrative body set up to support them was left underfunded and overstretched.[41] The result was that Peru's filmmakers became even more pressed to compete with the Hollywood blockbusters while attempting to portray issues and tell stories of national interest. The fact that locally made cinema is now experiencing a phase of growth, with 30 features covering a range of genres released in 2015, indicates that the role of cinema is no longer simply to be a marker of the nation's commercial and technical maturity, but more profoundly to be a symbol of creativity and freedom of expression. As Robles Godoy has revealed, for him:

> It doesn't matter whether my films are seen or not by thousands of people …; the only thing I want is to have the freedom to create cinema and I believe that all those who do the same – whether to make money or to express themselves – should have the right to do so.[42]

Despite the difficulties and pressures, many of the films that have been made by Peru's filmmakers since the late 1980s, when the protective Cinema Law of 1972 began to flounder, have continued to use the art of film to challenge the political status quo and draw awareness to issues of cultural diversity. They confront their spectators with ways of thinking about Peruvian culture and identity that sometimes contradict official political discourse, and act as reminders of the divisions that are prevalent within Peruvian society, refusing to offer cinematic illusions of unity. Indeed, while it is not the aim of this project to cover every feature film made in Peru since the release of *La boca del lobo*, those discussed are linked not only by the stories of their production contexts, but also by their references to a specific period of violent conflict that highlighted the racial and ethnic tensions between Peru's different social groups, and that tore apart any pretence of national cohesion. They serve as an antagonistic reminder of a deeply traumatic conflict, challenging the 'relatively coherent and stable structure of memories' upon which the exercise of national power is reliant.[43] Echoing Higson, I argue that rather than working to 'construct imaginary bonds which ... hold the peoples of a nation together as a community', they threaten to expose the lack of such bonds in a nation where so many feel themselves excluded from opportunities, resources and political agency.[44] They refuse to fulfil the early role of national cinema (in Peru as elsewhere) as nation-builder by, as Jarvie suggests, contributing to the socialisation of 'newly emancipated populations away from radicalism and towards acceptance of the *mores*, outlook and continuing hegemony of the governing and cultural elites'.[45] Instead, these films reveal the nation's 'masquerade of unity' and draw attention to the deep-rooted cultural fragmentation.[46] As such, they work against 'the underlying principles of nationalism and [act] at cross-purposes with the originating idea of the nation as a unified identity'.[47] In sum, the analyses that follow should demonstrate the extent to which individual feature films have the capacity to provoke debate amongst audiences, industry and policy-makers alike, and shed light on the way that national and transnational developments of socio-economic and political scope might affect the reception of such films.

2

Cinema, Transition and Turmoil

This chapter focuses on three Peruvian feature films made between 1988 and 1991, during an important period of political transition and turmoil: *La boca del lobo/The Lion's Den* (Francisco Lombardi, 1988), *Ni con dios ni con el diablo/Neither with God nor the Devil* (Nilo Pereira del Mar, 1990) and *Alias la gringa/AKA 'La gringa'* (Alberto Durant, 1991). The analyses of these works and reference to the few others that achieved public release during this period set them in their political and cultural contexts, and highlight their shared concerns with themes of identity and violence. Some of the key features of Peruvian identity, including issues of diversity and differentiation, are explored further through these analyses, which suggest that violence is framed and presented via these landmark fiction films as apparently integral to imagined notions of the Peruvian nation.

During this period, Peruvian society experienced an acute economic crisis, including intense hyperinflation, which resulted largely from the chaotic administration of President Alan García's regime (1985–1990) and the heightening of the campaign of violence by the guerrilla group Shining Path. Increasingly frequent insurgent attacks on the capital city made it impossible for the political and social elite of the nation to ignore a conflict that until then had been acted out mainly in rural parts of the country.

García's term ended in 1990 and a surprise election triumph followed for the previously unknown academic turned politician from a Japanese migrant family, Alberto Fujimori, who defeated author Mario Vargas Llosa, the favourite of the ruling classes. Fujimori's appeal was based in large part on his political independence and on the strident promises he made to reform the government, defeat Shining Path and improve the living conditions of the poor majority of Peru.

As for national cinema, the protectionist law established in 1972 by the military nationalist administration of Juan Velasco was still in place, although its flaws had been acknowledged and revisions were underway jointly between the cinema representatives and government policy-makers. In particular, there was growing concern that the 'guaranteed screening' feature of that policy had led to a degree of complacency amongst Peruvian filmmakers and a decline in the quality of films supported by the law, which disappointed audiences and infuriated exhibitors. Moreover, it had become evident that little of the money that was returned to the production companies was being used to develop the infrastructure needed to sustain a serious film industry. From the late 1980s, various groups had collaborated on a new project with the support of García's administration, and hoped that Fujimori would help them bring this plan to fruition.

Inevitably, given the political climate and the tendency of Peruvian filmmakers – in the tradition of Latin American cinema production more broadly – to create work that explored the main issues that affected different sections of society, violence would be a key concern of the few films that were made during this economically difficult period. Deep social rifts based largely on Peru's colonial past had been exposed by the media and state responses to the conflict with Shining Path. Such tensions gave rise to a surge in cultural production, including cinema, that readdressed questions of national identity, acknowledged and interrogated the heterogeneous nature of the Peruvian peoples, and considered the specific place of *mestizaje* within Peruvian culture, emphasising hybrid cultural experiences and the associated relations of power that stem from families with interracial identities.

La boca del lobo was the first Peruvian feature film to highlight the differences between soldiers and villagers, and to consider such differences as important factors motivating much of the violence enacted by the military.

Ni con dios ni con el diablo follows an indigenous protagonist who joins the wave of conflict-induced internal migrants, flees his village and seeks prosperity in the city. His encounters with different social and cultural groups come under scrutiny and it is argued here that the film thus draws attention to some of the more complex elements of Peruvian national identity. On the other hand, *Alias la gringa* presents the accounts of a man who was imprisoned for delinquent behaviour during the time when many Shining Path suspects were being locked up without trial. Like Lombardi's film, it uses a confined setting that is framed as a microcosm of the nation in terms of the range of social types portrayed within it. Through its concern with the capacity of creative activity, in this case writing, as a catalyst for individual and social change, it is suggested by this analysis that Durant's film also considers the broader role and responsibilities of cultural production at a time of deepening national crisis.

Conflicting Identities and National Crisis: *La boca del lobo* (Francisco Lombardi, 1988)

The politically motivated conflict between Shining Path and the Peruvian state resulted in close to 70,000 victims – dead or 'disappeared' – at a time when the country was also in the throes of socio-political and economic collapse. Peru's filmmakers avoided tackling this potentially fertile but sensitive topic of political violence during most of the 1980s, perhaps mindful of the anti-terrorism legislation restricting public debate that might be perceived as arousing sympathy for the Shining Path cause.[1] They may also have been affected by a desire to put a little distance between past and present – between real events and their cultural representation – perhaps to give time for reflection as well as to establish the individual and collective mechanisms required to cope with such trauma.[2] Nevertheless, in 1988, the release of Francisco Lombardi's *La boca del lobo* brought to cinema screens a critical perspective on violence, in the form of a fiction feature film that enjoyed acclaim from domestic and international audiences. This landmark cinematic work explores the emotions and actions of soldiers sent from Lima to fight the insurgents. It draws attention to their encounters with the Andean inhabitants they have come to defend, as well as to the varied responses to the violence they are forced to confront. Indeed, it was the first national film to deal with what one critic noted as 'one of the most serious problems that confronts Peru today'.[3] It thus provided a benchmark for those directors across many different parts of Peru who thereafter offered their own cinematic responses to the worst political conflict and social crisis to affect the nation in decades.

This analysis unravels the approach of Lombardi's film to the representation of physical and psychological conflict, addressing the ways in which it explores the complex relationship between violence and national identity in Peru, including the interconnections between masculinity and institutional violence. In common with his earlier films, *La boca* explores the various effects of fear, claustrophobia and confinement on the collective and individual human psyche, and these universal themes will be discussed with regard to the way they impact upon and interweave with the film's more local and topical concerns.[4] It is likewise important to note that this was the only film made by Lombardi to be located in the Andes. Hence, it is useful to consider how the director utilises the rural landscape to emphasise the gradual subordination of a group of soldiers whose only experience has been of an urban way of life and who assume a certain cultural superiority on their arrival in the village they are sent to defend. As such, the analysis looks at the implied dominance of Lima in terms of defining and framing the image of the nation, and the subordinate position of the Andean region within that image. Finally, it looks at the manner in which the film highlights various aspects of difference between the soldiers and the villagers, and considers these factors as at least part of the motivation for much of the violence portrayed.[5]

Production Contexts

When *La boca del lobo* was released in 1988, the García regime had launched a disastrous economic 'shock' programme that caused misery for Peruvians everywhere, and 'guerrilla violence was escalating throughout the country and the capital'.[6] Pressure was mounting on the government to eradicate the Shining Path 'enemy', but the President was aware of fierce international opposition to the use of excessive military force directed against what the dominant Spanish newspaper *El País* referred to as 'the oppressed classes and cultures' of Peru.[7] In particular, the public outcry after the state-led prison massacres of 1986 (depicted in *Alias la gringa*, discussed later) threatened to undermine government plans to crack down more harshly on the insurgent group. Lombardi himself was undoubtedly aware that any film that dared to tackle the Shining Path conflict without conveying unquestionable support for the military, and hence the state, would risk falling foul of the 1981 anti-terrorism legislation, and would attract criticism from those more interested in promoting sympathy for an increasingly harsh counter-insurgency strategy. On the other hand, those concerned about violations on the part of any government, elected or otherwise, were bound to be frustrated by a film that seemed to offer a form of rationale for such abuses, and which thanked the armed forces for their co-operation in the closing credits.[8] Lombardi gave a large of interviews around the time of the release of *La boca* in late 1988, in which he set out to articulate his intentions and defend his position. The Lima-based current affairs magazine *Debate* published perhaps the most extensive statement given by Lombardi just before the film was released commercially on domestic screens, after a tense period of negotiation with COPROCI – the state institution that administered national cinema activity between 1972 and 1992. In this statement, Lombardi begins by revealing that he wanted to 'reflect and force others to reflect upon the violence that our country has suffered over recent years'.[9] He was, he stressed, eager to prompt discussion on the methods used by all sides in the violent struggle, and to force all Peruvians, especially those living in Lima, to be aware of what was happening to their fellow citizens. He continues thus:

> The film tries to say: this violence which you all want to keep at a safe distance is in reality brutal and terrible. And the people who are suffering this situation the most are made of flesh and blood, like you and me. It wants to make the citizens of the cities appreciate the violence suffered by those in the small mountain villages.[10]

Despite its humanist objectives, there was concern on the part of COPROCI representatives about its ideological impact: that the film might be dangerously effective as pro-Shining Path propaganda due to its apparently critical portrayal of the actions of its military characters. Since censorship did not officially exist in Peru, there were no overt attempts to ban the film, but for the first time in its history COPROCI invited specialist groups, including military representatives, to view it and comment upon it in advance. In fact, as confirmed by one commentator at the time, the film could have been banned for up to 10 years for 'defying the state of emergency' established by the government during the conflict with Shining Path.[11] The Peruvian authorities were particularly concerned that the release of the film would coincide with a groundswell of resistance to the state's harsh counter-insurgency campaign, as well as with a deepening economic crisis that dealt a further blow to public confidence in political leaders. It was the first time that a Peruvian-made feature film had dared to show members of the armed forces, here acting as representatives of the state, in pursuit of and killing apparently innocent civilians.[12] There were protests that it offered criticism of the armed forces at a time when national unity and belief in the power of the state to defeat the enemy were considered crucial, especially as the rebels seemed stronger than ever and attacks had begun on Lima-based targets, including government posts.[13] Furthermore, the authorities would have been aware from press reports that they risked losing the faith of the public in the efficacy of their efforts to combat Shining Path. As Peralta explains in his study of press reporting on the conflict from the end of 1986 until the early 1990s, at the time of this film's release, 'discourse was turning steadily towards the possibility that this group might take power'.[14]

Nevertheless, although military chiefs were undoubtedly uncomfortable with what they saw depicted in *La boca del lobo*, they were at the same time reluctant to prevent the screening of this latest work by Peru's most famous director at a time when the battle for public support was critical, and when yet another restriction might have proved counter-productive. Furthermore, it was the first of Lombardi's films to be co-produced and financed by a Spanish partner, Televisión Española (TVE), in an arrangement that guaranteed that the production would attract considerable press attention, both domestically and internationally. The film was finally approved for release but only with a classification equivalent to the UK '18' certificate, which in Peru is usually reserved for pornographic works. This angered Lombardi, who was keen for his film to be seen by the widest possible audience, especially by young people, whom he felt should be at the centre of any debate on violence and collective responsibilities.[15] In the end, the film was one of his most successful in terms of ongoing critical acclaim, and is considered by many to be the highlight of a remarkably consistent career.[16]

Framing Nation and Violence

The film opens with a prologue sequence that follows a young shepherdess as she leads her animals through a desolated village square laden with signs of death and destruction. The text that precedes these poignant images establishes the quite specific time and place of the action as being early 1983, at the beginning of the 'dirty war' between the military and insurgents, in a village in the Peruvian sierra.[17] The narrative then begins by positioning the audience so as to follow the drama from the point of view of its young military protagonist, Vitín Luna (Toño Vega). It thus privileges his voice-over and his gaze out onto the unfamiliar terrain to which he has been sent, and highlights its difference and subordinated status from the outset. Luna is presented at first as an idealistic cadet who is keen to advance his military career: inspired by the apparently glorious career and reputation of an esteemed uncle, a high-ranking and decorated military officer, he has requested a transfer which has led to his arrival in the fictional Andean village of Chuspi. The surrounding area has been officially declared a newly 'liberated' zone following successful military intervention, but the newly formed regiment soon discover that the threat of Shining Path prevails and that the villagers are further threatened by this fresh intrusion.

Luna and his comrades have evidently arrived in a dangerous place, but although they are advised by their superiors to remain on the lookout for signs of insurgent attack, they fail at first to take the warning seriously due in part to the invisibility of the supposed enemy. The newly formed and largely inexperienced regiment is under the command of Lieutenant

Basulto (Antero Sánchez), who believes they must confront the enemy with aggression but at the same time retain their integrity and humanity. His democratic leadership style upsets and confuses some of the younger men, who had expected a more decisive approach. Shortly after arriving, however, Basulto is brutally murdered and his body is mutilated by Shining Path rebels while on his way to deliver a villager suspected of terrorism to the nearest town. Basulto is replaced by Lieutenant Roca (Gustavo Bueno), a more authoritarian leader who insists on absolute discipline and obedience from all his men, whatever their private feelings or views, and insists on support from the villagers. Roca redefines the regiment's response to the terrorist threat, invoking the primitive hostility of the soldiers towards an unknown enemy, which results in a widening of the cultural gap between them and the villagers by drawing on racist sentiment borne out of ignorance, frustration and fear (as seen in Plate 3).[18]

The rape of a local woman by one of the younger soldiers, and the chaos created by an unofficial raid on a wedding party, provoke an intensely frustrated Roca to order a massacre of civilians in what appears to be a last-ditch attempt to reassert his authority and to restore some sense of order and dominance. Luna is both disgusted and disappointed by this officer's brutal conduct and refuses to shoot the villagers. He is taken prisoner, and then challenges the sneering Roca to a life-or-death game of Russian roulette. Luna feels he has nothing left to lose and deliberately forces the lieutenant to relive a similar moment from his past, the traumatic memory of which he has struggled to repress and had earlier revealed to the younger man. In the end, neither soldier is killed, but the experience changes their relationship irrevocably. In the final scene, Luna abandons his post and disappears into the mountains, watched by the shepherdess from the prologue sequence.

Having viewed and discussed the film before making a decision about its commercial release, the military finally insisted only upon a slight modification to the text that is placed over the images of the prologue sequence. Hence, Lombardi was forced to remove his preferred opening title, 'Masacre en Soccos', which referred explicitly to the real attack by the military on the Andean village of Soccos in 1983, during which about 40 people – mostly innocent civilians, including women and children – were executed, without trial, on apparent suspicion of collaboration with the 'enemy'. The rest of the text remains unchanged, informing its audience that the drama is set in 1983, by which time the central Andean region of the nation had already suffered three years of violent repression. The text is fairly lengthy, mindful no doubt of the responsibility to inform its audience in a balanced way of the key details of a complex conflict. It relates the main developments that led to the beginning of the so-called 'dirty war', when the military became actively involved in putting an end to the groundswell of insurgency that at first was largely dismissed by President Fernando Belaúnde Terry's regime (1980–1985) as the mindless acts of delinquents. As well as implicitly referring to the failure of the state to protect its citizens, the text explicitly points out that 'terrorist attacks on rural communities and police posts ... had become everyday occurrences', thus confirming the film's central message that Shining Path was the main perpetrator at this stage.

However benign it might appear, by agreeing to remove those three words that refer specifically to the real tragedy suffered by the village of Soccos, Lombardi conferred upon his film a broader metaphorical dimension that is suggestive of the brutality faced by many such communities located in remote rural areas of Peru. Rather than simply reconstruct the specific events leading up to one act of slaughter and its consequences, the film instead confronts the general terrorist phenomenon of Shining Path. It draws attention to the great pressure on the armed forces to bring the escalating violence across the central sierra to a swift end.[19] In the event, it seems that such pressure led to what Manrique describes as a 'merciless campaign of repression'.[20] This was characterised by a desire to 'isolate Shining Path by demonstrating that the army could exert even greater terror than the guerrillas', thus drawing on North American doctrines of counter-insurgency that were readily absorbed by key Peruvian military personnel during training.[21] As a result, more inhabitants of the Sierra were killed by both sides during 1983 and 1984 than at any other stage of the conflict as the military's strategy was based on an indiscriminate use of terror that for a while was difficult to distinguish from Shining Path tactics.[22]

Although *La boca*, Lombardi's sixth feature, was intended as a fictional account, it does refer implicitly to a specific historical episode (the slaughter at Soccos) and states explicitly that it is based on what the director considered to be 'true' events of the conflict (that is, the abuse and indiscriminate killing of innocent villagers by military forces as part of a semi-official counter-insurgency strategy), which goes some way to prevent audiences from dismissing out of hand the brutal scenes depicted as mere products of the director's imagination or political bias. The film therefore confronts spectators with the disturbing possibility that the state and its armed forces might find it necessary to attack its own citizens. It thus refuses to let them ignore, or wilfully forget, the possible violations committed by the military, on behalf of the state, in their determination to overcome the terrorist threat.[23] Since the film's release, extensive research conducted throughout the 1990s has confirmed that 'the lack of direct civilian control or formal oversight mechanisms … produced massive human rights violations'.[24]

The release of *La boca* coincided with a renewed period of violation, including disappearances of suspected Shining Path sympathisers (knows as *senderistas*) and apparently indiscriminate executions of local community leaders (referred to as *comuneros*).[25] The general approach and sympathies of the film also chime with what Hortensia Muñoz describes as a 'turning point in sensibilities' regarding such occurrences.[26] She suggests that the testimonies of survivors revealed the perverse and impossible situation within which the villagers were placed, caught in the crossfire between army and Shining Path. Indeed, the community portrayed in *La boca* had clearly already suffered at the brutal hands of the insurgents, as highlighted by images of bodies and graffiti shown in the prologue sequence, as well as by the fear of those villagers who survived – the traces of trauma are already marked upon them. The subsequent narrative depiction of rape and slaughter of villagers by the soldiers sent to defend them thus emphasises the director's own desire to express particular concern with officially sanctioned acts of violence. Moreover, critics such as Bedoya acknowledged that the film should be interpreted at least in part as a 'denunciation of the policies adopted by the government and an indictment of the inhumanity that resulted from the "dirty war" between Sendero Luminoso and the Peruvian Army'.[27]

However, the tension between the topical and the perennial, the thematic and the dramatic aspects of the film, confused and disappointed some critics who expected the film to deal more directly and explicitly with specific contemporary events. For example, filmmaker and commentator José Carlos Huayhuaca observed that:

> on one hand (the 'thematic'), everything seems to be centred around the historical focus made up by the slaughter of the civilian population of Soccos, and, on the other hand (the 'dramatic'), the centre gradually moves towards the relationship between the two main characters whose end is the sequence of the duel playing the Russian roulette game – through which the importance of such an event (the slaughter of some innocent people as part of the dynamic of the 'dirty war') becomes relative and the real topic of the film is finally the old motive pursued by Lombardi since his first films: the turn from a friendship based on admiration (of masculine values) to a breakdown when these are revealed as false and deceptive.[28]

Nevertheless, there were many who applauded the interweaving of specific socio-political references with broader concerns and who considered this combination to be the real strength of the film. For example, Chilean critics Cavallo and Martínez stated that, for them, the specific historical context by which the film's diegesis is framed contributes to its sense of 'tragic universality', and argue that while without reference to the Shining Path conflict the film would have been admirable, 'with it, it becomes exceptional'.[29] Without doubt, the approach to representation of conflict and its relationship with issues of masculine and national identity seem to have provoked as much debate amongst critics as amongst politicians and military officials. It is pertinent therefore to take a closer look at some of the main features that continue to give rise to such discussion.

The Peruvian state is represented in microcosm within the film by the small detachment of soldiers. Such an implicit yet strongly felt connection suggests a desire on the part of the director to emphasise the perceived continuing dominance of the military within the democratically elected regime of Belaúnde, and perhaps also, though less overtly, of García. In doing so, he also highlights the dominance of a patriarchal structure and a certain type of macho identity that dominates many images of the Peruvian nation. The detachment that is depicted has been sent out from Lima (the centre) to one of the most remote parts of the Andean sierra (the periphery), where the soldiers arrogantly expect to assume control with ease, an attitude that is suggestive of the dominance of the capital in perceptions of the nation-state and as the centre of law and order. The influence of the state is further reinforced by intermittent radio conversations conducted by officers with the nearest base, which consist mainly of orders from outside on how to behave. The chain of command is thus clearly established as being directed from the nation's symbolic centre, albeit one that remains visually absent throughout.

Despite their bravado, it is clear that the soldiers are bewildered to find themselves defending such unfamiliar terrain, with its apparently hostile inhabitants. Exchanges between the men reveal that the village is supposed to have been 'liberated' and cleared of terrorists, but the threat of Shining Path is present in every scene. Cinematically, this impression is conveyed by the sombre musical composition that underscores the atmosphere of tension, by the tight composition of each frame that gradually acts to lock its characters in, and by focus within the *mise-en-scène* on evidence of the aftermath of terrorist intrusion. The identity of Shining Path attackers remains a mystery, and the level of collaboration with the insurgents by the villagers remains unclear.[30] Shining Path, as actor Gustavo Bueno, who plays Roca, has attested, 'is present in the film but in a ghostly way'.[31] Meanwhile, all radio requests for additional supplies and backup, or even to leave the post, are denied, and the regiment is largely abandoned in a quest that becomes one of survival rather than protection or attack. The men are shown shivering in the cold as they guard the garrison by night, and maintaining morale by dancing, drinking and recalling more comfortable times in Lima. In this way, the film neatly guides its spectators to an appreciation of the extreme situation faced by the soldiers, several of whom are fresh out of basic military training.

Nevertheless, while invoking sympathy for the regiment, the film is equally careful to provoke debate about the soldiers' varied responses to the fear they face and the paranoia they feel. For example, the eagerness of the young recruits to submit the first suspected terrorist they catch to torture is rebuked by Basulto, who represents a humane approach to law and order that is portrayed as commendable yet ineffective in this context and which ultimately leads to his own death. They openly condemn his apparent weakness and indecision, failing to understand that Basulto stopped the questioning because the suspect seemed not to understand Spanish. Subsequent scenes reveal ongoing military abuse of villagers, including rape, robbery and racist verbal insults, but they also suggest that the men who perpetrate such brutal acts are in some ways themselves the victims of neglect by the military authorities who have abandoned them. It seems we are invited to reflect upon the intense frustration felt by each of the men when confronted by an enemy that refuses to reveal itself and whose actions seem to carry no logical explanation that would enable them to pursue a considered line of attack. Basulto's killing may be the pivotal act of apparently unjustified violence that triggers a determination to take revenge and that lays the groundwork for an initial acceptance of Roca's less humane attitude by the men. However, it also seems reasonable to suggest that the men have been pushed to the very edge of (self-)destruction by the fear that is intensified by abandonment. Moreover, the film seems also to pursue the line of thought proposed by Freud, that 'the inclination to aggression is an original, self-subsisting instinctual disposition in man [which] constitutes the greatest impediment to civilisation', with its emphasis on the absence of civilised behaviours throughout.[32]

While the action remains hermetic, and the principal actors few, it might be considered that the conflict against Shining Path and its impact on the national image are presented here in microcosm. On a broad level, the depiction for example of internal conflict of opinion regarding how to respond to the insurgency is suggestive of the lack of political and military consensus throughout much of the 1980s, which in turn 'reflected deep conflicts among differing state elites over the role of the state in society and even the nature of Peruvian society itself'.[33] However, the film's dramatic approach focuses as much on complex character development as on the authenticity of the socio-political context, and the set of conflicts that develop within and between the male characters is arguably one of the film's main points of interest. Many of the film's most intense scenes set out to demonstrate the fragile emotional and psychological state of its protagonists, locked in a situation 'exacerbated by fear, loneliness, cultural difference and the irrational threat of an invisible enemy'.[34] Much of the controversy regarding portrayal of the military may stem from the number of different character types representing different attitudes towards conflict and violence within the military itself, as well as throughout the nation at large.

The Characterisation of Violence

Lieutenant Roca, for example, is the flawed father figure, a charismatic but fanatical leader of men. He is a ruthless, authoritarian and morally questionable leader, whose actions draw attention to the less humane approach taken by the military to the enemy and to those innocents caught in the crossfire. Alberto Flores Galindo, in his study of the development of violence in Peru, described how several senior military officers were openly prepared to deploy any means necessary to defeat subversion, even if that led to high death rates of innocent people. He cites a spokesman of the more conservative faction of the armed forces who revealed that, in their view, any human collateral damage was unfortunate but sometimes inevitable.[35] Roca's status as official state representative is further reinforced by images of him saluting the national flag and leading the singing of the national anthem, seen framed by a long shot remote from the crowd and almost engulfed by the church building that itself forms an oppressive centrepiece to the village. It should be noted, however, that his position with regard to the nation-state is complicated by his confession to Luna that he was demoted for unjustified violence against a comrade during a previous mission and had requested a transfer to Chuspi so as to prove his worth. Thus, instead of acting as an honourable upholder of state values and defence, it seems that he set himself a more individualistic goal that leads to his total isolation. It could also be suggested that Roca's seniors, aware of his excessively violent instinct, decided to deploy him as their killing machine with the single aim of enforcing their brutal policy of counter-subversion.

Luna's so-called friend, Quique Gallardo (José Tejado), is portrayed as similar in temperament and purpose. He too has a history of bad conduct in the army, lacks discipline but constantly seeks Luna's approval. His ignorant, racist attitude towards the villagers, in particular his objectification, harassment and subsequent rape of Julia (Berta Pagaza), betrays a deeply felt fear of the apparently inferior and abject Andean (especially female) 'other' on the part of an immature, middle-class young man from Lima, and a desire to overcome this fear by destroying its cause. He has little sense of where to draw the line ethically; he believes he has the right to take food from the community, to run up debts to satisfy his drinking habit and to invite himself to a private wedding party. He relies on alcohol to ward off the cold and fear, which in turn makes his behaviour more aggressive and irrational. He is unwilling to admit to his wrong-doing and expects to be able to act with impunity. Such an attitude ominously echoes that held by many fearful, inexperienced and angry young soldiers who perpetrated abuses during the 'dirty war' and expressed no regret for so doing. Gallardo is representative therefore of those officers who seemed to believe that their military status alone placed them beyond reproach and that their 'uniform seems to place them beyond the reach of judicial order'.[36] Moreover, Gallardo seems to feel he is justified in attacking Julia, 'authorized by an ideology of [patriarchal] supremacy'.[37] His assumed position of dominance based on a specific approach to gender extends also to racial hierarchy. This is most clearly seen in his disdainful and ignorant attitude towards the villagers, his eagerness to torture individuals suspected of *senderista* activity, and his ability to rationalise the slaughter of innocents by accepting and repeating militaristic discourse on the need to wipe out the enemy using all necessary means. For him, absolute violence is the only way to achieve this and hence to rid the nation of fear. He has no concern for the subsequent threat posed to democratic values nor for the protection of civil liberties at a time of grave danger for national stability. This view, shared by many in Peru at the time of the film's release and since, is called into question by the development of Gallardo as an increasingly unstable character. This perspective is further compounded by comparison with Luna, whose own instinct for aggression is held in check by an emerging sense of morality that is profoundly affected by the events he witnesses, and by Luna's eventual rejection of Gallardo altogether.

Apart from Luna, Sergeant Moncado (Gilberto Torres) is the only soldier depicted who attempts to challenge Roca's brutal methods, albeit with little real force and without success. His protests are dismissed and he appears powerless to prevent the atrocities, eventually choosing to remain silent instead, like those who chose to turn a blind eye to crimes against innocent civilians. Roca seems to recognise Moncado's weakened instinct for aggression, as well as his reluctance to report any wrong-doing, and dismisses him as passively emasculated. Moncado's different approach further emphasises the film's critical message about the connection between a macho form of masculinity, patriarchal authority and violence that dominates the image of the nation. Moncado is not chosen to participate in the shooting of villagers, so is not actively involved in the killing, but nor does he seem willing to speak out to his superiors. He appears disillusioned by the apparent abandonment of the regiment by the state and frustrated by the lack of an alternative solution; he has also seen the unfortunate result of Basulto's more benign strategy. As Bedoya points out, the sight of Basulto's body undermines the regiment's faith in rational and lawful methods of conflict resolution, and leads soldiers like Moncado to accept, albeit grudgingly, values pertaining to aggressive authority.[38] Moreover, experience would perhaps lead him to surmise that the appointment of a leader of such dubious temperament and reputation would signal the covert intention of the armed forces to step up their campaign of brutal violence at any cost.

Until the killing of Basulto and the arrival of Roca, the soldiers are portrayed as a unified group, diverse in appearance and ethnic background (for example, one is of Chinese descent, another Afro-Peruvian), but unified by their shared experience of life in Lima, which contrasts so greatly with the harsh conditions of the Andes. Drawing on Gellner's definition of national identity, they share the same culture and they '*recognise* each other as belonging to the same nation'.[39] In the scene that occurs just before the discovery of Basulto's body, the soldiers gather together to sing, dance and reminisce about the food, music, landscape and everyday rituals of life in the capital. Through this sense of shared understanding and mutual opposition to an unfamiliar rural culture, a strong bond is formed that serves to reinforce the gulf between them and the Andean villagers. As such, the film highlights the impossibility of a nation somehow imagined by all Peruvians and emphasises the dominance of the capital in its efforts to construct, or to impose, a sense of nationhood that fails to acknowledge the different cultures, backgrounds and experiences of its citizens. As such, it is an example of a national cinema that seemed, increasingly, to 'problematise a nation – by exposing its masquerade of unity'.[40]

After Basulto's killing, the differences within the group and between its members become clearer as each man reacts differently to the all-encompassing fear of attack and death, and the bonds between them begin to unravel. Some find comfort and stability by continuing to obey orders blindly, others hesitate or question but then submit to authority, while only one character, Luna, openly refuses to participate in the barbaric slaughter of innocent villagers ordered by Roca. His failure to shoot could be considered a passive reaction, an unplanned response of disgust, as opposed to a decisive action that he knows will endanger him greatly. Roca would not have been sure of Luna's defiance had he not insisted that Luna fire the final shot alone. Nevertheless, this is the point of no return for a young man who has been forced to grow up fast in the harshest of conditions.

If considered as a kind of fictional testimony of his military experience, it is possible to see how the film traces Luna's 'submission to the loyalties of an insular community and strictly organized life, through to his disenchantment with the system'.[41] He begins as a committed soldier, determined to help wipe out the rebels, and identifies the apparently self-disciplined Roca as a role model, catching up with him on his morning run and revealing his ambition to be a great military man. A multi-faceted character with many flaws, Luna undergoes a journey of self-discovery. His initial blind confidence in the institution is complicated by his experience in the field, and his shock at the killing of comrades marks a turning point in his attitude towards the mission – from viewing it as a potentially glorious opportunity for career development to realisation of the danger they all face as well as the excessive actions they are required to carry out. At first it seems that he will, like Moncado, remain silent about the abuse committed by his comrades as he fails to speak out to confirm and condemn the rape committed by Gallardo. Nevertheless, the revelation that the man he thought he knew well and whom he considered to be a flawed though decent friend might be capable of perpetrating violence without remorse comes as a great shock. Amongst other things, it confronts Luna with the possibility that he and his comrades are no less capable of terrible behaviour than the terrorists they are hunting down.

Spectatorial identification with Luna as a more humane character is encouraged by depicting him idealistically as the only soldier who attempts to make an emotional connection with members of the local community. Indeed, it has been reported that, in reality, troops failed 'to create a rapport with the local population … finding it almost impossible to distinguish between *senderistas* and *non-senderistas*, they therefore treated all with equal suspicion'.[42] Luna thus stands out, for example, by showing sympathy for Julia's plight and disgust at Gallardo's treatment of her. Although he fails to speak out to support her, he later tries to make amends by appealing to Roca not to harm the villagers he has locked up after the raid on the wedding party. It is perhaps also significant that Luna is not involved in the second interrogation scene in the film, in which torture methods of an increasingly brutal nature are encouraged by Lieutenant Roca. A further sign of the tentative beginnings of a mutual bond of kinship comes when the villager who has acted as the regiment's mountain guide begs Luna personally to save them, as if he recognises that this young man differs from his comrades in his attitude towards the community. In the end, Luna seems bitterly disappointed with himself for failing to defend and protect those who have shown kindness towards him at various points, but even this demonstrates his willingness not to regard the village as one homogeneous enemy. Moreover, by presenting the evolution of its key protagonist towards humanity and kindness, the film draws attention to a desire for the differences within rural indigenous communities to be understood. Luna's more liberal attitude in a context of war is appreciated as more complex, perhaps bewildering and even dangerous, but his sensitivity towards others regardless of their background is offered as an admirable quality.

The emphasis on Luna's experience as crucial to the film's overall message is further emphasised by the manner in which Roca, already depicted as crazed, hysterical and out of control, chooses to regard Luna's decision not to shoot as a sign of weakness and impotence – as a crisis of masculinity. This emphasises again the questioning of a hard, brutal, violent form of masculinity as the only way forward. Luna's ability to commit to the struggle is questioned, and hence also his identity as macho soldier. He is imprisoned as a traitor, and the physical confinement he endures is aggravated by a growing realisation that his disgust at the escalating brutality marginalises him from the rest of the group. The others may not appreciate Roca's inclination for excessive violence, but they can see no alternative, whereas Luna reasons that such a solution is unjustified whatever the circumstances. The slaughter of the community hence triggers a different but no less important episode of conflict between the two main protagonists, the culmination of what Bedoya describes as a battle between:

> A conscience in a state of becoming – caught between fidelity to his personal beliefs and complying with the authoritarian requirements of the institution – the symbolic paternal order.[43]

It may also represent a battle between different types of masculine identity, and thus by extension a questioning of their relationship with violence and the dominant national image. By challenging Roca to Russian roulette, Luna forces his superior to relive the traumatic event that triggered the psychological breakdown that he has tried to repress by consignment to oblivion. Sneered at by his comrades for his apparent weakness, Luna thereby tries to take control of the situation and reassert a different kind of moral and emotional authority. In so doing, he performs his own act of rebellion against the system of patriarchy, represented by Roca, which he had admired but which has failed and oppressed him. The Russian roulette game thus serves as a dramatic device that draws the two men to a similar level, by forcing each of them to confront their own mortality at the same time and within the same space. By leading the challenge with determination, Luna proves to himself and to his comrades that he is capable of facing up to his fears. In contrast, close-ups of Roca's face and hands reveal a trembling vulnerability beneath the surface of the tough image he prefers to project that is fundamental to his sense of self. As the 'game' progresses, Luna draws attention to his lack of respect for his lieutenant by addressing Roca using the informal 'tú' form, and ensures that the whole regiment observes the spectacle of Roca's degradation. While the former thus reasserts his macho masculinity before the group, the latter suffers a loss of self in the most humiliating way. In order to triumph, Luna needs to resort to the tactics of violence, but then rewrites the rules by walking away.

Luna's character is suggestive of a generation of young men in Lima who committed themselves enthusiastically to the counter-insurgency campaign, but who ended up as reluctant perpetrators of acts of extreme violence themselves and murderers of thousands of apparently innocent people.[44] His bold decision to refute the orders of the authorities, and to distance himself from the rest of the group, is what makes him remarkable and hence a perfect protagonist. Meanwhile, the representation of Roca's behaviour as excessive and irrational might be interpreted as a critical comment on the state's increasingly desperate response to spiralling insurgent attacks. After all, the main test for the existence and survival of a nation is based upon 'the ability of the state to impose order and monopolize violence within established boundaries'.[45] The film's overall message of anti-violence is confirmed when Luna does not kill Roca, despite the pressure to do so. By refusing to kill another human being for the second time in the film, the young man is seen to reject violence altogether as a solution to conflict.

One of Lombardi's stated aims with this film was to make Peruvians living in Lima aware of what was happening in the more remote parts of their own country, in keeping with the ideology of *indigenismo* that developed in Peru between 1930 and the 1950s.[46] The village depicted is caught between two forces of violence, and as a result of the extreme tactics of each, is barely able to distinguish which is the enemy and which the protector. As far as the villagers depicted can see, the army uses violent methods of repression (torture, abuse and apparently random executions) that replicate those of the terrorists. Moreover, the apparent inability of the soldiers to defend even themselves from attack, as well as their aggressive and disrespectful attitude towards the villagers, prevents the development of any degree of trust.

Attention is drawn to this notion of cultural difference and lack of mutual recognition from the opening scenes, when Luna is instructed to raise the Peruvian flag and is watched by huddled groups of apparently uncomprehending villagers. There are no cries of patriotic jubilation in honour of the regime, and no warm welcome for the soldiers who represent it. The problem of lack of national unity as part of the overall conflict is hence signalled by the film from the outset, as the remote community depicted fails to recognise one of the 'conventional symbols of particularity' of the Peruvian nation.[47] Luna is confused by the apparent defiance of the villagers, as shown by their resentful gaze upon the flag and by their refusal to sing the national anthem when that flag is raised for the second time.

Instead of appreciating that the anthem itself would seem irrelevant – and perhaps linguistically incomprehensible – to a community that, since independence from Spain, has been largely excluded from participation in the development of a unified and single sense of national identity, the soldiers interpret the behaviour of the villagers as anti-state hostility.[48] Only Luna comes to realise that there might be other reasons for the villagers' silence that have more to do with centuries of fear, suffering and oppression inflicted by outsiders, of which these soldiers from Lima might be perceived as the latest. The decision taken by Lombardi to focus attention on the protagonists' growing awareness of and respect for cultural differences would seem to confirm that the film is committed to exploring the enormous divide between Peruvians of different social and ethnic backgrounds as depicted between those familiar with life in Lima and those whose with experience of life only in the sierra.

Even before the audience is introduced to Luna and despite the contextual titles, the prologue establishes the film's intended sympathies with the Andean community in a powerful visual sense. It opens with a long tracking shot that follows a young shepherdess leading her flock through the empty village and culminates with a poignant close-up of her face. As she passes the church, she stops to look at the corpses piled up in the village square. She then gazes directly at the camera, before walking on. In the closing scene, the same young woman gazes at Luna as he flees. In both instances, her facial expression is ambiguous. The young soldier pauses and seems to want to speak to her, to explain, to justify his actions, to apologise even for what has happened to her community, but leaves without uttering a word, unable to communicate and rationalise what he has been part of. The enigmatic character of the shepherdess may be read as broadly symbolic of the few Andean survivors of the 'dirty war' who would eventually – 12 years later – get the opportunity to testify about the brutality they witnessed, but who at this point have no recourse to justice. By contrast, Luna's inability to articulate his experiences in the final scene perhaps helps indirectly to confirm and explain some of the ugly complexities of the conflict. His lack of words here points to the apparent difficulty of communication and understanding between the different communities of Peru, drawing further critical attention to the divisions and differences that mark Peruvian national identity.

As a director, Lombardi tends to develop his stories by placing an ensemble of characters within a confined and bordered physical space that, given the broad symbolic nature of his films, could be read as suggestive of national borders. This approach then allows for the development of tense dramas that explore the psychological impact of the given environment on human behaviour.[49] *La boca del lobo* emphasises the way in which the actual ambiguity of borders and uninhabited spaces can add to the impression of fear. The film is broadly located in the expansive setting of the Andean mountains, and the regiment's lack of familiarity with the sierra landscape, which seems to hold so many secrets and to offer so many hiding places for the enemy, intensifies their fear and plays on deep-rooted anxieties about the potential threat of the unknown 'other'. In fact, the film is situated in an ambiguous no-man's land, where Peruvian army meets Shining Path guerrilla control. The soldiers assume that the area has already been cleared of terrorists before they arrive, but they soon discover that the village is under siege and that the emergency zone has become a liminal space where traditional rules of engagement do not apply and where the boundaries of moral standards have likewise become blurred. At first, the soldiers do little more than gaze fearfully at the ominous mountain terrain, hardly daring to venture beyond the edge of the village. Later on, Roca makes it a priority to reclaim physical and psychological dominance of the terrain and to restore confidence by taking his men out on training exercises across the sierra, penetrating deep into what was perceived to represent the imperious heartland of the enemy. As such, the struggle against confinement and entrapment becomes an 'essential condition of the action'.[50]

By portraying the sierra as a battleground, the director goes against the more lyrical and romantic stereotypical view of the Andes. As one critic noted, the film 'portrays the mountainous territory without falling into the trap of exoticism; on the contrary, it is used to generate a climate of tension, abandonment and desolation within which characters and conflict evolve'.[51] Rather than offering an idyllic and mystical impression of the sierra, reminiscent of many more sentimental portrayals of indigenous life as peaceful and harmonious, it is presented here as hostile and menacing, a place of death and destruction.[52] Instead of freedom and space, the mountains evoke restriction and oppression, and the soldiers are shown as virtually paralysed by the almost palpable impression that the invisible beast of terror is roaming close by, and by the impossibility of discovering the landscape for themselves. While Shining Path remains invisible, its 'otherness' is constantly reflected in the physical surroundings and, as such, the mountains come to represent the terrorist enemy itself.

The film's dramatic tension is shaped by the tight framing of every image, by the desolate sounds of high winds and by the sombre musical composition. Most of the on-screen action takes place in the remote village the soldiers have been sent to defend, with its small indoor spaces and narrow, winding streets. Hesitant travelling shots and slow pans are suggestive of a nervous surveillance gaze from the point of view of the soldiers, who cannot be sure where the danger resides. As they patrol the village armed with machine guns, close-up shots of their frightened eyes reveal a fear of what might lurk round the corner. Night and day are made to look equally threatening, with the harsh Andean light of dawn and dusk being manipulated so as to benefit from menacing shadows formed at either end of the day. The intense blue sky locks in further the characters and action, contributing to the multi-layered effect of confinement and the apparent impossibility of escape. This in turn adds to the atmosphere of overwhelming claustrophobia that serves to heighten the frustrations and fears of the soldiers, and to accentuate divisions between them and the community. Doors of village houses remain closed and the local wedding proceeds in an enclosed high-walled garden, serving to infuriate and alienate the soldiers even further.

This developing atmosphere of imprisonment, isolation and paralysis is emphasised in several key moments of the film's narrative: for example, when Roca arrives by helicopter to assume leadership of the garrison he is dropped as if from nowhere and appears with no further backup or supplies. Before that, Luna literally stops in his tracks when he sets out for his first early-morning run and spots that the national flag he had raised over the garrison the day before has been replaced by one bearing the Shining

Path symbol. He goes no further than the opposite side of the square before turning back. Unable to leave, the soldiers are forced to conclude that the new flag was raised by guerrillas who slipped in during the night from a hiding place close by, and thus they are confronted with the probability that the village borders are porous to the Shining Path threat.

Luna does finally leave the village, despite his acute awareness of the dangers he will probably encounter beyond its boundaries. In contrast to the upbeat images of the group's arrival by truck via the main road, with protective armour and supplies, the film's closing images show him ripping off his uniform, and running out of the village along a winding track. He pauses as he encounters the young shepherdess before continuing his journey. He then disappears into the same wilderness that, for the soldiers, shelters the enemy they hoped to destroy. He renounces his position as a member of the armed forces and defender of the state, and faces an uncertain future as a deserter. He also renounces violence as part of his personal identity and more broadly as integral to the image of the nation.

Rejecting Violence

La boca del lobo functions effectively on a number of different but interrelated levels: as a political indictment of contemporary events in Peru and the national image connected with violence and machismo; as a critical observation of the tense relations between members of the armed forces and the inhabitants of remote Andean communities; and as a psychological drama which explores the reactions of a group of men 'confronted with themselves, at the edge of death'.[53] Through the portrayal of increasingly brutal encounters between soldiers and villagers, it reveals deep-rooted racism based on ignorance and intolerance towards people who live within the same country but who do not recognise each other as sharing the same national identity. It was also the first national film to invite debate on the methods a democratic state might use to defend itself from threats such as those posed by Shining Path. When released in 1988, the concept and indeed practice of democracy in Peru was still in its infancy and the García regime struggled to retain control over the military. There remained little opportunity for participation in public life by those other than the social elite, most of whom were based in the capital city. The film implies not only that indigenous communities remained isolated from a collective concept of the Peruvian nation, but also that cultural diversity was viewed as a threat to coherence and stability, rather than as a cause for national pride.

La boca gives expression not only to horrific acts of violence, including rape, torture, mutilation and slaughter of soldiers by guerrillas as well as of villagers by soldiers, but also to the psychological effects of fear and violence on a group of men sent by the state to defend national territory at all costs from a nebulous enemy that remained impossible to locate and identify. Indeed, the impact of such brutality affected their sense of self as well as their place within the nation. Made at a time when the García regime was struggling to contain the Shining Path threat and was under increasing pressure to pursue more brutal counter-insurgency methods, the film's overriding message is one of condemnation of the pointless use of violence at any cost. Although the film was criticised by some in Peru for presenting a negative view of the military and the director was accused of displaying pro-*senderista* sympathies, it seems more useful to consider the film as a statement against the futility of violence as a means of reinscribing nationhood, and as recognition of the problems of a society in crisis. While the film offers a complex insight into the dilemma facing a small regiment under extreme pressure, particular sympathy is reserved for the indigenous community, which becomes the victim of abuse at the hands of both terrorists and the military forces.[54]

Actor Gustavo Bueno explained on the film's release that for him 'one of the messages of this film is to make us realise that these military actions will not destroy Shining Path – there has to be a different way'.[55] *La boca del lobo* is a film that promotes the values and achievement of social justice, equality of opportunity, and national stability without bloody attacks and abuses of basic human rights. The director and his screenwriters professed concern to reveal 'the essence of violence in Peru and how it seems to continue to disturb our daily existence'.[56] The film offers no specific solutions to the conflict, but in trying to understand the root causes it succeeded in drawing attention to it on a national and international scale.

Moreover, while the film draws its inspiration from topical material events, its core dramatic interest remains, as Bedoya suggests, 'the repercussions of a violent event on the conscience of one young man'.[57] Protagonist Luna rejects Roca's strategy of victory by any means. Having been locked up for disobedience, he leaves because otherwise he risks being incarcerated (or worse) for treason; his military career is over. (See Plate 4) More significantly, he is perhaps also terrified of what kind of person he might become if he were to remain with the regiment and submit to Roca's aggressive rule. It is a pessimistic ending in so far as the film seems to suggest both that there is no place in the military for the will of the individual, and that the instinct for aggression is an inevitable aspect of human behaviour that one must constantly struggle to contain. Lombardi presents a joyless world, one where the individual is forced to succumb to the institution.[58] The manner of Luna's departure, watched by the orphan shepherdess, signals a loss of faith in the institution he had cherished and – more broadly – in the state (as represented here by the military), which is portrayed as abandoning the marginalised communities.

Despite the restrictions placed on its release and the growing reluctance of exhibitors to show national films anyway, *La boca del lobo* was a great success and remains a landmark film for Peru. It raises questions about the military response to the Shining Path conflict, and presents a provocative portrayal of a highly fractured Peruvian nation. It attracted international acclaim and notoriety even before its release in Peru, and became the focus of much discussion in the domestic mass media. Indeed, this was the first time that Peruvians had been able to watch a feature fiction film based on the Shining Path conflict, which was still raging throughout their country. Its reflective, critical approach provided an opportunity for public debate about issues that affected Peruvians in remote areas on a daily basis. Lombardi was criticised by more radical viewers for having created an entertaining work of classical cinema that rejected the more overtly political aesthetics and philosophies of his Third Cinema predecessors. Nevertheless, he was applauded by most for having carefully interwoven topical and local themes with the perennial and the global. The act of making and screening this film while the civil war was ongoing was described by one critic as an 'act of civic courage': Lombardi rejected pressure from the authorities to delay the screening until a 'more convenient moment', and secured screening of it at the renowned and influential Havana Film Festival, where it won numerous prizes and international recognition.[59] Shortly afterwards, the film was cleared for screening on domestic screens and this polemical fiction about contemporary Peruvian reality and identity was placed at the very heart of public debate.

The Hybridisation of National Identity: *Ni con dios ni con el diablo* (Nilo Pereira del Mar, 1990)

Ni con dios ni con el diablo was the first Peruvian feature film after Lombardi's landmark *La boca del lobo* (1988) to deal explicitly with issues raised by the political conflict between Shining Path revolutionaries and the Peruvian state. It was also the first in Peruvian film history to offer direct representation of the rebel group on the cinema screen. In contrast to Lombardi's portrayal, which alludes to the constant presence of the attackers but leaves them as an invisible threat sheltered by the Andean mountains, and perhaps therefore partly a response to that production, Pereira del Mar's debut fiction film gives a face to the insurgents. It depicts them barking orders and preaching ideology at their new recruits, and carrying out attacks on urban and rural targets. Like *La boca del lobo* to a certain extent, the central concern here is with the portrayal of the experience and perspective of one individual and his interactions with the different groups and environments with which he comes into contact. The analysis examines the extent to which *Ni con dios* draws attention to the conflicting elements of Peruvian national identity and offers a vision of a fragmented nation in crisis, revealing some of the seemingly unassailable rifts between the diverse social and ethnic communities in Peru. It also considers the impact of political conflict in forcing social changes with complex consequences during this important transitional phase in Peru's recent history. In particular, the film's depiction of the specifically topical social phenomenon of human migration from rural periphery to urban centre is explored in relation to intra-cultural conflicts based on ethnic, racial and class divisions that arose during a traumatic episode of political violence and which are emphasised in the publicity poster for the film. (See Plate 5)

Production Contexts

As already noted in the discussion of Peruvian national identity in the introductory chapter, several writers have remarked upon the increasingly hybrid and heterogeneous nature of Peruvian culture since the end of the Spanish colonial era, with studies focusing mainly on the tension between indigenous and European communities. While problems relating to ethnic and class differences as well as social exclusion clearly remain a key feature of Peruvian society, the movement of communities and individuals into and within the nation have led to a complex system of social exchange in which new and different cultural groups have emerged. For example, the plantations that developed during the nineteenth century encouraged indigenous people to move away from the highlands and brought them into more sustained contact with white Peruvians, leading to the strengthening of a distinct *mestizo* culture in coastal areas. During the first half of the twentieth century, such industries were largely replaced by state administration as the main employer of coastal *mestizos*. This in turn led to the creation of an urban middle class with increased political agency, and a separation between this new social group and the still largely impoverished manual and peasant workers. A wave of economic migration in the 1950s further isolated the Andean and Amazon communities, and saw the development around Lima of enormous shanty towns, whose inhabitants organised themselves politically in their struggle for resources. Meanwhile, a burgeoning informal sector of employment encompassing domestic service and fringe commerce provided further opportunities for interaction between different social groups.

    Lima quickly became the main focus for cultural exchange, a lively meeting point for Peruvians of all ethnic and social backgrounds. *Ni con Dios* foregrounds this feature of the city while showing also how boundaries separating the different social groups remained difficult to transgress. For example, the film shows elite Peruvian households clinging onto their 'European culture as a means to reaffirm what they perceive as their superior "white" racial origins'.[60] *Mestizo* men are depicted labouring on construction sites while *mestizo* women work as housekeepers, serving the dominant *criollo* and gringo cultures. They were anxious to distance themselves from their indigenous roots and to be associated with a more modern, urban and apparently sophisticated way of life, but there appears little possibility of them being treated as equals by their employers. Meanwhile, the protagonist, a newly arrived immigrant from the highlands, is shown struggling to fit into a culture that seems alien and that treats him with added suspicion given the imagined identification of the indigenous culture with Shining Path in the minds of Lima's inhabitants.

Perhaps the most important aspect of Peruvian identity relating to the story presented in this film is that of *choloficación*, the process of 'becoming *cholo*'. *Cholo* is the term used (usually in a derogatory sense) to refer to those who have migrated from the country to the city, who set out to 'whiten' themselves so as to fit in with the dominant culture and wish to eliminate the stigma of difference and inferiority bestowed upon them by others. It refers to the process of cultural transformation from identification as someone of an apparently inferior and barbaric indigenous background, to association with a supposedly more civilised *criollo* social and cultural identity, through the gradual acquisition of the habits and customs shared by the urban majority, usually stemming from the white elite. The term *cholo* does not always define a specific group of people, but is often a relational term, used by one individual or group to deprecate others perceived as inferior or not-quite-*mestizo*. As Wade points out, in Lima, 'terms such as indian and *cholo* were used by some migrants to describe other migrants'; and all migrants would be labelled *cholo* by those outside their circle.[61] Categorisation, with associated meanings, remains an important part of everyday urban life, however fluid the status of the individuals concerned. The main difficulty and indeed danger comes, as seen here with the protagonist's tragedy, when the immigrant remains strongly identified by others, and hence marginalised, in terms of his indigenous heritage. Unable to rely upon the protection of the community that he has left behind, he is also rejected by others in a similar position who have already embarked upon their own journey of personal and cultural transformation.

Framing Nation and Violence

The narrative structure of *Ni con dios ni con el diablo* is divided into two parts, with the first concentrating on the incursion of a Shining Path cell into a highland Andean village. The traumatic consequences of this event for one of the young villagers, Jeremías (Marino León de la Torre), are foreseen in a 'reading' of the coca leaves by the village shaman. Soon after, the insurgent group executes the community leader on trumped-up charges of corruption and Jeremías, because he is known to have had at least a basic education, is nominated as Shining Path's reluctant local representative, along with his friend Ofelia (Ivonne Fraissinnett), as tax collector. When the armed forces arrive, Jeremías is forced to flee, since he is now officially an enemy of the state. He leaves for Lima with the aim of finding his patron (*padrino*), a white North American who once visited the village and promised to look after him. On his long journey to the capital, he is forced to earn money by labouring in the highland mines and for the first time is confronted by examples of modernity and technology – from mechanised transport to capitalist labour divisions and the printing press – that have not yet reached his own remote community.

The second part of the film is signalled by the arrival of Jeremías in Lima and the deceptively upbeat tone of his first encounter with life in the capital. He tracks down his patron, who reluctantly offers him work and shelter on a new building site. Before long, a series of misadventures causes Jeremías to lose both his job and the support of his white protector. Further confusion at the house of a police chief where he next finds employment leads to him being suspected of involvement in a terrorist attack, despite being at a neighbouring house with his girlfriend Victoria (Patricia Cabrera) at the time. As he leaves that house, he is shot by security forces and his dead body is photographed with a gun placed in his hand. This carefully constructed image is used on the front page of newspapers the next day, with headlines celebrating victory over the 'enemy'. The very last image is a freeze-frame on the face of Ofelia as she passes the news stand and the image of Jeremías, failing to notice the image of her deceased friend. Having earlier refused to leave the highlands with Jeremías, she is now dressed in Western-style clothes and walking the streets of Lima. Nothing is shown of her journey into or around the city, but such an ending implies that the problems of urban migration are perpetual and endemic.

Ni con dios ni con el diablo was Pereira del Mar's first feature-length film, after a consistent career as a short filmmaker. His early work benefited from the economic incentives of the 1972 Cinema Law (discussed in Chapter 1). After making this film, he took a leading political role representing national filmmakers as President of the Asociación de Cineastas del Perú/Association of Peruvian Filmmakers. He campaigned for revisions to the Cinema Law that were designed to develop further the infrastructure for a national cinema by building on the strengths and dealing with the flaws of the previous legislation. The failure of that venture and its redirection by the Fujimori regime led to disappointment and anger on the part of the director, sentiments that align with the anti-establishment tone of this feature film. Indeed, the comments he made during a speech delivered in November 1996 on the occasion of the first awards ceremony under the 1994 Cinema Law railed against the perceived restrictions to freedom of expression for Peru's filmmakers. For example, he expressed regret that so few short films, including several international award winners, were granted funding awards by the state, and hoped such decisions were not based on judgement of content rather than on artistic merit alone.[62]

He suspected the government of taking a more sinister role than previously in the development of, or restrictions to, national cinema, and suggested that films illustrating signs of political dissent and social critique continued to be institutionally ignored. His speech sheds some light on the filmmaker's views on the freedoms he believed should underpin a democratic regime, and on the role of national cinema to challenge the political status quo. The following analysis of his film indicates the extent to which Pereira del Mar's known political sympathies inform his portrayal of this particular episode of national transformation.

With *Ni con dios*, Pereira del Mar highlights an issue of direct concern to much of the Peruvian population – that of 'forced migration to Lima by a young man from the mountains who has been displaced as a result of the conflict with Shining Path'.[63] As David Wood explains in his study of the complexities of Peruvian society, although migration from rural communities to urban centres had been under way for most of the second half of the twentieth century, the 1980s witnessed a much higher level of migration as well as a different kind of social movement that affected the entire nation. Whereas migration in the 1950s–1970s had coincided with economic expansion in the coastal cities, with corresponding deprivation in provincial areas of the mountain (*sierra*) and jungle (*selva*), most of those arriving in Lima and other coastal centres in the 1980s were forced to do so for political reasons. Wood summarises that 'they were more like refugees from extreme political violence than migrants: their passage to the city was neither premeditated nor gradual but most often a desperate escape'.[64] It is precisely this category of refugee-migrant that is represented in *Ni con dios* by protagonist Jeremías, who represents a type of Peruvian who would have been familiar to many urban audiences in the 1990s, from images in the national press if not from everyday life. It is the journey taken by this young man from the highlands, and the behaviour towards him of those already living in the capital and thus familiar with urban culture, that provide the main narrative focus and centre of conflict within the film. The film thus conveys a point of view on the problem of urban migration that is largely critical of the state response and blames its lack of foresight and planning rather than the Shining Path conflict for much of the social tension in the capital.

Ni con dios ni con el diablo is set during the early 1980s, at the point when the ferocity of the Shining Path campaign of violence began to present a serious threat to both the Belaúnde regime and to national stability more generally. While the insurgency group's first decisive action took place in May 1980, it was not until December 1982 that Belaúnde declared the highland region of Ayacucho to be an emergency zone and ordered the military to enter it. This decision resulted in a dramatic increase in the death toll, not only of insurgents and the armed forces but also of civilians. Many of the latter fled rural areas to escape from military and Shining Path reprisals, partly to shield young members of families from suspicion by military or recruitment by revolutionaries, as well as to escape the extreme poverty intensified by the conflict.[65] An example of one such Shining Path incursion and military response, depicted in the first part of *Ni con Dios*, forms the motivation for the protagonist's flight from his village. In fact, the period represented by the film's diegesis can be pinpointed more precisely to early 1983. The narrative makes specific reference to TV and newspaper reports of the massacre of eight journalists in Uchuraccay by highlanders whose motives were the subject of much press speculation and public debate. At the time, Peralta notes, such media reporting included heated assertions about the supposed 'primitive reactions' and 'the instinct for collective violence on the part of the indigenous communities', inflaming racist resentment of those of Andean origin.[66] *Ni con dios* offers a challenge to that dominant perception of indigenous peoples as uncivilised and instinctively violent by portraying them instead as innocent victims caught in the crossfire of an increasingly 'dirty war' orchestrated in large part by the state.

The year 1983 also heralded the beginning of violent attacks in the capital city itself, with electricity blackouts and car bomb explosions, both of which are incorporated into the film's plot. Such events ensured that the inhabitants of Lima began to take the Shining Path conflict more seriously and to appreciate the threat it posed to national stability. Moreover, it was during this year that economic austerity measures were introduced, resulting in a GDP drop of 12%, with mass unemployment and the beginning of spiralling inflation that would last a further 10 years. Economic deprivation is presented as a serious concern for some, though by no means all, of the characters in this film. Extreme inequities in wealth distribution are highlighted by contrasting images that emphasise the poverty of the highlanders and the exploitation of the mining community with those that draw attention to the decadence of the wealthy Lima elite.

Ni con dios went into production at the end of the 1980s, a turbulent decade of economic and political crisis, and the film provides a reflection and critique of events that continued to traumatise the nation. Although it appears to look back to a set of particular events, it deals in fact with issues that pertain closely to the time of its making and release. By 1990, the violence affected the entire nation, and Shining Path had shifted its tactics to concentrate more on urban destruction than rural domination. The year 1988 in particular, when this film was in development, marked a turning point for Shining Path, with a shift from a rural to an urban-based revolution with the proclaimed aim of, as Aliaga puts it, speeding up 'destruction of the state and the creation of a new democracy based on the peasants and urban workers'.[67] Attacks became bolder and more visible, with masked protestors attending political meetings to shout down speakers and to incite violence. Bombing attacks in Lima became a major feature of Shining Path's psychological war aimed at demoralising the population.[68] Meanwhile, the military continued to respond with such force that human rights groups such as Amnesty International observed that Peru had the highest number of forced 'disappearances' of any nation between 1987 and 1989.[69] Despite the consideration given to human rights and developmental issues during the first two years of the García regime, by 1987 the government's main strategy had returned to repression. By 1990, political violence was endemic and the country was in total chaos.[70] Dominant media outlets, including *El Comercio*, *Radioprogramas* and *24 Horas*, encouraged readers, listeners and viewers to support the military in its battle to eradicate the insurgents, who seemed bent on destroying the infrastructure of the Peruvian nation.[71] The more brutal actions of the government's 'dirty war' strategy were not officially revealed to the Peruvian public until 20 years later, in the report from the Commission of Truth and Reconciliation (2003). Even then, many continued to believe that such a harsh response had been a necessary step in the face of an overwhelming threat to law, order and national stability. The portrayal of conflict in *Ni con Dios* offered to the Peruvian public in 1990 would thus have set itself at odds with the hegemonic discourse advanced to tackle a political conflict that seemed to have spiralled out of control. Moreover, it illustrates the more antagonistic role played by national cinema at times of crisis in drawing attention to issues of difference and opposing injustice.

Pereira del Mar makes it clear to his audience where his own political sympathies lie: he positions the spectator to experience the film from the point of view of his young protagonist, a young man from the country who has been 'forced to flee the capital, a victim of abuse from all sides'.[72] Although Jeremías is instructed to become the local Shining Path representative after the execution of the village elder, it is clearly a role he has no desire to fulfil, and which leads to his subsequent tragic position as a target for both Shining Path and the military forces, and as a traitor to both causes. By assuming this role against his will, he also becomes broadly representative of the thousands of young people from the highlands who were caught in the crossfire between revolutionary fervour and military counter-insurgency. Youngsters aged 14 or 15 were the primary targets for recruitment to the Shining Path cause, since they were considered less likely to be tainted by life experience and more susceptible to the Mao-Marxist ideology and idealism of the revolutionary group. Moreover, an increasing awareness of their exclusion from the dominant Lima-centric Peruvian identity made them particularly vulnerable to the alternative offered by Shining Path. Nevertheless, Jeremías never actually makes the transition to Shining Path sympathiser, let alone armed recruit, since his sights are set on finding wealth in Lima and entering the capitalist system that Shining Path so despises. Unlike his cousin who becomes passionately inspired by the insurgent campaign, Jeremías feels no self-sacrificial commitment to the Shining Path cause. His ambitions lie not in helping to create a radically new social structure, but in leaving the harsh subsistence life of the village behind. His childhood encounter with a kindly rich gringo has convinced him that other solutions are possible.

Jeremías is in fact portrayed as an outsider in every social context. In his village, he is more interested in reading and fantasising about Lima than in tending his sheep, and like many teenagers is unable to appreciate fully the potential value and complexity of his community's way of life. Later, he fails to fulfil his Shining Path responsibilities and rejects the solution for change offered by the revolutionary group. He lacks the strength and skills to work effectively in the mines and is bewildered by the communication technology, organised labour and authoritarian oppression he finds there. (See Plate 6)

Once in Lima, he is treated with some impatience by his patron, whose priorities have clearly shifted from the social idealism of his own youth to more capitalist commercial interests, and who appears irritated by Jeremías's lack of understanding of social and cultural difference. On the building site, older colleagues mock his accent and skin colour, even though several of them clearly share a similar ethnic background. Having lived longer in Lima, however, they have learnt to assimilate and adapt to the dominant culture, as well as the perceived merits of distancing themselves from the newcomer from the highlands, whose very presence serves to remind them of an identity with which they no longer wish to be associated. Several may indeed be second- or third-generation migrants to the city, in which case their identity is likely to be even more closely aligned with the culture of urban *criollismo* than with their indigenous roots.

The final section of the film completes the social marginalisation of the protagonist. When he enters the household of the police chief to begin work in domestic service, Jeremías is utterly bewildered by the alien nature of elite Peruvian culture. The costume of white tuxedo and gloves he is forced to wear restricts his movement and emphasises the darkness of his skin, thus highlighting his position as inferior, a dangerous 'other', and providing, as James Snead argues, 'blatant linkage of the idea of the black with that of the monster'.[73] His confusion with the gadgets and household implements he is expected to use further illustrates his estrangement from modern life. Moreover, his lack of awareness of social boundaries triggers suspicion in the mind of the police chief, who is concerned to find that Jeremías has answered the private telephone in his office and has thus had access to papers relating to the counter-insurgency campaign. When the boy's name is discovered subsequently on a list of traitors, hysteria breaks out as the police chief and his wife believe they have allowed the enemy to enter their home. Jeremías's tragic fate as scapegoat is sealed when the car bomb explodes moments later.

The bewilderment felt by Jeremías at every situation he encounters emphasises his daily struggle to negotiate survival in this new urban environment, and the extent to which he feels alienated from modern life. The 'othering' of Jeremías by all of the characters he meets marks him out as inferior, even from the other indigenous men and women working as house servants in Lima. Like the building labourers, they also look down on him for lacking the skills and know-how that stand for modernity and civilisation and for having failed to come to terms with the dominant white culture. They distance themselves from him for fear of being reminded of their own position as subjects of economic deprivation, social injustice, exploitation and abuse, and of being marked out as Shining Path suspects. As Sarah Radcliffe has noted, 'the indian migrant from the highlands of Peru who becomes a domestic maid in Lima is on her way to becoming a *mestizo* woman, but her background is not forgotten'.[74] Any wilful distortion of ethnic affiliation, in the name of integration, assimilation or a new cultural identity, is not made easier by constant reminders of origin and inferiority in the form of new migrants such as Jeremías. The shift away from a culture associated by the dominant elite with savagery, towards a *mestizo* identity that marks progression up the social hierarchy and a blurring of ethnic difference, might be socially, economically and politically desirable, but is likely also to be slow, traumatic and fraught with difficulty.[75] *Ni con Dios* mourns the erasure of social boundaries and the loss of distinct indigenous cultures. It points out that a hybrid *mestizo* identity conceals somewhat the differences of origins and thus holds the potential to create the illusion of a new sense of social unity. Hence, it is perceived as less threatening than one that has come to be associated with terrorism, poverty and social exclusion.

The two social groups that pose the greatest physical threat to Jeremías, the security forces and the Shining Path cell, are represented largely as monolithic entities in ways that reinforce sympathy for the protagonist. The military, for example, is shown only as a homogeneous violent force, entering the highland village and assassinating or 'disappearing' all those suspected of sympathising with the enemy. In contrast to Lombardi's *La boca del lobo*, nothing is shown of the different ways in which the soldiers might have interacted with the community, and their abusive behaviour is more overtly portrayed as part of a general military strategy rather than as the errant actions of a few renegade individuals. Likewise, little differentiation is depicted within the Shining Path cell, and the rebels are also represented as ruthless perpetrators of violence who make no effort to forge a relationship with the villagers. Neither group shows any regard for the cultural practices of the indigenous people; both are determined to impose their own solution for social change without considering the impact upon others. Audience sympathy for the plight of those unsuspecting villagers caught in the crossfire is thus activated through representation of both the military and Shining Path as brutal, inhuman agents of violence.

The Peruvian state is further represented in the film by a political leader and a police chief, briefly shown in heated debate about how best to tackle the violence that has begun to make its presence felt in the capital city. Behind the politician, a portrait of independence fighter Simón Bolívar (*El Libertador*) is caught in the background as an indirect reference to the birth of the independent Peruvian nation-state in 1821 – a much-debated turning point for Peruvian identity, when violent confrontation and unfulfilled promises reinforced rather than eradicated many of the divisions and inequalities in a society that had developed during the colonial era.[76] This visual cue offers further evidence of the director's desire to challenge the state's ambivalent attitude towards Peruvians of Andean ethnic origin. The memory of the freeing of the nation from colonial rule is ironically undermined by the way the film draws attention to the numerous everyday restrictions, exclusions and inequalities that exist for many contemporary Peruvian citizens, and the strong ethnic and class-based hierarchies that remain in place.

The state's position is undermined more forcefully via a sustained and critical portrayal of the head of the elite security force responsible both for controlling law and order within the capital and for overseeing the general counter-insurgency strategy. He is thus shown to be leader of an institution that is struggling to contain and overcome the Shining Path threat and fearful of losing public support. He is also a member of the wealthy coastal elite, and the depiction offered of his household, with clear demarcation between owners and servants, reinforces the stereotype of this social group. As Radcliffe also outlined, the incorporation into the household of an indigenous migrant 'in a subordinate position in terms of class, ethnic, and gender ranking entails the systematic denial of peasant ethnic identity and the substitution of middle-class norms of the mestizo nation.'[77] He is quick to suspect Jeremías, a newly arrived dark-skinned boy who is behaving strangely in his house, as a member of Shining Path. It is at this point that Jeremías is understood as an unfortunate outsider who has no sense of how to protect himself in the urban jungle of Lima. During his short time in the city, Jeremías has become the victim of beatings, verbal abuse, unfair dismissal and false accusations of robbery. As far as the police chief is concerned, however, Jeremías is the perpetrator of violent crime. From the point of view of the dominant culture, the boy's obvious social, racial and ethnic difference mark him out as barbaric other who represents a threat to Lima-based constructs of the Peruvian nation.

The Shining Path cell that infiltrates and 'liberates' the highland village from which Jeremías flees is depicted as focused, determined and fearless. The female leader of the group is shown setting out the Shining Path message calmly and clearly. She articulates the group's vision of an alternative society that prioritises a collective way of life that promises indigenous communities a greater role in public debate, and offers them greater visibility in the political life of the nation. Her sense of control serves as a counterpoint to the more hysterical behaviour of the chief of the security forces. Moreover, her leadership of the rebel group draws attention to the important role played by women in the revolutionary conflict, an aspect that is explored in greater depth in Marianne Eyde's *La vida es una sola* (1993).[78] *Ni con Dios* begins with the incursion of Shining Path members into the village and their disruption of life there. The Shining Path vision was imposed as the only possible solution to social inequality, and wiping the slate clean was considered the first necessary step regardless of the trauma involved.[79] They root out the community leader, accuse him of collaboration with the capitalist enemy and stage a mock trial, during which villagers are forced to vote for his execution. Such a scene draws attention to the Shining Path strategy of destroying existing organisational structures and imposing new leaders selected by the party.

The visibility of the Shining Path rebels decreases during the second part of the film, but their impact on characters and narrative events remains strong. For example, after Jeremías's arrival in Lima, the narrative cuts on several occasions to brief sequences that show the Shining Path cell in pursuit of their traitor that serve to reinforce the protagonist's position as a helpless victim and object of oppression from all sides. Even though Jeremías has fled from the village, abandoning his position as Shining Path-appointed community leader, he is unable to break free from his forced affiliation with the terrorist group and it is this that leads to his tragic death. In the final section, an example of Shining Path's urban campaign is shown, thus emphasising a strategy which aimed 'to identify key figures, assist, co-opt, intimidate or kill them'.[80] In this instance, the attack involves blowing up the police chief's house while other 'key figures' from the security forces are gathered there, and when Jeremías's presence puts him in the frame as the key suspect. Portrayal of the rebel group serves on the whole to emphasise the status of the protagonist as a victim, to provide narrative motivation for his flight from the highlands, and to reinforce the debate about the relationship between individual desire and collective responsibility.

Many of the issues pertaining to social and cultural identity and difference discussed above are reinforced by the film's creative use of space and place. In the first instance, the physical journey taken by Jeremías offers spectators the chance to explore visually some of the diverse geographical locations inhabited by Peruvians and to consider the ways in which space and culture interrelate. Moreover, the various modes of transport taken by Jeremías as he makes his way to Lima link each space and draw attention to the way in which different cultures interact and overlap. The movement between rural and urban spaces, between traditional and modern cultures, is shown mostly in the direction of the capital city as Jeremías makes his way to Lima. Nevertheless, portrayal of the incursions by the army and the Shining Path cell into the highland space suggest that everyday life in the remote Andes experienced considerable interruption and interference during the conflict.

Ni con Dios opens with a classic establishing shot of the empty and barren Andean landscape, with its snow-topped mountains and seemingly unpopulated highlands. The hostility of the terrain is reinforced by a diegetic soundtrack of whistling high winds. A group of indigenous villagers comes into view, slowly taking one of their dead to be buried amongst the rocks. As these villagers pay homage to their mountain deities, reference is thus made to the distinct belief system and language of the Andean people, as again in the scene when the village elder solemnly takes a 'reading' of the coca leaves. The perceived failure of the Peruvian state to look after all its people is suggested by such images of intense deprivation in the Andean community and, later on, by more images of the hardship and exploitation faced by those working in the mines. The spectator is thus encouraged at an early stage to sympathise with the plight of the indigenous and lower social classes of Peru, especially when contrasted with the consumerism, technology and waste of urban spaces, symbols of modernity that have yet to make their mark on remote highland communities such as the one shown here.

The initial section of the film indicates that the highland villagers are totally unprepared for their traumatic impending fate at the hands of the rebels. They are offered no protection from the state and the prediction by the village elder of dangerous times ahead provides little comfort. On the other hand, the close relationship between the villagers and the natural world suggests that the ancient traditions, which are an essential feature of such communities, might offer alternative strategies to deal with the contemporary situation. Rather than domination and control of the savage 'other', the Andean approach to nature is portrayed as one that emphasises respect and co-operation in the hope of receiving guidance and protection in return. However, young Jeremías is slow to comprehend the deeper significance of the rituals and, while he does not absolutely reject the beliefs and practices of his elders, he clearly has dreams of a different way of life in Lima. As in most communities, attitudes differ from one generation to another, and such tensions are exploited by the Shining Path cell, depicted in their mission to recruit disillusioned young villagers.

The image of the village elder reading the ominous prediction from coca leaves recurs at key moments during Jeremías's journey to the capital city. These flashbacks act as a reminder both of his origins and of the reason for his urgent need to flee from the village. They suggest that the way of life he left behind remains integral to his identity and that he might draw upon the knowledge, skills and beliefs he acquired there in his struggle to survive in Lima. Part of his failure to adapt to urban culture appears to result from his inability to understand how the traditional and the modern might interact and integrate productively, and might offer him tactics to negotiate his path through the minefield of cultural encounters he faces. Instead, he rejects the culture with which is he familiar and heads towards another without appreciating the challenges of assimilation and integration.

As Jeremías enters the city, the screen fills with colour and the upbeat music suggests that his fortunes are about to take a turn for the better. For him, the metropolis is associated with excitement, comfort and wealth as a result of the fantasies triggered by his childhood encounter with his patron. However, images of him dressed in peasant clothing and overwhelmed in the frame by oppressive colonial buildings emphasise his disenfranchisement from a colonialised cultural heritage that impregnates life at all levels in Lima. The composition of the *mise-en-scène* that emphasises the protagonist's alienation from his surroundings signals fundamental differences and inequalities between rural and urban culture. It also indicates conflicting ideas of Peruvian history and national identity that work along problematic binaries that separate highland/rural and coastal/urban dwellers, however differentiated and unstable each of these geographically defined groups might actually be. The notion that such communities might 'imagine' themselves belonging to one nation, as Benedict Anderson suggests, is called into question by images that draw attention to Jeremías's struggle to find a place for himself in Lima.[81]

Ella Shohat and Robert Stam, in their study of 'Eurocentrism' in the media, discuss how land and space are represented in films of the classic Western genre in such a way as to reflect and reinforce divisions between indigenous and European Americans. For example, they draw attention to the following important distinction:

> For most Native American cultures, land is not real estate for sale but is sacred both as historically consecrated and as the 'mother' that gives (and needs) nurture.... For the European, on the other hand, the land was a soulless conglomeration of exploitable resources, and the Indians a wandering horde without a sense of property, law, or government.[82]

Similarly, *Ni con Dios* highlights differences between the indigenous and the European approach to land. It evokes nostalgia for the Andean way of life, and mourns what is presented as the gradual eradication of traditional practices and belief systems that promote productive engagement with the sierra. For example, the opening burial ceremony and sacrificial offerings emphasise the 'reverent attitude towards the landscape' adopted by traditional indigenous communities.[83] By contrast, later scenes on the building site in Lima portend a desire for control, transformation and commodification of land on the part of the North American property developer. Meanwhile, the protagonist's lack of engagement with the natural world, despite his work as shepherd, and his dreams of a different way of life suggest a shift in priorities amongst the younger generation that potentially destabilises perceptions of the hitherto enduring nature of indigenous traditions.

The binary structure that is tentatively suggested by the way that space and place are initially presented is further disrupted by the portrayal of Lima as a city replete with cultural and social difference. Distinct districts have developed particular identities in terms of the socio-economic and ethnic status of their inhabitants, some of which are shown directly as Jeremías travels around the city discovering that he is unwelcome in most of those spaces. When, for example, he arrives at the gringo's luxurious house in a wealthy part of Lima, his initial excitement is tempered by the sight of impenetrable high gates and fences, and the suspicion of the maid who greets him. This time he is able to transgress the physical and the symbolic barriers and is invited to enter the living quarters of the white man. To her great irritation, the maid is ordered to serve the boy with food and drink. She is insulted at being required to serve someone of a lower social and cultural status to herself, thus illustrating the hierarchical structure that prioritises both whiteness and Western notions of urban progress. The meal with the gringo ends with Jeremías being quickly made aware of his inferiority and rejected from that milieu. He is forced to work and sleep amongst the rubble of the building site, where expensive new houses are being constructed for the elite of Lima, who have been fortunate in benefiting from international investment and co-operation. When he does eat with others, it is in a dingy, poorly lit bar located in a run-down area of the city where the electricity blackouts caused by Shining Path have little impact on the lives of those with very limited resources.

The most explicit episode of cultural conflict takes place when Jeremías enters the house of the police chief. He is expected to dress in restrictive formal waiter's attire and to use a range of basic domestic appliances. That he is unfamiliar with all of them is perhaps exaggerated, but his ignorance and confusion serve to emphasise the film's critique of the inequalities embedded within Peruvian society. Each new space bewilders the protagonist and upsets his sense of self more and more, while his failure to adapt and to assimilate puts him in a position of danger. In the end, he is gunned down while alone in the street on which the police chief's house has just been attacked. The still image of his body, cropped for use by the press, further isolates him, and denies him any cultural context or connection with his surroundings. This image also 'double-frames' him, reinforcing and complicating his position as 'othered' object of the gaze.[84] The implication is that he will be viewed as a dangerous, savage 'other' by the film's fictional newspaper reader who is fearful of another Shining Path attack, but with sympathy by the film's omniscient spectator, who is aware of the tragedy of Jeremías's fate.

Resisting Change

When *Ni con dios* was released on a commercial domestic basis, it was screened at nine cinemas in Lima. Judging by the lack of material to be found on that film within the meticulously kept archives of the National Film Archive, and the single review offered by Bedoya's authoritative and comprehensive study on Peruvian cinema, Pereira del Mar's first attempt at feature filmmaking went largely ignored by the national press.[85] Even Bedoya paid scant attention to the film's efforts to offer critical comment on some of the social consequences of the nation's worst political conflict since the Wars of Independence. It is worth considering, therefore, some of the compelling socio-economic, political and aesthetic reasons for this apparent indifference towards a national film, during a year when only four others were produced.

The year of the film's release, 1990, marked the start of a new decade that held little sign of change from a state of seemingly perpetual national crisis. The conflict with Shining Path was the most obvious manifestation of this crisis, and the one highlighted in *Ni con Dios*, but other aspects included spiralling inflation, severe economic austerity measures and high unemployment. The consequences of mass migration from rural to urban areas represented by the tragic story of the film's protagonist were keenly felt in the capital city and were in fact the cause of further conflict as previously disparate groups were forced to confront each other in their daily lives. The date also coincided with a national election campaign, which the population hoped would bring a new leader who would alleviate the crisis and offer the chance of a better future for all. It was perhaps too soon for the domestic spectator to be expected to appreciate a film about the consequences of a political conflict that was ongoing, the physical and psychological effects of which were still keenly felt.

A further set of problems for the film's reception lay in the largely monolithic portrayal of both Shining Path and the state, as well as in the film's clear nostalgia for an indigenous rural identity that not only reminded urban *criollos* of their disenfranchised origins, but which was also associated in the popular conscience with terrorism. Moreover, despite acknowledging diversity, in fact it reduces social groups to a limited set of reified stereotypes. Amongst these is the portrayal of the protagonist himself as an innocent and tragic victim of oppressive forces and circumstances beyond his control rather than as a hero who actively chooses to confront the 'enemy' – whether Shining Path or military – and to sacrifice himself in the face of evil. In addition, Jeremías is more interested in pursuing his own goal of self-improvement than in putting his life on the line for the sake of a remote collective cause. Identification with him by national spectators at the time would have been further complicated by his position as a pitiful disenfranchised, emasculated, poorly educated and unskilled young man who struggles to find a role in Peruvian society. Although he undertakes an arduous physical journey, there is no sign that he has any appreciation of the need to embark on a much more profound psychological journey, finding a place within the liminal ethnic and cultural identity of *mestizaje*, if he is to survive and achieve his goals.

Despite the indifference shown towards this film by national critics, audiences and institutions, *Ni con Dios ni con el diablo* fulfils one of the key criteria of a national cinema as outlined by Andrew Higson, by drawing attention to issues that are pertinent to contemporary Peruvian society and culture, especially those concerned with 'questions of nationhood'.[86] In particular, it focuses on the phenomenon of mass migration arising from political conflict, while more generally it tackles the subsequent crises in individual and collective forms and processes of identity formation. Aspects of 'banal nationalism' abound in the visual and aural aspects of the portrayal, from the distinctive images and sounds of Andean landscape and everyday life, to the more cosmopolitan and culturally blurred spaces and practices of the capital city.[87] The film highlights issues of national cultural identity by concentrating on a Peruvian protagonist from one part of the country (the periphery) and by following his long journey to and within Lima (the centre). Jeremías's bewildered gaze, and the point-of-view shots that seek to position the spectator so as to share his confusion, draw further attention to intra-cultural differences, tensions and inequalities. The film deploys 'contrastive cultural elements' in order to contest the assumption that any uniform, stable and cohesive national identity might exist in Peru.[88]

Moreover, it draws attention to specific issues of identity raised by incidents of political conflict, forced migration and cultural encounter. Divisions along racial, ethnic and class lines are linked in the film to questions of power, dominance and exclusion. The unlawful killing by the security forces of the indigenous Jeremías harks back to episodes of violence between indigenous and European Peruvians at several points in national history. With a differently coloured skin and an accent that exposes his provincial origins, and lack of money, skills and education, Jeremías is marked out and marginalised on multiple levels. The final sequence of the film reinforces the tragic view that rural-to-urban migration in times of political conflict is fraught with difficulty and danger both for individuals and for society in general. In his study of political violence in Peru published just two years after the film's release, David Scott Palmer pointed out that:

> The racial divide amongst white, *mestizo*, and Indian appears to be the decisive factor that keeps the center from responding effectively and keeps the periphery paying a disproportionate human toll in the ongoing struggle.[89]

Ni con Dios offers a dystopian vision of Peruvian society that warns of the further entrenchment of social injustice and racial division. The dominant white culture in Lima is portrayed as reluctant to enter into a conflict that initially was hardly felt, let alone seen, in the capital city. In reality, it was only when rural migrants began to arrive in significant numbers, and when key state figures were attacked, that the response became serious. Even then, the need to apportion blame and to maintain political and social equilibrium emerged as a greater priority than addressing the underlying social causes of the conflict. The indigenous culture, represented here by the emblematic Jeremías, became both the collective victim and the scapegoat. The film pessimistically suggests that achieving triumph over prejudice is unlikely and the challenges of cultural diversity remain the target of the film's central critique.[90] The film finally suggests that its tragic protagonist's failure to recognise these difficulties is the real reason for his death, and that the various forms of physical and psychological violence that he has been forced to endure are symptomatic of the deep-rooted social divisions and resentments that remain at the heart of Peruvian national identity.

Identity, Violence and Social Responsibility: *Alias la gringa* (Alberto 'Chicho' Durant, 1991)

Alias la gringa/AKA 'La Gringa', the only Peruvian film released in 1991, is a prison drama set amidst a backdrop of political conflict.[91] The film took five years to make and was a project that suffered, as did *Ni con Dios*, from a lack of funds and state support for national cinema. While the 1972 legislation for promotion of the national film industry was still officially in place, faith in it as an effective and efficient system had diminished significantly and relations between exhibitors and producers were tense. Indeed, the former reneged on their commitment to screen all national films approved for domestic exhibition by the government-sanctioned administrative body COPROCI. As a result, Durant drew upon international funding and co-production support from six different investors, including TVE (Spain), ICAIC (Cuba) and Channel 4 (UK), resulting in a more complex arrangement that could have disrupted the film's status as a national film. Inspired by two sets of topical events, and tackling perennial themes such as friendship, loyalty and betrayal, Durant offers a pessimistic vision of Peru during the mid-1980s in a film that achieved domestic box office success as well as critical acclaim, alongside a clutch of international festival awards.[92] By addressing the film's themes, narrative structure and character development, this analysis explores the representation of political conflict and associated issues of national identity and culture. It also compares the instantaneous reporting of events by the mass media with the retrospective semi-fictional representation of those events in the cinema, and considers the capacity of each mode of expression to shape public opinion. Finally, it considers more generally the role and responsibilities of the intellectual and of cultural production at times of crisis, and explores the self-reflexive aspects of this film which allow for interrogation of the process and purpose of creative activity.

Production Contexts

The primary topical level of Durant's drama is loosely based on the unpublished memoirs of Guillermo Portugal, to whom the film is dedicated, and who escaped from prison for the last time in 1985, after 17 years in total behind bars. While the film appears to take the more objective form of a typical third-person narrative, it in fact adopts the literal and ethical point of view of the protagonist, known as La Gringa (Germán González).[93] The narrative focuses upon a key episode of transformation for the main character, anachronistically contrived in the film so as to coincide with a momentous episode in the Shining Path conflict. Moreover, the film follows La Gringa as he embarks upon a reluctant voyage of self-discovery and experiences the awakening of a sense of collective responsibility as a result of the surprising relationships he forges while imprisoned. His story also provides an explicit critical reflection of the prison conditions that he and his fellow inmates are forced to endure. This is achieved by voice-over readings from the notebooks in which he records the day-to-day events of prison life, and which are suggestive of the importance of creative activity, to this character and more generally. The film also offers implicit comment on Peruvian society from the viewpoint of an individual who has been excluded from it for several years. La Gringa hence becomes the increasingly sympathetic vehicle for the film's fundamental themes of compassion, friendship and social responsibility, as shown via the publicty poster.

The second topical element of *Alias la gringa* deals with the dramatisation of events that were widely reported and debated in the national media and serve here to provide action, spectacle and a sense of social realism for the protagonist's personal narrative. These were the riots instigated by Shining Path captives on the prison island of El Frontón in June 1986 and the military reprisals that were carried out under the orders of President García himself, which resulted in the deaths of hundreds of prisoners.[94] By fabricating a connection between the personal and the collective, and by flagging up places and events of national significance, Durant prompts reflection on the broad responsibilities of citizens in times of social crisis. Indeed, one reviewer interpreted the film as a vision of Peru in the 1990s and compared it with the films of Lombardi, which had a similar tone of despair and futility with regard to social commitment in Peru.[95] It is suggested here that the film might be read as critical of a perceived social lethargy and as a plea for the awakening of a collective conscience that might commit to identifying an alternative solution to crisis in the light of growing lack of confidence in an apparently ineffective and abusive regime.[96]

Framing Nation and Violence

In terms of generic categorisation, *Alias la gringa* combines a prison drama, one that draws attention to the structural violence and claustrophobia of Peruvian institutions, with the spectacular elements of the action-adventure genre, such as escape attempts, bomb attacks, basketball matches and fights that contribute towards the development of tension and anticipation. The film begins with an escape sequence that prompts early audience interest in, if not immediate sympathy with, the protagonist, La Gringa. After being briefly reunited with his loyal girlfriend Julia (Elsa Olivero), La Gringa is captured after betrayal by the prisoner he left behind, Loca Luna (Juan Manuel Ochoa), who henceforth becomes his mortal enemy. There follows a long section on the prison island of El Frontón, during which a range of interactions with other prisoners and the governor are shown, including La Gringa's encounters with the inmate "Professor Montes" (Orlando Sacha), whose plight eventually pricks his conscience. (See Plate 7) This is followed by the second escape, and a short spell in a safe house where plans are made for a new identity and further escape to Guayaquil in Ecuador. This time, however, La Gringa decides to return to the prison island in a bid to rescue the Professor, who earlier saved his life and encouraged him with his literary endeavours. The rescue bid goes wrong and La Gringa is locked up in solitary confinement until a sudden bombing attack on the island by the military provides him with a further opportunity to escape. The final image of the film shows La Gringa swimming away from the island after having witnessed the slaughter of Shining Path prisoners who refused to surrender, and the killing of the Professor, who wanted to be saved. The final voice-over conversation between La Gringa and Julia signals that they have made it to Ecuador, and that he plans to publish his diaries so as to make public the abuse he has seen committed in Peru's most infamous prison.

The specific political context of the Shining Path conflict and the nation's social and economic problems are introduced in the opening scene, when La Gringa becomes involved in an argument about torch batteries, during which mention is made of the electricity blackouts caused by the violence. As La Gringa wanders through the city, he notices several more acts of delinquency. Having been in prison and thus removed from everyday life for some time, he seems genuinely surprised by the general level of anti-social behaviour all around him. As Crabtree explains, during the mid-1980s the 'climate of violence was ... enhanced by social as well as explicitly political forms of violence and was especially evident in the cities'.[97] When La Gringa takes a taxi, he hears a radio news report that refers to him as a dangerous and cunning criminal and that causes him to bristle with some pride at the notoriety he has achieved. The same report then gives news of terrorist action (the killing of the parliamentary deputy and the subsequent rounding up of 15,000 suspects, events which actually occurred), which contrasts sharply with his own materialistically motivated crime of armed robbery. The taxi driver reacts with depressed familiarity rather than shock at this news; this early sequence thus serves to draw attention to the entrenchment of violence and delinquency in everyday life, and to the resignation of citizens to such situations over which they appear to have no control. Instead, the film shows the emergence of alternative survival tactics, such as theft, bribery and deceit, that threaten to atomise society and lead to the collapse of a fragile democratic state.

In fact, the return to democracy in Peru had taken place only in 1980, after 12 years of military rule, when it was welcomed with high expectations of social transformation amongst the mobilised masses. Nevertheless, such high hopes were quickly dashed by several factors, including the legacy of the previous regimes, Shining Path subversion from 1980, international debt crises from 1982, the environmental impact of the El Niño phenomenon on valuable sea resources in 1983 and the Belaúnde government's failure to react adequately to any of these challenges.[98] Historical tensions between the main political parties and a heightened sense of social division added to these difficulties, 'as did the classic weakness of the State in its approach to formulating, organising and implementing coherent decisions'.[99] García's regime (1985–1990) was arguably worse than that of Belaúnde in terms of its impact upon social conditions and its response to the political crisis. It took a controversial approach to counter-insurgency, which included the mass rounding-up of suspects and the targeting of intellectuals as perceived sympathisers, as illustrated in this film. It was also responsible for economic collapse, which became the second worst example of hyperinflation in world history, bringing poverty and misery to millions of Peruvian citizens. Although by the end of 1989 the situation had improved a little, real wages were still low and prices high; indeed, as John Crabtree concludes, 'an unprecedented proportion of the labour force was officially categorised "sub-employed" by 1989'.[100] Consideration of this contextual detail is important for appreciation of the film's depiction of entrenched cynicism on the streets of Lima, and the suggestion of a greater degree of social inequality and dislocation resulting from the economic crisis. It also aids understanding of the heightened paranoia and selfish behaviour on the part of the main as well as the secondary characters, who appear to have lost all respect for authority.

The classical approach to filmmaking – with its invisible editing style, third-person narration and linear structure – enables directors to focus spectator attention not only on the drama but also on the relationships and emotions of the film's central characters. Durant's film adopts this apparently neutral and omniscient style that in fact encourages a specific, preferred reading of *Alias la gringa* that emphasises the point of view of the protagonist, La Gringa, a flawed character whose position in relation to the world is transformed by his experiences in prison. His friendship, for example, with Professor Montes, who has been convicted mistakenly of being a Shining Path sympathiser, is of particular interest to this analysis. It provides the key to an appreciation of what Durant is trying to convey about the military's counter-insurgency strategy, as well as the emphasis he places on collective responsibility over individual freedom. A further contrast is drawn between the ideology of self-sacrifice as extolled by Shining Path for the sake of revolution and the single act of sacrifice taken by La Gringa in risking further imprisonment and possibly even death in order to save another human life and thereby repay a moral debt.

In order to appreciate fully the significance of this final act of sacrifice, it should be noted that La Gringa is initially presented as an unscrupulous, egotistical individual who cannot bear confinement and wishes to escape not only from the physical constraints of prison, but also from the 'parameters of social and legal life'.[101] He behaves like a caged animal that instinctively seeks freedom as soon as it is locked up. Moreover, he shows no sense of loyalty nor compassion towards fellow prisoners, leaving one (Loca Luna) for dead during his first attempt at escape, and indirectly causing the death of two others as punishment for aiding the second attempt. And yet, despite his obviously flawed nature, La Gringa emerges as the character with whom the audience feels most sympathy. This is largely achieved by the tracing of his moral transformation, and in particular by the portrayal of his relationships with Montes and an older man, Viejo (Enrique Victoria), whose own moral codes offer La Gringa a more socially responsible way of living. As Bedoya points out, 'the dramatic relations, focused on the triangle of friendship between La Gringa and two prisoners ... contribute to the psychological, social and cultural transformation of this one prisoner'.[102]

Meanwhile, both Sendero and the state, variously represented by the prison governor and guards, military and politicians, are depicted in an irredeemably negative light, the former as emphatically dogmatic and irrational, and the latter as unscrupulous, fraudulent and murderous. It quickly becomes clear that the film is critical of both sides of the political conflict, while reserving its sympathies for those in society who are excluded from participating in debate. Despite facing difficulties with disruptive Sendero inmates, the dictatorial prison governor (Gonzalo de Miguel) continues in his efforts to maintain order on the island. He acts with impunity: the abuse of prisoners goes unpunished and is indeed encouraged at the highest level. Faced with the sharp-witted La Gringa, however, his power is tested and undermined and his corruption further exposed as he tries first to have him killed, and then resorts to bribery. Yet physical maltreatment only strengthens the protagonist's desire to escape, and subsequent promises of better conditions merely serve to make him feel that he has the upper hand. La Gringa's overtly anti-authoritarian stance infuriates the governor, to the extent that he is willing to order his elimination. This troublesome prisoner represents a threat to the governor's professional future, in that one more attempt to escape by the former will result in a loss of promotion, and the longed for escape from the island, by the latter. The governor is bound by a destiny which has been shaped by conflict and corruption, and over which he has limited control, given the ultimate intervention of the military high command, and thus might also be understood as a prisoner of the state he is ordered to protect, with violence if necessary. He tries to compensate for this lack of power by heaping abuse on his prisoners and by constantly reminding them of who is in control.

By explicitly emphasising and inviting critical comment on the abuse meted out to common criminals, Durant implicitly challenges the response of the military to the rioting of the political prisoners held on the other side of the island in their own block. At the time (1986), public opinion was shaped largely by press, TV and radio coverage, which encouraged the population to understand why the attack had been ordered, if not to agree with the action necessary to regain control of the Shining Path rebellion. For example, Peralta's study on press reporting of the conflict informs us that editorials in the dominant national daily newspaper *El Comercio* expressed regret for the high number of casualties but considered this outcome as 'inevitable given the need to put an end to the Sendero threat'.[103] This view was compounded at the time by reports that a ship packed with weapons had been apprehended on its way to the island, where it was to have provided ammunition for the prisoners, to strengthen their campaign of violence. The view advanced by the military, according to Gorriti's historical study based on visits to the prison just before the attack, was that the prison had become a Shining Path centre for training, internal advancement, planning and indoctrination. It was feared that conquest of the prison by the insurgents was 'an encapsulated version of what the Shining Path insurrection was trying to achieve throughout the country'.[104] Indeed, the press even speculated that Shining Path activity nationwide was being masterminded from the prison cells.

The film's prison governor acts as the mediator of the dominant counter-insurgency discourse that held such views, and articulates the hegemonic point of view regarding the conflict on several occasions during the film. In so doing, this character assumes a more emblematic status as symbolic of the state that denies him (like his prisoners) any individual freedom, and the prison island he seeks to defend thus becomes a microcosm for the nation itself. The governor's bullying behaviour and relative impotence in controlling the prisoners, however, reinforce the film's intention for audience identification with a protagonist whose attempts to escape threaten the governor's retirement plans, and emphasises the director's attempt to critique the violent methods of the state in seeking to quell insurgent behaviour. The emotive depictions of the violent deaths of apparently innocent inmates Montes and El Viejo, the former gunned down by soldiers as he walks out with a white flag of surrender, and the latter as a result of a severe beating ordered by the governor, add further weight to the ideological force of the film and its condemnation of violence as integral to national identity.

At the same time, the film falls short of evoking sympathy for the revolutionary cause, since the Shining Path group is portrayed as a slogan-chanting undifferentiated collective, with a crazed leader who will tolerate neither negotiation nor surrender. Instead the film reserves its empathy for the unfortunate prisoner, Professor Montes, who is portrayed as having been caught in the political crossfire.[105] Through conversations between Montes and La Gringa, the Professor's story is recounted in some detail and he is presented thus as the victim of political paranoia. He acts to a large extent as the moral conscience of the film, a bridge between the political and the petty in criminal worlds, and a sounding board for La Gringa's ideas and ambitions. He is despised by the Shining Path group with whom he is locked up, and subjected to the 'constant pressures, routine insults and permanent hostility' that Gustavo Gorriti reports were faced by prisoners who refused to give themselves to the revolutionary cause.[106] Nevertheless, the Professor is labelled a terrorist by the prison guards and separated from the common criminals. His murder by the military is depicted as a cruel act of aggression given that he was waving a white flag and his tragic demise thus draws critical attention to the collateral damage that the armed forces were willing to commit for the wider national cause. It also shows that, like Jeremías in *Ni con dios*, the Professor's failure to affiliate himself with a particular social group serves to isolate him from protection and places him in a dangerous position of liminality.

Rather than cast blame on one side more than the other, the film's downbeat portrayal of Peruvian society damaged by 10 years of political violence and economic mismanagement suggests that both sides of the conflict caused terrible damage to the Peruvian people. The film conveys an overwhelming feeling of social entrapment by criminality and despair, and La Gringa's story becomes a metaphor for 'a country taken by fear, where freedom is a constant threat'.[107] The general atmosphere of fear and claustrophobia is emphasised by the film's portrayal of both Lima and the prison island as restrictive spaces, bounded by walls and rocky beaches, within which violence could erupt at any moment. (See Plate 8) The depiction of the city as an extension of the prison space creates the effect of a '"national prison" where the worst behaved are not necessarily those who are "inside"'.[108] Furthermore, the film's reflective moments – shown mainly when La Gringa is writing about his experiences or watching city life go by from the anonymity of the rooftops – articulate the depressing idea that it will be a long time before Peruvian citizens are ever free from economic, political and social chaos. The juxtaposition of city and prison life reinforces the notion of the prison as a microcosm of a nation in which opportunities are restricted, and resentment, disorder and desperation are the overriding sentiments.[109]

Thanks mainly to the initiative of his girlfriend, Julia, La Gringa is offered the opportunity to renounce his life of violent crime. She negotiates her way through the demands of the state institutions that inhibit her partner's freedom, persuading the judiciary to forward his appeal for release, only to find that he rejects any concept of negotiation by escaping during the journey to the court. Meanwhile, she continues to work to acquire the resources they need to leave the country in their joint bid for a different kind of freedom beyond the national borders. In spite of her support and their plans, however, he returns to the prison once more, this time of his own volition. It is as if the very real chance for physical escape triggers a realisation that wherever he goes, he will remain trapped by his selfish behaviour. In order to set himself free on a more profound psychological level, inspired in part by Julia's selfless actions, he determines to risk his own life for someone else. Her determination to find a way out of a situation of relative impoverishment through negotiation and hard work offers a challenge to the more macho approach adopted by La Gringa.

The plan to leave Peru was one that many citizens shared in the late 1980s and early 1990s, when democracy and economic fortune seemed to have reached an all-time low. As Emilio Bustamente points out, 'many Peruvians left the country out of fear for terrorism and the economic crisis',[110] *Alias la gringa* points to the general suffering of Peruvian society at the end of a traumatic decade, and La Gringa's story of resistance and escape, from prison and from the nation, serves as a metaphor for social trends at the time. Moreover, his eventual rejection of the criminality and anarchic behaviour that he had accepted as an integral part of his nature suggests the possibility of change, and the rejection of violence generally as a constituent part of national identity. An alternative model based on negotiation is offered by Julia's story, which shows her contributing to society and engaging with the authorities in a way that emphasises responsibility, solidarity and constructive dialogue over conflict and destruction. The function of her character on a broader, symbolic level is more interesting than many female characters in Peruvian fiction films to that date. On the one hand, she is portrayed as an attractive woman and dutiful partner who affirms La Gringa's active, macho identity in accordance with traditional interpretations of gender in classical cinema.[111] The deliberately erotic display of her body further reinforces her position as object of the male gaze and her willingness to wait for La Gringa to return as subject to patriarchal forces. On the other hand, however, her confidence and intelligence, her ability to assume agency and power, and the framing of her body as sexually liberated all serve to suggest an alternative behaviour that is modern rather than reactionary.[112] As such, the film complicates the notion of Peruvian identity as dominated by repressive machismo and points gently to the possibility for change via non-violent means, a theme that is further pursued in the later films discussed in this study.

The Peruvian population, whether locked up in El Frontón or trapped within the streets of Lima, is presented as oppressed, restricted in terms of life options, and possessing neither the motivation nor the inclination to behave in a more socially responsible way. Indeed, it is the prison which is the space where lines of solidarity are forged. By contrast, within

Lima all sense of solidarity is shown as having collapsed and criminal behaviour has become ingrained into the daily life of the capital. As Crabtree notes, by the late 1980s 'criminal violence, especially armed assault and robbery, became particularly common as a result of the fall in living standards ... [and contributed to] creating a climate of fear not just among the wealthy and the middle class, but also among wide sectors of the poor'.[113] Indeed, de Cárdenas argues that the main strength of the film is its development of a sense that there really is no escape from such desperate times, except perhaps for those who, like La Gringa, have the option of leaving altogether.[114] Indeed, his nickname suggests that the best opportunities (for physical or economic escape from deprivation and violence) are reserved for those of European or North American descent. Moreover, the element of disguise refers specifically to the construction of a preferred identity for the sake of social integration and advancement, if not by changing skin colour then by adapting everyday practices, attitudes and appearances.[115]

The loss of social cohesion and sense of belonging is perhaps the film's main concern and, in some respects, the bonding between different social groups within the prison offers an alternative to the fragmented society observed by La Gringa as he watches from the city's rooftops. It is by contrasting how the different groups respond to their circumstances that the protagonist comes to appreciate the responsibility he has to help those he left behind. It dawns on him that, like Montes, he needs to become actively engaged in the struggle for a better society rather than focusing all his attentions on himself. Hence his dangerous return to the island to pay an honourable debt of gratitude to the men who helped him, and his despair at being unable to save their lives as they did his. By closing the narrative with an act of self-sacrifice that demonstrates the extent of La Gringa's moral transformation, the film ends on a note of subdued optimism. The message that seems to be offered is that it is better for the development of a nation if its people act as caring and responsible citizens rather than as selfishly competitive individuals, whatever their background. It also suggests that change is possible, and that identity – whether personal or collective – is fluid. Just as La Gringa changed himself once (superficially) to escape the confines of prison, so he succeeds in changing again, on a more profound level, in order to break free from a personality that is apparently addicted to criminality, violence and narcissistic behaviour.

La Gringa traverses a rich terrain of ambiguity and liminality with his actions of escape and return and, more symbolically, by his refusal to conform to social stereotype. In her discussion of thematisations of nation, Mette Hjort suggests that a depiction of issues and events of national interest will often be used, 'not to affirm some inherent and enduring [national] identity … [but to emphasise the notion that] human beings forge their own destinies and can become the vehicles for change'.[116] This, she further suggests, might be achieved by focusing critical attention on current national identities. Indeed, La Gringa's encounters with Montes and Viejo force him to reassess his own relationship with the world around him. Explicit change can be detected in the growing awakening of a moral conscience in La Gringa. Through his experience of topical events of national importance, his story becomes an appeal for a more general shift in collective attitude. The 'real' story on which this fiction film is based therefore becomes subordinated to its main political concern, to provoke a broader debate about social responsibility.

Revealing Structural Violence

In summary, Durant's third feature film offers a critique of Peruvian society at a time of crisis, oppression and depression. It challenges aspects of the state's economic and counter-insurgency strategy specifically, through reconstruction of the adventures of an individual who defied the system and refused to become a victim of it. It acts, hence, as a film of protest both against institutional and structural violence and against social lethargy on the part of individual citizens, at a time when acute poverty and political violence had given rise to feelings of despair and hopelessness. Although Fujimori had just claimed victory as the new President when this film was released, everyday life was still dominated by the economic crisis and political violence that had characterised the 1980s. By identifying with the anti-authoritarian protagonist, domestic spectators could participate in an escapist fantasy wrapped in topical detail that was specifically targeted at their own situation. Meanwhile, the film urges collective action and creativity in facing up to difficult times that seem out of control. It appeals to citizens of all backgrounds to reclaim power and control at a community level and to promote positive human relations as fundamental to the rebuilding of a better society.

Moreover, it claims a stake in the important role of cultural production in shaping national identity, while it appeals to intellectuals and artists to become active in the struggle to rebuild a society, and to apply their skills and talents to the political cause. For Durant, a national cinema should be regarded as 'the face of a country', depicting and exploring issues of national concern.[117] Indeed, the very existence of 'national film' at a time of crisis for Peru and Peruvian cinema may even be considered as an act of protest in itself.[118] While *Alias la gringa* is not a film that interrogates in detail the complex social and political reasons for the chaos of contemporary Peru, it nevertheless provides a critical snapshot of a society in collective decline. It reveals a picture of systematic abuse and structural violence in Peruvian prisons and on the streets, and suggests that the only real options are to get out or work together for a better future. La Gringa himself defies the system one last time by fleeing the country; his redemption in narrative terms is secured by a commitment to publish his prison memoirs, linking cultural production with social justice. By closing in this way, the film seems finally to suggest that since a government engaged in dubious counter-insurgency and ineffective economic policy cannot be trusted to guarantee the safety of its citizens – whether in prison or on the streets – then individuals of all backgrounds must take on that responsibility themselves.

3

Cinema, Oppression and Ideology, 1992–2000

This chapter examines the context and outputs for feature cinema made in Peru during the mid to late 1990s, a period that spans the first and second terms of President Alberto Fujimori's increasingly oppressive regime and a time when freedom to debate difficult issues of national concern was gradually stifled. In early 1992, Fujimori enacted a shocking *autogolpe*/self-coup and created a new constitution and government structure that was welcomed by many of the electorate who felt isolated by and marginalised from the ruling elite at that time. This move, which included the strengthening of anti-terrorist legislation, also served to counter any apparent sympathy in more rural communities for the *Sendero* campaign that set out to destroy the authorities and institutions of Peru before creating a new system that promised to address issues of injustice and inequality. Moreover, later in 1992, Fujimori's security forces succeeded in capturing the *Sendero* leader and produced memorable media images of a humiliated Abimael Guzmán, caged, bound and dressed in prisoner's uniform. There swiftly followed a cessation of violence and the end of Shining Path as an organised group. Fujimori quickly took the opportunity to endorse and promote a neoliberal approach to economic development, welcoming foreign investment and introducing policies that seemed to prepare the nation for future growth.

Within this context, filmmaking in Peru floundered as the plans for a revised cinema law were abolished by Fujimori's regime; a new project was unilaterally developed by the Finance Minister and approved by government without any consultation with filmmakers or producers. This new legislation did away with guaranteed screening and associated revenue and introduced a competitive funding mechanism which emphasised the need to look for matched funds beyond the state. Most Peruvian filmmakers expressed alarm at the speed and tone of these developments and their fears appeared to be borne out when the funds to support such a scheme failed to materialise. Indeed, the three films addressed in detail in this chapter were made during the period when state resources had dried up completely. Meanwhile, in the mid-1990s, a new pan-regional venture called Ibermedia was set up in a bid to encourage filmmaking in Latin America through the pooling of resources, but Peruvian directors were unable to benefit from this until 2001, due to Fujimori's failure to fulfil the required national contribution.

Films that dealt explicitly with political issues struggled to find support, and even Lombardi's work took a turn to the symbolic, tackling less directly the contemporary Peruvian situation. Nevertheless, it is argued that thorny themes of violence and identity remain at the heart of each of the films under discussion in this chapter and gender identity is shown to play an increasingly important and nuanced role, with female protagonists brought to the fore variously as warriors, protestors, survivors and victims. Indeed, there is a blurring and shifting of the boundaries between these labels as more complex characters are developed that resonated with the increasingly multi-layered political, social and cultural contexts framing these films. For example, Marianne Eyde's *La vida es una sola/You Only Live Once* (1993) was the first Peruvian feature film to look closely at the position of women in the conflict and hence to interrogate and complicate the relationship between patriarchy and violence in the contemporary Peruvian context. Her fictional depiction of events located in the Andes provoked more hostility than any of the other films addressed in this study, and the detail of that controversy is explored. Two years later, Augusto Tamayo released *Anda, corre, vuela…/Walk, Run, Fly …* (1995), a film that draws on the socialist ideologies and neorealist intentions of productions by the Chaski Group, and highlights some of the injustices and prejudices of the counter-insurgent campaign, emphasising models of social development that reject violence.

Coraje/Courage (Alberto Durant, 1998) is discussed in terms of its representation of a controversial woman, a real-life defiant community leader, who is presented as an iconic figurehead for non-violent social change. The issues explored within this film and the media debates that ensued offer the possibility to probe further both the political role of cinema to activate public debate on events of national concern, and its capacity to provoke opposition to the prevailing hegemonic discourse of neoliberalism and oppression.

Female interventions: *La vida es una sola* (Marianne Eyde, 1993)

La vida es una sola highlights the experiences of the inhabitants of Rayopampa, a fictional Andean community caught between Shining Path and the Peruvian armed forces.[1] The film, like Lombardi's *La boca del lobo*, with which it shares some similarities of approach, is set in 1983, one of the most significant years in the conflict. It marked a crucial turning point in terms of the state's response to the guerrilla threat, and a heightening of danger for those living in parts of the sierra that had been declared 'liberated' by *senderistas*. Military intrusions were part of the army's new, more brutal counter-insurgency strategy, which saw the conflict referred to more generally as a 'dirty war'.[2] By focusing on the interaction between villagers and soldiers as well as between villagers and *senderistas*, Eyde's film, like Lombardi's, draws attention to the fragmented nature of Peruvian society and national identity. It emphasises the part played by the state in much of the violence perpetrated against innocent villagers as a result of its determination to eliminate an invisible enemy. Moreover, the specific community and conflicts depicted in *La vida* take on a broader representational significance in terms of symbolising the nation in crisis. Unlike Lombardi's work, Eyde's feature foregrounds issues of female identity and links them to alternative ways of framing national and violence. It is considered to be 'one of the freshest and most intelligent cinematic portraits of rural insurgency from any region'.[3]

Production Contexts

La vida was distinctive for devoting narrative space to detailed articulation of the ideologies and motives of Shining Path. It depicts individual rebels as complex characters whom the audience is invited to get to know and understand. Already dealing with controversial material, the film suffered from being completed at about the same time as the capture of Sendero leader Abimael Guzmán in September 1992. His long-awaited capture gave cause for national celebration for the relatively new Fujimori regime, since it marked a possible end to one of the nation's darkest eras of violence. However, it also triggered a period of widespread denial, repression of debate and collective amnesia regarding collective responsibility for victims of the violence, as well as the extent of the armed forces' involvement in torture, disappearance and other forms of abuse. Influential sectors of the domestic mass media appeared to turn a blind eye to the nature of the military's brutal counter-subversion strategies, for the sake of national unity and preservation of the political status quo.[4] As Susan Hayward suggests, 'nationalisms are forged in part in a ... remodelling of the past',[5] and it was undoubtedly in the political interests of President Fujimori to remodel certain memories of the military's involvement in the conflict so as to secure greater confidence in the regime's strategy for the future.

Nevertheless, testimonies from survivors reveal that the need to keep alive a more rounded memory of the struggle remained strong. Indeed, amongst families and communities that had suffered the greatest loss, the very act of speaking about loved ones tortured or disappeared by the military as well as by Sendero represented a 'stubborn refusal to acquiesce to the state's desire to erase the use of terror from collective memory'.[6] Eyde's film, eventually sanctioned for release by COPROCI as part of the national cinema approval system, confronted Peruvians of all classes and cultures with some of the uncomfortable and complex realities of the battle against Sendero, as well as the problems of national identity. In the event, the controversial representation of the political conflict offered by

Eyde's provocative film led to it being regarded by many as an ideological threat to the state, and even to the new era of relative peace that was being proclaimed by the media on a daily basis. The film was debated within the context of the 1981 anti-terrorist legislation; as a result, its release was delayed by a year, the director was accused of betraying pro-*senderista* sympathies, and some commentators demanded that those few cinemas that dared screen it be burned down.[7] This analysis sets out therefore to examine the key features of the portrayal of conflict in *La vida* and the context of its reception in order to help understand why this particular depiction of events provoked more hostility than any of the other films addressed in this study.

Framing Nation and Violence

The film opens with images of the annual carnival celebrations of Rayopampa, with a young llama being sacrificed and offered to the mountain deities. Three students, two men and one woman, arrive in the village ostensibly to learn about Andean culture. It is later revealed that they are Shining Path comrades who have come to lay the groundwork for the recruitment of village youngsters to the rebel cause and hence to secure the 'liberation' of the area from military (state) control. One of the *senderistas*, Aurelio (Jiliat Zambrano), seduces a local girl, Florinda (Milagros del Carpio), as a strategy to infiltrate the community, while his comrades befriend other young villagers whom they suspect might be vulnerable to ideological persuasion. As suspicions are aroused about their real motives, the three comrades disappear back into the mountains, just before a regiment of the armed forces based nearby arrives to remind the villagers of their duty to the state. The rebels return later, this time without disguise, and execute the community leader who they believe betrayed them to the military. They nominate two new leaders, then leave again, taking most of the young people with them. Florinda joins them out of misguided love for Aurelio but is soon repelled by the brutal methods used by the group, and deeply hurt by Aurelio's deception. When she is called upon to execute a deserter, someone she has known since childhood, she feels she has no choice but to run away herself, despite the danger to her own life. On her return to the village, she finds her home devastated and her presence is clearly a cause for concern for the few survivors of military reprisals. Florinda's father persuades her to leave again and, like *La boca*'s Vitín Luna, she finally disappears into the snow-capped mountains. The focus here on a female protagonist and her rejection of violence suggests a different vision of the nation that challenges the notion of an assumed link between machismo, patriarchy and national identity.

Eyde's film thus places the Sendero group at the centre of the drama and gives them a set of identifiable faces and distinct identities. Moreover, the film provides, through its three Shining Path characters and their recruitment mission, a detailed articulation of the rebel group's justification for their campaign of violence. Frequent references are made to their belief in the need to destroy the current state structure and build a new, more equitable and socially inclusive system of governance in its place. Critic de Cárdenas compares the multi-faceted portrayal of Shining Path offered in this film with that in *La boca*, in which the enemy remains invisible, and with Durant's *Alias la gringa* (1991), in which the rebels are depicted as savage madmen.[8] In Eyde's film, rebel comrade Roger (Javier Maraví) sets out to enlighten a select group of young villagers about the need for change by debating their plight while they are working on the land together. He urges them to consider rejecting the notion of private land ownership and instead to work together more closely to provide for the whole community. He stirs up antagonism within the younger villagers towards the older generation. Meanwhile, one of the village leaders refuses to work on the land with the group and insists on tilling his own plot in a gesture of defiance. Such scenes demonstrate how ordinary, generation-related frictions were exploited by Shining Path in such a way as to destabilise the unity on which such a community depends for its survival, both in fighting poverty and in combating violent attacks. Later on, Roger urges the same young villagers to rise up against the so-called exploiters and oppressors – both within and outside the community.

By articulating Shining Path ideology in this way, Roger highlights the rebel group's main public discourse, which promoted 'equality and justice for the peasants'.[9] Steve Stern has reported that one of the main reasons for Shining Path's initial focus on the Andean communities rather than other rural areas of Peru was that this was where 'state support for the hacienda system and ethnic domination continued to reign'.[10] In contrast, efforts to enhance social inclusion in coastal areas had been more vigorous and successful since the 1960s. In her study of relations between Shining Path and the inhabitants of the Andes, Isabel Cordero further points out that the rebel group sought to relate to the Andean people 'through a discourse of change, of a new society without poor or rich people, and with a new state'.[11] This echoes José Carlos Mariátegui's studies of conditions for the indigenous people of Peru, in which he advocates the need to reformulate social structures and, in particular, to renegotiate issues of land ownership.[12] The guerrilla ideology argued that a people's war was the only way to achieve the desired new state structure, and in *La vida*, Roger further reveals his Shining Path credentials by promoting the value of armed struggle. There is evidence to suggest, however, that those in charge of the guerrilla group despised the poor almost as much as the rich, accusing the most vulnerable of being 'parasitic burdens, useless and disposable'.[13] Indeed, the cruelty of the group's later treatment of the villagers of Rayopampa reveals a determination to achieve power at all costs, showing no particular respect for the *campesinos* on whose behalf they profess to fight.[14]

The film is further distinguished from the others included in this study by its emphasis on a female *senderista* leader, Comrade Meche (Rosa María Olórtegui). While commentators on gender and violence such as R. W. Connell have pointed out that 'most episodes of major violence ... are transactions among men', *La vida* highlights the reality that within the Shining Path hierarchy, women were offered some of the most active and demanding roles.[15] In his analysis of terrorism in Peru, David Whittaker speculates that 'women overcame the subordinate role and status historically ascribed to them in Peruvian society when they participated as equals in the Shining Path apparatus and led many of its initiatives'.[16] According to Isabel Cordero, however, female participation in guerrilla warfare was not necessarily a sign that Shining Path proposed a radical new agenda for women in Peru, but rather that 'their presence derived more from their own expectations and desires to enter new spaces of participation'.[17] Their involvement in this way would have presented a challenge to gender stereotypes and might thereby have made the group even more threatening to a state system based on patriarchal order. The presentation of Comrade Meche as rebel leader is especially provocative in this regard. (See Plate 9) Even Cordero's more measured report acknowledges that 'women [in Shining Path] achieved a visibility never before seen in any political party in Peruvian history'.[18] While most women were restricted to traditional duties of attending to the survival needs of male recruits, others were involved in more logistical and propaganda activities. As the conflict continued, Shining Path leaders sought in fact to turn many more of its female members into brave *macha* warriors, and the character of Meche embodies this aspect of female participation in the Shining Path campaign. Nevertheless, this strategy largely imitated existing patriarchal structures and reinforced the dominance of machismo as one of the dominant features of national identity. It therefore contributed little in the long term to the development of a meaningful alternative position for women within the social hierarchy.

Cordero further argues that there were two basic requirements for the acceptance of women by Shining Path: 'capacity for leadership and readiness to give oneself over to party activities, to the point of renouncing responsibilities such as work and study and renouncing familial and affective ties'.[19] Meche is an idealised representation of such a woman. Critic Fernando Vivas described her character as 'a woman of the ultra-left with the asexualised aura of bliss that all fanatical leaders tend to have'.[20] She exudes contentment with and devotion to her chosen path in life, and embodies the spirit of personal sacrifice that was fundamental to Shining Path philosophy.[21]

Alongside the traditionally ultra-masculine qualities of warrior-like courage and a fierce determination to succeed, Meche is depicted as intelligent and articulate. Little is offered regarding her background except that she was a university friend of Aurelio and Roger. She assumes the role of indoctrination of the youngest villagers, interrupting their lessons to instruct them about an alternative version of their nation's history that emphasises the deep-rooted struggle between exploiters and exploited of Peru. She thus attempts to reinvent national history in such a way as to prevent the development of any emotional tie for those children to the official state version of the founding of the nation. She is aware that 'history is …

a crucial player in the construction of nation'.[22] Moreover, she demands absolute commitment to the party from those around her, and throughout the film issues orders that constantly test that devotion. As Cordero suggests, women like Meche were 'characterized by their total identification with the project and their great will to work and to struggle'.[23] The creation of such a compelling female insurgent character as someone to be reviled for her actions, but perhaps also admired for her commitment, defiance and transgression of cultural boundaries, might have contributed to the hostility displayed towards Eyde's film by audiences, critics and authorities alike.

A further controversial aspect to Eyde's film lies in its condemnation of the violence perpetrated by the military. While Lombardi's *La boca del lobo* was also critical in this regard, Eyde's film risked upsetting the state by neglecting to offer much discussion of the reasons for the actions of the armed forces. Moreover, the film offers only a single character, Tigre (Aristóteles Picho), through whom to portray the approach taken by the military to both the Shining Path enemy and the Andean communities. Indeed, some critics believed this to be the most controversial aspect of the film, due to the context of its release in early 1993, when Guzmán had been captured and certain other advances in the anti-subversive campaign had been made.[24] At this point, the military's much debated and criticised counter-insurgency strategy 'based on the indiscriminate use of terror against the peasantry' was more or less forgotten and the press was discouraged from discussing it.[25] Hence, this big-screen depiction of a lieutenant leading his regiment against Sendero by striking fear into the rural inhabitants they had been sent to protect jarred with the official discourse of triumphant state victory and apparent restoration of peace.

Moreover, Tigre is depicted ambivalently as both perpetrator and victim, subject to the demands of the military institution and the nation-state to which he has committed his life, together with the fierce desire to win a conflict that has come to define him. He reveals to the community leader that he considers himself dead inside, thanks to his time spent battling against the largely invisible Shining Path enemy with an ill-equipped and underprepared army. He, like Lieutenant Roca in Lombardi's film, has been driven mad by the apparent impossibility of curbing the violence of the guerrillas, and by the reluctance of the villagers to collaborate with his efforts. He considers their refusal to name traitors, to take down the Shining Path flag and to bury a villager murdered by the rebels as acts of betrayal on the part of the whole village. As a man who has given himself to the protection of the state and its institutions, he derides the villagers' fears and is intensely frustrated that they prioritise a duty to the community over loyalty to the state and defence of the nation. He reacts angrily to their passive defiance and uses insulting language that betrays an attitude of racism towards the villagers. Rather than defend them, he is quick to accuse them all of having joined the Shining Path cause, and selects at random a group of villagers for punishment, who are then 'disappeared' for good. He thus embodies all that was despised about the armed forces by those who fought against human rights abuses committed by the military during the struggle. Like most of the soldiers in *La boca*, he does not recognise the villagers as sharing the same sense of national identity as himself; he fails to acknowledge them as fellow citizens of the nation-state it is his mission to protect.

La vida stirred up further controversy by focusing much of its sympathy on the Andean community of Rayopampa, around which the drama revolves. Most of the villagers are depicted as the indisputable victims of forces that are beyond their control, whether those are the indoctrination tactics of Shining Path on the young people or the brutal threats of the military on the older generation. (See Plate 10)

Such an approach resonates with the director's documentary work of the 1970s and 1980s, which casts a generous spotlight upon the daily lives of indigenous Peruvians. Through careful framing and use of soundtrack, the film develops an impression of a tight-knit rural community that in many ways becomes the real protagonist of the film, trapped between Shining Path terror and military abuse. The importance of internal unity and homogeneity in the daily lives and functioning of the community is emphasised through the use, for example, of high and wide angle shots that refuse to let the camera rest upon one individual character. César Pérez, director of photography and a key collaborator on Eyde's documentary work in the Andes, allows his camera to glide over the top of the action and thus take in the whole community in a single frame, as in the scene of mourning for the executed community leader. In early scenes, the viewer is introduced to the rituals of daily life in the sierra, with colourful, idealised images of animals, rural customs and festivities, and collective agricultural work, thus emphasising the community's closeness to the land and harmonious existence with nature. Such scenes contribute towards placing the rural community at the heart of the drama, and help to establish a sense of equilibrium which is disrupted moments later. They also contrast with the approach to the Andean landscape in *La boca del lobo*, which emphasises the harshness of life in the mountain terrain, for newcomers and inhabitants alike. Eyde's vision is romantic, lyrical and slightly nostalgic, more in line with the vision of the Andean way of life promoted by the indigenist movement of the 1930s to the 1950s. Certainly it shares with that movement a desire to 'question the hegemonic concept of national identity based on Lima's creole population' and a move to refocus attention on the diversity of Peruvian identity that includes the rural and the indigenous.[26]

The film emphasises its view of the tragic nature of the degradation of an ancient way of life by the forces of modernity by alternating scenes of peaceful tranquillity with scenes of brutality, the latter eventually overwhelming the former as the narrative progresses and the penetration of Shining Path members into rural life becomes deeper. What begins as manipulative ingratiation with and feigned respect for local customs and traditional way of life on the part of Roger, Aurelio and Meche turns into sadistic domination of and intrusion into all of the community's rituals. School lessons are interrupted by speeches on Shining Path ideology, and the teachings of Guzmán and his followers are spread amongst the adults as they work the land. The younger villagers remain the primary target, however, since their lack of experience makes them more susceptible than their elders to the promises of a better way of life offered by Shining Path. The fictional highland village of Rayopampa thus stands emblematically for all those Andean communities that found themselves trapped between two violent groups: between 'the military's offensive, principally against youth and leaders labelled terrorists, and Shining Path's efforts at forced recruitment, which targeted the same groups'.[27] Moreover, the older *comuneros* realise too late that they should have shown greater resistance, by organising themselves into a civil defence committee, and reference is made to other communities that have already done so. The tragedy is hence compounded for the inhabitants of Rayopampa as they come to realise that if only they had been provided with the basic resources with which to defend themselves and some backup from the military, they might have been able to save the village from total destruction.[28]

The villagers are depicted on the whole as terrified victims of violence from all sides, accused by Shining Path of collaborating with the army, and suspected by the military of collusion with the rebels. (See Plate 11)

However, the plight of one individual, Florinda, is highlighted above all others, by placing the story of her traumatic transition to adulthood amidst a context of violence within the broader political framework of the film. As Vivas pointed out, the whole drama is embodied in the personal dilemma Florinda faces in deciding whether to participate in the action by joining Shining Path's campaign.[29] Arguably, her decisions are initially dictated by the manipulative Aurelio, but she assumes a more active and defiant position by fleeing the group in the end, despite his pleas. At the same time as contributing unwittingly to the collapse of her community and the destruction of her family home, she also experiences an intense initiation to love and death. Bedoya went further than Vivas, by drawing attention to Florinda's important symbolic role in conveying the film's themes. He suggests that she is herself emblematic of all those communities devastated by the political conflict.[30]

The depiction of Florinda as primarily submissive to the demands of Shining Path leaders seems to have been influenced by Eyde's understanding of the treatment of Andean women by the guerrilla group. Her portrayal contrasts with the respect and superiority accorded to a figure like Meche, differentiated from the *campesina* by her university education and familiarity with life outside the sierra, and thus suggesting a familiarity with a supposedly more modern way of life on the coast. Cordero notes that, despite some effort by Shining Path to address gender relations, interaction by its male members with indigenous women betrayed its preference for patriarchy and its lack of respect for inhabitants of the Andes. She notes, for example, that Shining Path used romance as a strategy for recruiting women, a tactic that is highlighted in the film by its focus on the control that Aurelio exerts over Florinda.[31] Their encounter also draws attention to the fluidity and ambiguous complexity of Peruvian identity. It becomes clear that Aurelio was born and grew up in Rayopampa, yet has become differentiated from his childhood friends as a result of his education, life in a modern urban environment and participation in politics. His absolute allegiance to the Shining Path dream of revolution, with the promise of a total redefinition of Peruvian society, suggests that he is prepared to oversee the destruction of his own community. Moreover, Aurelio, like all Shining Path members, was obliged to renounce his name and emotional ties with the past, including family and friends, thus sacrificing himself totally to the revolutionary cause. Indeed, he tells Florinda she should be proud to do the same. At first she grudgingly accepts this, as her belief in his love for her holds sway, but the order from Meche to kill first a dog and then a friend who is accused of desertion, 'as proof of her radicalisation', tips her over the edge and causes her to flee.[32] Her emotional bond to her community and family is too great to allow her to tolerate such separation and destruction, which makes it all the more tragic that when she does return home, her father urges her to leave and carry on running. Her time with Shining Path has changed her irrevocably; having been forced to make the transition to adulthood more sharply and intensely than other girls in the community, she now has to leave it. Meanwhile, her rejection of violence, central to the film's ideological message and linked to her identity as female, further emphasises the apparently tight link between masculinity and violence and their prominent position as integral to the prevailing national image.

In common with the young protagonist of Lombardi's film, we last see Florinda running into the Andean mountains, fleeing from both the military and Shining Path. Her situation is dangerously ambiguous, as she is now considered a traitor by both sides of the conflict. Although her future is far from certain, one miserable possibility is that, if she is lucky, she will join the masses of *campesinos* migrating from the country to the streets of Lima, like Jeremías in del Pereira's *Ni con dios ni con el diablo*. Her dream of romance is shattered along with her youthful innocence; her family cannot protect her, and the state now regards her as an enemy of the nation. And yet she refuses to embrace the option offered by Shining Path, turning her back on an approach based on destruction and an image shaped by violence.

The projection of sympathy onto an Andean community devastated by conflict and abandoned by the state excluded from the national-building project was at odds with official discourse of the 1990s. To a certain extent, *La vida es una sola* revived debates that had been sparked by the likes of cultural commentator Alberto Flores Galindo, who examined the apparent rupture between Peruvian state and society in the 1980s, drawing attention to the lack of solidarity, common national image and shared collective projects in his country.[33] Like Lombardi's film, *La vida* also illustrated the tensions that arise from the formation and projection of a Peruvian national identity that continued to be controlled by a social, economic and cultural elite that was shaped largely by notions of macho masculinity and violence.

The release of Eyde's film was fraught with difficulty, due in large part to important socio-political changes in Peru at the turn of the 1990s. The political and economic climate had hardened as the terrorist attacks persisted and began to affect Lima with greater frequency. The authorities hence proved unwilling to accept a film that portrayed the rebels in such detail. One consequence was that the release of the film was delayed as it underwent close scrutiny by the nervous members of COPROCI, who took the unprecedented step of sending the film to the Ministry of the Interior before voting on its suitability for release. Furthermore, the co-screenwriter, respected national playwright Alonso Alegría, insisted on the removal of his name from the credits for fear of persecution by the state and hostility from audiences that might damage his reputation. The director herself was accused by many of revealing and pursuing a pro-*senderista* agenda. According to interviews given in 1992, she was angry that the very institution set up to oversee and promote national cinema was reluctant or scared to approve the film's release, on ideological grounds.[34]

In response to the accusation that she was a terrorist sympathiser, Eyde drew attention to what she perceived as a lack of collective responsibility for a national problem, and called for institutions such as COPROCI to enter publicly into this important debate. She considered her treatment by the state as insulting, degrading and as an oppressive attack on freedom of expression and creative production in general. Several of the nation's most renowned and respected filmmakers signed a letter to COPROCI in support of the film, and the debate continued for over a year.[35] It is suggested here that Eyde's identity as a female director originating from Norway might have been part of the reason behind the treatment she received from the press and authorities in particular. Moreover, she received no funding from the Peruvian state. The $150,000 budget was instead financed by grants and facilities hire from Norwegian, Dutch and Venezuelan organisations as well as through personal loans. This brings to mind the tension between a concern for cultural authenticity and the tendency still to dismiss those films ' "tainted" by extra-national elements and influences' despite the need for cross-cultural collaboration in order for national films to be made.[36] It seems, perhaps above all, that this national topic was not to be dealt with in such a provocative manner, if at all, by someone who, despite having actively confirmed her affiliation to the Peruvian nation, was still considered an outsider.[37]

The Pain of Remembering

La vida was eventually released in November 1993, but its critical reception nationally was ambivalent despite acclaim at a number of international festivals. Furthermore, whereas *La boca del lobo* had been released at a time when a protective cinema law guaranteed exhibition on the national cinema circuit, by the time Eyde's film was released, the law had been abolished and national films were forced to compete on the open market – in a battle weighted heavily on the side of popular and highly polished Hollywood products. Moreover, while Lombardi's film was able to rely upon considerable domestic state support and co-production funding from Spain, Eyde was forced to draw on more meagre resources. When her film was finally approved for release, it opened at only four cinemas in Lima, and national TV channels refused to incorporate it into their schedules for a further 10 years.

Meanwhile, renowned critics Bedoya and León Frías came to the film's defence in separate reviews, suggesting that the director's clear, distanced and reflective approach to her subject was to be applauded.[38] Fernando Vivas reminded potential viewers that the 'dirty war' really did take place and that many innocent civilians were indeed caught in the crossfire.[39] Nevertheless, all three critics were careful to put some distance between events as they were shown on screen and the political climate of the time. They were also reluctant to make any statement on the possible continuing relevance of this film's message to the Fujimori regime of the early 1990s.

For her part, Eyde, as Lombardi had done five years earlier, insisted in interviews that her film should be interpreted on a broad level as a call for peace, a rejection of violence, an expression of a passion for life and a statement on human rights for all, as well as a historical text that draws attention to an important period in the nation's recent history. The director claimed to have been motivated by a firm belief that commitment to human rights must mean, above all, a commitment to the right to life, acknowledging that Shining Path violated that right just as much as the state. She was particularly shocked by the elaborate discourse about death used by the guerrilla group to indoctrinate youngsters, and by their strategic use of violent imagery and language, which included emotive references to ancient Inca traditions in order to seduce the new recruits.

When looking for evidence of her intended message of humanity within the film itself, it seems pertinent to cite the emotional drama that revolves around Florinda and thus the choice of a female protagonist as bearer of the film's message against violence. Although much of the film deals with the political struggle, her story emerges as the central thread and her character as the one to whom the audience feels most attached and for whom we feel most concern. Like Vitín Luna, she is flawed in many ways – naive, foolhardy and impetuous – but her deep emotional bond with her family and her community is what distinguishes her. Her realisation that these ties are what matter most is what saves her ethically. At the end of the film, Florinda, having been forced into the position of killer, accepts the greatest sacrifice, leaves her family and 'flees for her own salvation'.[40] The focus in the final sequence on her escape into the mountains, rejecting violence, despite the risks and personal loss involved, is what finally marks her out as heroic and iconic. Her traumatic experience thus symbolises the dilemma faced by a generation of young people growing up in the Andes in the 1980s of how to locate themselves in relation to the armed struggle. It embodies the film's message as a rejection of violence at the time of a regime that had proved itself to be 'efficient in the control of terrorism' but which did not respect 'democratic institutionality'.[41] Finally, what the film achieves is a focus on the deep-rooted divisions and fragmentations of Peruvian national identity, with the consequent complex process of affiliation to and movement across different social groups, as well as the tensions emerging as a consequence of the struggle by each for recognition and inclusion.

Identity, Agency and Social Development: *Anda, corre, vuela* .../*Run, Walk, Fly* ... (Augusto Tamayo, 1995)

Anda, corre, vuela ... is situated temporally between the *autogolpe* and the arrest of Shining Path leader Abimael Guzmán, a significant period when daily life in Lima was profoundly affected by violence, fear and oppression from both sides of the conflict. In April 1992, the President arbitrarily closed down Congress and sacked the Supreme Court in the face of resistance to his 'government's desire to grant far-reaching new powers to the military, ostensibly to fight the war against guerrilla subversion'.[42] He thus reaffirmed the prominence of the armed forces in national political life. Tamayo's film shows how the daily lives of marginalised young people living in Lima were affected by such events, rooting itself in a topical reality, and yet also tackling such perennial themes as friendship, loyalty and love. Unlike most of the films discussed in this book, it strikes an affirmative note about the important role of individual dreams and ambitions, whatever one's circumstances. Moreover, it suggests that the abandonment of personal plans to work on collective projects is more desirable and fulfilling for both the individual and society, and is indeed the only long-term and sustainable way to make change for the better. It also highlights an ineffective state infrastructure that is so engaged in broad counter-insurgency and economic shock policies that, ironically, it is unable to protect its citizens from the very violence and poverty it seeks to erase, and indeed intensifies their impact on them.

By way of counterpoint, the film celebrates the solidarity and resilience of those communities that find creative ways not only to defend themselves from physical attack and economic decline, but also to give them hope for a brighter future. In this sense, it offers an optimistic solution to the breakdown of traditional social order, by calling for a new type of solidarity that allows individual and collective desires to co-exist. This analysis explores the film's approach to these themes and discusses its response to issues of concern to Peruvian society in the early 1990s. The various critical reactions to several scenes depicted in the film at the time of its commercial domestic release are also explored. Finally, it focuses on the connections between violence and national identity, and on the possibility for new forms of political agency and social development.

Production Contexts

Although directed by Augusto Tamayo, this film was really a producer's project in that it was Stefan Kaspar, the Swiss founder of Peruvian production company Casablanca Films and a former co-founder and director of the filmmaking collective known as the Grupo Chaski, who drove the plan to complete what he envisaged as a trilogy which had begun with *Gregorio* (1984) and *Juliana* (1989), two of the most iconic national films of the 1980s.[43] (See Plate 12)

These earlier feature films, and their sympathetic prototypic protagonists, were thus already very much a part of the collective national cinematic memory, with their tales of the life of street children in the poorer districts of Lima during that decade. With them, the Chaski collective had begun its cine-sociological mission to document the marginalised communities of Peru through feature and documentary filmmaking and to provoke the social conscience of the spectator.[44] They aimed to give a sense of the general chaos in Lima by drawing attention to the everyday experience of many of its more invisible citizens in a way that provided a counterpoint to the increasingly common perception of such young people in urban areas as delinquents responsible for a new wave of street violence. As Sophia McClennen has observed, when the Chaski Group began their work, 'Peru's marginalized social sectors had no history of seeing themselves reflected on screen'. She further notes that while the most of the rest of the filmmakers discussed here present a more middle-class perspective on Peruvian politics and society than the politically engaged Chaski Group, it is through their shared 'interest in representing local circumstances that they have come to find solidarity' with each other.[45]

While the same actors are used to reprise their characters from the earlier films, and even though similar themes are developed, the representational style of *Anda, corre, vuela* ... is different and the tone of immediacy and urgency, so compelling in the first two, is subordinated here to one of sentiment and spectacle. In fact, the unashamedly political imperative of the earlier works gives way to the demands of entertainment. *Anda, corre, vuela* ... is more clearly a fictional (melo)drama in which action-adventure (Tamayo's cinematic speciality) vies for position with social realism (the preferred Kaspar/Chaski approach).[46] In fact, the film intertwines and draws on a range of generic forms. Hence, there develops a sentimental love story between the two protagonists; a heart-warming tale of survival amidst adversity on the streets of Lima; and an action-packed series of scenes of explosions and escape attempts. Romance, adventure, crime and social realism are thus mixed to create an ambitiously hybrid cinematic concoction, in which the cine-sociological mission is downplayed.

Framing Nation and Violence

As the film begins, Gregorio (Marino León de la Torre) is depicted working at a petrol station and taking his entrance examinations in an attempt to achieve a university place to study electrical engineering. Juliana (Rosa Isabel Morfino) lives in a shack on the cliffs on the margins of the affluent Miraflores district of Lima, within walking distance of the plush hotels and shopping centres, and has ambitions of eventually living in the US. Both hail from similar ethnic backgrounds, are marked racially by their dark skins, and take care of younger children who work as shoeshine boys and flower sellers respectively. Juliana meets Gregorio by chance one day when she is out pick-pocketing, and reports back to her drug-dealing acquaintances on how they can break into the safe at the petrol station where Gregorio works.

The dramatic turning point of the film takes place with a bomb attack at the petrol station. This occurs just after Juliana has warned the manager of the impending robbery, as her conscience had been pricked by an argument with Gregorio about honesty, ambition and responsibility. However, the police go in search of both Juliana and Gregorio as suspected accomplices of the bombers, while the drug dealers also pursue the pair of them for apparently having sabotaged their planned break-in. Juliana and Gregorio escape and then hide with the help of the children, but Juliana is eventually captured by the police. However, the police captain (Carlos Danós) is forced, by the children's ingenuity, to admit he is holding the wrong suspect and she is freed. In the end, Gregorio and Juliana put their own personal ambitions to one side and instead use the money they had been saving to help them escape life in Lima to build the neighbourhood music venue that is desired by their young friends. The film concludes with a jubilant long shot of a community rock concert opened by the recently liberated Juliana.

This film shares with its Chaski predecessors a similar vision of the Peruvian social infrastructure as chaotic and dysfunctional. As Jon Beasley-Murray noted, the film's central problematic is 'the difficulty of convincing anyone of your innocence in a context of social chaos, official incompetence and paranoia, and generalized fear and distrust'.[47] Moreover, blame for this is placed again on state institutions such as the police and the judiciary and their failure to look after all national citizens. The breakdown of family life due to economic hardship, and the overwhelming atmosphere of fear, resentment and prejudice after a decade of political conflict are also referred to throughout. The nation was, after all, in a situation of crisis that some commentators believed could end in total atomisation.[48] The subsequent weakening of social bonds and lack of coherent, consistent moral guidance that, according to Durkheim's vision, could lead to privileging of the individual over society were direct consequences of ineffective government.[49] Indeed, in *Anda, corre, vuela* ... the young protagonists struggle with their lack of any sense of belonging to a dominant social structure as they are denied access to those very systems that are designed to promote the notion of a collective bond: education, judiciary, employment and so on.

Juliana and Gregorio are at first presented as victims of this social chaos, unable to pursue their dreams within Peru, nor to envisage a possibility of escape through education or travel. As the producer, Kaspar, points out: 'The main characters are marginalised youths who are left to face an urban world that does not offer them the necessary conditions to realise their dreams and projects'.[50] Gregorio persists, but repeatedly fails to gain access to and recognition by conventional society through diligently carrying out his low-paid job at the petrol station and through his thwarted efforts to gain a university place. Meanwhile, the others, even the smallest children, all survive on the fringes of society by working in the informal service sector as shoeshine boys and flower sellers, while Juliana supplements this by resorting to criminal activity such as pick-pocketing and assisting drug-dealers. While the younger characters display a stoic acceptance of their lot and enjoy each other's company, Gregorio and Juliana long for escape. The film's opening establishing shot shows college students celebrating news about university entrance, while Gregorio is devastated to discover that he has missed out yet again. Meanwhile, Juliana is frequently shown staring out to sea – that is to say, away from Peru and Lima – in despair at her wasted youth, with nothing to look forward to. Their sense of failure is compounded by the signs of Western-style progress that surround them, indicative of the nation's Western-inspired ideas of development more broadly, and their treatment as invisible by fellow Peruvians of a higher economic status.

In a leading study of Peru's so-called informal economy, undertaken at the end of the 1980s, Hernando de Soto argued that the very existence of such a high proportion of activity taking place outside the law was evidence that the state was generally deemed not to be a protector of the poor, but a 'systematic obstacle' to progress.[51] He described the state as unresponsive to the needs of the majority of its citizens and hence responsible for the kind of structural poverty and violence that arise from a lack of social cohesion, that become engrained in everyday life and that result in routine violation of laws.[52] De Soto's study concluded that activities contributing to the burgeoning informal economy might be more fruitfully considered as creating an alternative route to national development, rather than simply denounced as falling beyond the legal limits of governmental authority. Indeed, Tamayo's film reminds its audience that there are many Peruvians who have had little choice but to survive by ignoring or violating laws, and by putting up with a range of violent situations, some of which might be blamed on state neglect. At the same time, the motivations, decisions and actions of his characters suggest that different ways of considering social structures, community development and a more cohesive sense of identity might be possible, and that violence as a means through which to enact such change is not inevitable.

For example, *Anda, corre, vuela* ... depicts new social bonds as emerging in spite of the lack of a relevant and acceptable framework of guidance, and goals are achieved through collective efforts rather than individual ambition. Gregorio and Juliana are not left as individuals to find their own way in the world. As well as finding each other, their eventual strength and survival come from the formation of a new type of community, held together by a solidarity that is adapted to the Peruvian context of informality, and represents a rejection by the young characters of state-sponsored corruption and abuse. Rather than responding to any legal structure of punishment, Juliana comes to realise with the help of friends and her own experiences that criminal deviance is not the way towards sustainable fulfilment. Juliana risks freedom and her life by choosing to remain with her new family rather than taking the chance to escape. Moreover, when they realise that the judicial system has failed them, the younger characters use their initiative to find an alternative way of proving their friend's innocence that circumvents the need for money or knowledge of an overly bureaucratic legal system.[53] Instead they rely on the more old-fashioned values of honesty and integrity, persuading the police to listen to the eyewitness account of the petrol station manager, once he has recovered from the injuries he suffered from the bomb attack. There is a child-like optimism to the film's exposition of the determination and creativity of a new generation working together for common goals that eschew the cynicism and apparent acceptance by the older generation of violence as an inevitable feature of national life and image. This, after all, is a utopian socialist, pacifist and humanitarian vision for Peru that reveals the influence of the Chaski Group's philosophical legacy that leans towards social solidarity and rejects violence in all its forms.

The narrative of *Anda, corre, vuela* ... is not based on particular real events but is rooted nevertheless in the context of mid-1992 when the conflict between Sendero and the military seemed to be spiralling out of control, with reports of murders, car bomb attacks and blackouts on a daily basis. As Peralta confirms: 'Between June and July 1992, Shining Path

1. *El candidato* (Álvaro Velarde, 2016, Velarde Producciones) – President Fujimoto rages from his prison cell

2. *La hora final* (Eduardo Mendoza de Echave, 2017, La Soga Producciones) – Filming on location in Lima, with the actor Pietro Sibille

3. *La boca del lobo* (Francisco Lombardi; 1988, Incan Film/Tornasol Films) – Lieutenant Roca looks on at the bodies of traitors on the steps of the church

4. *La boca del lobo* (Francisco Lombardi, 1988, Incan Film/Tornasol Films) – Sergeant Vitín Luna is locked up for having defied orders from his lieutenant

5. *Ni con dios ni con el diablo* (Nilo Pereira del Mar, 1990, Urpi Producciones) – publicity poster

6. *Ni con dios ni con el diablo* (Nilo Pereira del Mar, 1990, Urpi Producciones) – Jeremías joins the miners in his search for work

7. *Alias la Gringa* (Alberto Durant, 1991, ICAIC/TVE) – 'La Gringa' takes up arms

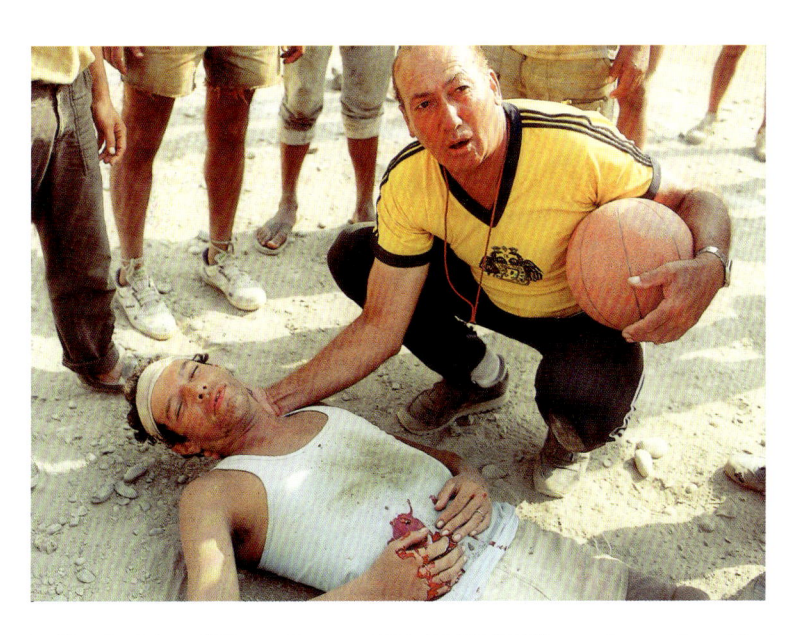

8. *Alias la Gringa* (Alberto Durant, 1991, ICAIC/TVE) – an inmate is stabbed during a game of basketball

9. *La vida es una sola* (Marianne Eyde, 1993, Kusi Films) – Shining Path rebel Comrade Meche leads her group into action

10. *La vida es una sola* (Marianne Eyde, 1993, Kusi Films) – villagers are threatened with death by Shining Path rebels

11. *La vida es una sola* (Marianne Eyde, 1993, Kusi Films) – villagers are forced to become killers and mourn their dead

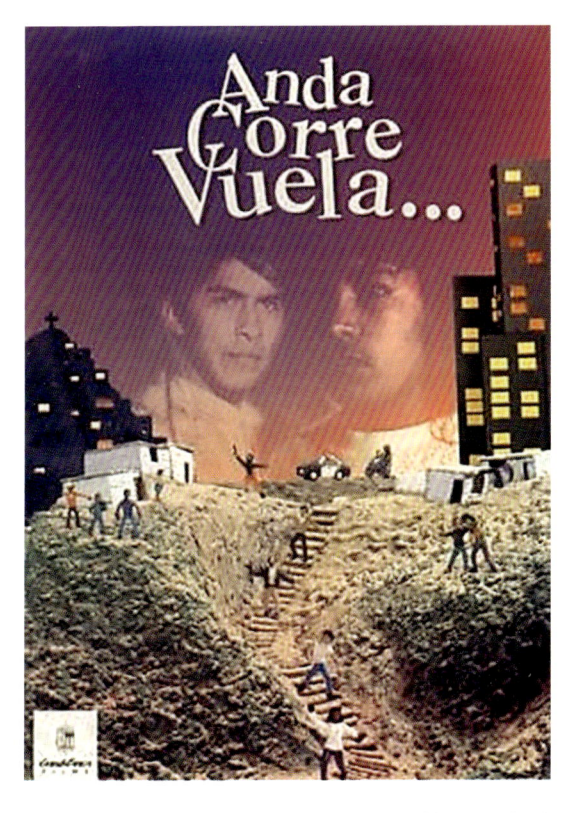

12. *Anda, corre, vuela* (Augusto Tamayo, 1995, Casablanca Films) – publicity poster showing Gregorio and Juliana running away from danger

13. *Coraje* (Alberto Durant, 1998, Agua Dulce Films) – María Elena Moyano galvanises her community of women into protest again Shining Path intimidation

14. *Coraje* (Alberto Durant, 1998, Agua Dulce Films) – publicity poster

15. *Paloma de papel* (Fabrizio Aguilar, 2003, Luna Llena Films) – young Juan is forced to take up arms

16. *Días de Santiago* (Josué Méndez, 2004, Chullachaki Producciones) – Santiago

17. *Días de Santiago* (Josué Méndez, 2004, Chullachaki Producciones) – Santiago and his former comrades

18. *Las malas intenciones* (Rosario García-Montero, 2011, Barry Films/Garmont Films) – Cayetana watches the world go by from her family's summer balcony, apparently distanced from real life and events

19. *Las malas intenciones* (Rosario García-Montero, 2011, Barry Films/Garmont Films) – Cayetana waits for her driver to arrive to take her home from school, protecting her from everyday life

20. *NN* (Héctor Gálvez, 2014, Piedra Alada Producciones/Séptima Films/Autentika Films/MPM Film) – Fidel searches for clues as to the identity of a victim of violence

21. *Magallanes* (Salvador del Solar, 2015, CEPA Audiovisual/Nephilim Producciones/Proyectil/Péndulo Films/Tondero Producciones) – Magallanes the taxi driver is confronted with the consequences of his past

22. *La última tarde* (Joel Calero, 2016, Factoria Sur/BF) – Ramón and Laura wander through the streets of Barranco as they wait for their divorce papers to be signed

23. *La última tarde* (Joel Calero, 2016, Factoria Sur/BF) – Laura

24. *La última tarde* (Joel Calero, 2016, Factoria Sur/BF) – Ramón

intensified their offensive on the Peruvian capital with car bombs, assassinations and armed attacks'.[54] He further explains that the distinguishing feature of these fresh attacks was the widening of the target to include middle- and upper-class areas of Lima, generating fear amongst an even wider and more influential portion of the population. The bombing in May of one of the main TV stations, Frecuencia Latina-Canal 2, which resulted in the death of one journalist and two security guards, caused particularly grave and widespread concern. Stringent anti-terrorist legislation was put in place that restricted many of the freedoms expected within the framework of a democracy, and which led to human rights abuses, as articulated by the disillusioned lawyer (Carlos Gassols) in this film.[55] Skidmore and Smith describe the new Fujimori regime as 'a textbook case of "illiberal democracy" – a regime that combines free elections for political office with systematic disrespect for the political and human rights of citizens'.[56] Newspaper headlines reporting on attacks and blackouts are shown in the film and commented on by the lawyer as contributing to a heightened sense of social hysteria. The pressure on the government to produce results intensified, and the film reflects this sense of urgency through the portrayal of a police force that is desperate to identify and lock up terrorist suspects, however flimsy the evidence. Meanwhile, the lawyer, representative here of Peru's disempowered and ineffective legal system, becomes so disgusted at his inability to protect the innocent and prevent further violence that he turns to drink and eventually kills himself. He advises Gregorio simply that there is no hope for Juliana, and that she is better off going into hiding to avoid imprisonment for a likely 20 years.

In fact, as in most of the films discussed so far, the sympathies, identifications and alignments are not clear cut, while violence is presented as virtually inevitable, as the only response on the part of both state and insurgents, with many caught in the cross-fire. Anonymous, hooded Shining Path attackers shoot indiscriminately at Juliana and the petrol station manager, and scatter ideological pamphlets bearing the group's sickle-and-hammer logo as they leave, having positioned their bomb to cause maximum destruction. Meanwhile, the police captain is depicted as a man determined to clamp down on terrorism and delinquency using any means necessary, and willing to lock up both protagonists as suspected accomplices to the attack. The need for visible results appears to justify the violence deployed to achieve them, with the clear implication that the imprisonment of marginalised young people who are flirting with criminality is far easier than dealing with experienced insurgents and drug-dealers. That the younger children are shown to have the courage, wisdom and moral determination to reject violence and look for different ways of changing their circumstances reinforces the point made about the ineffective nature of violence that pervades the state system and defines the national image.

The situation for Peruvians without identification documents, such as the youngsters in this film, is further complicated since it implies a lack of recognition by the state and the possibility of misinterpretation of their social status. Migrants from the Andes to Lima in the early 1990s were particularly vulnerable to accusations of terrorism, especially if their skin colour was noticeably dark and their economic status poor. This was seen with Jeremías in *Ni con dios* and again here, as Gregorio and Juliana, also migrants, are caught in the crossfire of delinquent and political conflict largely as a result of misrecognition, which was common at that time. For, as Alberto Flores Galindo observed, the Shining Path phenomenon deepened the distrust between different social groups.[57] The victimisation of Gregorio and Juliana draws attention to a deep-rooted racism in parts of Peruvian society that considers indigenous peoples as inherently and inescapably violent – as savage, uncivilised and primitive. As Víctor Vich suggests in his study of violence and culture in contemporary Peru, the military's counter-insurgency strategy seemed to be conceived as an extermination plan, 'where many of the main cultural tensions that structure Peruvian society general came to light'.[58] Such tensions are made evident here by the police captain's assumption that Juliana and Gregorio must be guilty of being part of the terrorist campaign, by virtue of their dark skin and their lack of official documents. Even the drug-dealers, white-skinned *criollos* who exploit and humiliate Juliana despite her efforts to help them out, are quick to distance themselves from her and label her *terruca* (slang for 'terrorist') when their plan to rob the petrol station is thwarted by the Shining Path attack. The cultural antagonism between them simmers away during earlier scenes, including one of attempted rape that brutally emphasises their assumption of macho cultural dominance. Blaming her for their misfortune, they then sadistically inflict further pain on her body and leave her to die. This episode illustrates the acute cultural distance between Juliana and the men: the visible difference of her skin colour combined with her status as a poor young female from a rural background make her, in their eyes, an object to be feared, reviled, punished and destroyed. As we have seen in all the films discussed so far in this study, gender, ethnic, racial and cultural difference are positioned here as dangerous, and particularly so if one character embodies all aspects of the marginalised.

By way of counterpoint, the film draws attention in a much more utopian way to the heterogeneity of the underclass of Lima in the 1990s, who themselves are represented as more broadly symbolic of the nation. The younger actors in particular were selected for the range of faces that they gave to the marginalised population of the capital. As in the Chaski Group's earlier feature films, however, these children are portrayed as survivors rather than victims, finding a social niche for themselves by providing unofficial services to the middle and higher classes of the city as shoeshine boys and flower sellers. They are depicted variously as wise, self-sufficient and resilient and, above all, aware that only by caring for each other will they be able to improve conditions for themselves. They also provide a link to a more traditional culture that underpins much of Peruvian society but which, in the early 1990s, was in danger of being erased from urban life. One of Gregorio's young shoeshine friends seems to possess magical powers that cannot be explained by the rationality that dominates a more Westernised sensibility. His interpretation of the whale sound which is heard diegetically at various key points during the film as an omen of good fortune and hope contrasts with the attitude of the North American marine biologist whose focus is on the whale's capacity to help him towards a better scientific understanding of the workings of the ocean. The discovery of the beached whale's carcass indirectly brings the youngsters money, which in turn enables them, once they have decided collectively how to spend it, to construct their own music venue, which they name La Ballena (The Whale). As with the reading of the coca leaves in *Ni con Dios*, this element of the film appears to serve as a reminder of the value of alternative, non-Western ways of understanding life, and as a warning not to disregard them as primitive and irrelevant. In particular, it draws attention to Andean culture and its emphasis on the interconnections between nature and man. As Vich points out, 'in the Andes, nature is integrated with the social world ... and the universe is conceived of as a living entity where there is no separation between humans and nature, individual and community, community and gods'.[59]

For those whose culture is rooted in Andean beliefs, animal and plant life is considered an ecological and a quasi-spiritual concern rather than the object of scientific research. Moreover, the Quechua magico-religious philosophy insists that the human and the natural worlds are interlinked in harmonious union.[60] The constant reference to this core feature of Andean cultural life applied to a coastal context through, for example, the mystical aural motif of the whale's call, points to the way in which such customs might still be relevant in offering means for dealing with social problems. It reminds the viewer of the existence of a world-view that by its very nature challenges the divisions and hierarchies that form the foundation of Westernised societies. For, as Rowe suggests, whereas on the one hand rapid modernisation has led to hybridisation of cultural forms and the fragmentation and dispersal of Andean culture, on the other hand the subsequent 'loss of traditional coherence for such modern hybridization gives Andean culture a new capacity to penetrate into the social fabric'.[61]

Anda, corre, vuela ..., perhaps more than any of the films discussed so far, constantly draws attention to its development of themes of nation and identity through casual and indirect reference to a range of elements of that are 'constitutive of everyday life'.[62] As Bedoya argues, the aesthetic principles of the Chaski Group were founded on 'the expression of the real the authentic, the "social"', and for Kaspar and his colleagues it was most important to depict 'the banal social experiences shared every day'.[63] First of all, the use of non-professional actors, of children from the streets and market-traders all talking directly to camera about their lives, creates the impression of a generalised, prototypic face of a marginalised society. An apparently neutral reportage style is used to film the latter group as they give details of their lives in a way that diverts attention from the central narrative. Rather than advance the narrative, this section exploits more apparently truthful documentary methods of representation and serves as a powerful testimonial of the harshness of life in the city. It thus further reinforces the idea of the film as sociological allegory and strengthens the impression of violence as an endemic feature of everyday life in Peru.

Again, as part of a body of work that is influenced by the methods of the Italian neorealists, location shooting is important. However, distinct spaces of regular social gathering, such as the national football stadium and the central fruit market, are used as the backdrop for key dramatic scenes that contribute to the establishment of a national image rooted in everyday life rather than in institutions. Juliana is often shown walking purposefully through the streets of various districts of the capital, at one point passing the yellow-painted walls of the colonial buildings of the city centre, for example, as she visits her drug-dealing acquaintances. For Bedoya, this very act of navigating the streets of Lima is suggestive of a kind of metaphysical merging on her part into the way of life in the city.[64] Meanwhile, familiar restaurants and hotels of the fashionable coastal area of Miraflores come into view as the flower sellers conduct their business amongst their wealthier neighbours. On the edge of this district are the clifftops where the girls live, which form a recurring backdrop to many of the film's more reflective moments. These clifftops, which are also the scene for the most dramatic chase and escape sequences, hold particular significance for the domestic spectator. As well as being familiar in themselves to most inhabitants of Lima and increasingly pictured on tourist websites about Lima, they had also already been used several times as a backdrop in national cinema, most famously in Lombardi's award-winning *Caídos del cielo/Fallen from the Sky* (1990). Moreover, the location provides a discreet reference, as did Lombardi's film more explicitly, to the short story *Al pie del acantilado/At the Foot of the Cliff*, by one of Peru's most important writers, Julio Ramón Ribeyro, whose work in general tackled themes of conflict, poverty and the effects of migration on cultural identity in the Lima of earlier decades.[65] The recurrence of these references through Juliana's escapades suggests that while context evolves, social conditions based on racial prejudice and socio-economic division remain much the same.

In a similar cultural vein, but with an eye to a more positive future, the choice of musical soundtrack to accompany the visual element of the film is important, since it serves to emphasise the producers' desire to draw attention to the creative potential of marginalised young people. The main theme tune is titled *Sarita Colonia*, after the most famous folk saint in Peru. With this overt reference to the national protector of the '"informals," taxi drivers, maids, job seekers, homosexuals, [and] migrants',[66] the lyrics further underscore the film's intention to focus on the 'lives of the common man/child, the ordinary character, the normal citizen' of Peru.[67] An original composition, it was written and performed by a local rock band, Los Mojarras, that went on to enjoy international success. As well as providing a non-diegetic soundtrack of protest to support the story of Juliana and Gregorio, the band enters the narrative world with their energetic rhythms and provide it with its jubilant closure. As in the earlier Chaski projects, grass-roots music is used here to reflect an atmosphere of resistance, and to help generate the solidarity missing from the children's lives in the early part of the film. Furthermore, it becomes another way of reinforcing a sense of everyday life that was so vital to the Chaski approach in their depictions of the hybrid mix of Lima culture.[68] Indeed, the ever-present 'chicha' soundtrack, with its 'flagrantly hybrid melody blending tropical, urban and Andean rhythms' becomes an expression of urban *mestizaje*.[69] It both represents and helps to shape that new sense of identity; it plays its part in the experiential process of identity formation and not only reflects the people but also 'produces them, creating and constructing an experience for them'.[70]

Music, as Simon Frith argues, 'is the cultural form best able both to cross borders – sounds carry across fences and walls and oceans, across classes, races and nations – and to define places',[71] and the final scene's wide overhead shot that pulls back to offer a view of the neighbourhood demonstrates the extent to which the rock sounds resonate across the whole *barrio*. Through the desire for a suitable venue in which to listen to and share the hybrid rock music that has emerged locally, new social bonds begin to be established that offer an alternative to dominant structures, and that help to redefine the space the protagonists wish to transform. This group of disparate and apparently marginalised young people are brought together by a mutual determination to improve their lives without relying on an ineffective state system that attacks rather than protects them. What is more, Juliana's position on stage as redeemed heroine of the drama, the bearer of the admiring and affectionate gaze, provides her with the status and self-respect that she has long desired and changes her self-perception as the film draws to a close. As she jumps off stage and mingles with the crowd, joined by Gregorio, her acceptance as part of the group is complete.

New Portraits of Society

Anda, corre, vuela ... was heralded as marking a new stage in national cinema production since it was one of the first to be released after the announcement of the new cinema law in 1994. In fact, however, it was filmed during the period when no law existed at all – that is to say during the hiatus between the two legislations of 1972 and 1994 – and relied upon overseas support, mainly from German co-production partners, to raise the budget of $320,000.[72] The film should have appeared on screens two years earlier, but delays in the Venezuelan processing laboratories meant that it took longer than anticipated to reach its audience. The consequence of this was that the film lost much of its resonance in the intervening years. Producer Kaspar notes that 'despite screening the film on eight copies via a circuit of the best screens, audience numbers were low and the exhibitors had to pull it from their programmes'.[73] The portrait of a 1980s Peruvian society in crisis offered by the story of Gregorio and Juliana was barely recognisable a decade later. It presents itself with the immediacy and urgency of a contemporary tale and yet the vision of Lima under attack was no longer deemed relevant. Kaspar himself seemed to realise the problem of a changed political climate that did not allow for memories of a violent national past. He insisted that the narrative and thematic focus on the marginalised youth of Lima remained valid, but acknowledged in interviews that he had not taken sufficient account of the way public interest would shift with changes in social context. 'In these times, people do not want to look back', he claimed, realising that it was too soon for audiences to be confronted with images of a nightmare that had only just ended.[74] Peru remained violent and issues relating to national identity were far from resolved, but the specific events and character types portrayed belonged to the past. While most critics pointed to other weaknesses in the film that had more to do with the film's stylistic approach,[75] Bedoya suggested that the disconnect between the period of production and date of release was a major problem.

On the other hand, the film was selected for screening at a number of international film festivals and won several awards.[76] Commentator Christian Wiener insisted that the film was made primarily with a European audience in mind, describing it as 'an action film which includes urban terrorism as part of a dossier of topics combining ecology, marginality and youth; politically correct themes aimed at Europe'.[77] This point is given some credence by the fact that the co-production agreement with Zweiten Deutschen Fernsehen (ZDF) included an obligation to screen the film as part of a German TV season on marginalised children around the world. It also fits with the accusation of paternalism and sentimentality directed by national critics at the earlier work of the Chaski Group, who dismissed the image of nation offered in their films as excessively sympathetic towards those living in poverty.

Bedoya, however, suggests another problem. He argues that the archetypal characters of Juliana and Gregorio, now adolescents, 'had lost the capacity to represent those social types who mixed marginality and resistance' as they had done in the Chaski films of the 1980s.[78] Here, they seem locked in a time warp and of far less relevance to society than their younger selves had been, as if their search for identity has stagnated for several long years. Furthermore, public perceptions of street children have always tended to differ from their perceptions of street teenagers, who are viewed as far more threatening, especially in the wake of Shining Path activity in the shanty towns.

Meanwhile, Peru – and Lima in particular – was in the process of becoming more integrated and pluralistic, more accepting of the diverse communities that together formed its national image. As the 1990s progressed, although many problems remained, there was a gradual movement towards a much greater level of participation by a wider range of social groups in the affairs of the nation. President Fujimori was also active in trying to include and address these traditionally marginal sectors during his first term in power, such that aggression based on a simplistic binary 'white/rich versus the rest' model of society was less easy to sustain. The multiracial and multicultural character of Peru was on its way, according to David Wood, to finding 'a greater recognition at national level',[79] none of which is acknowledged in this post-Chaski production. Instead, the young characters remain on the margins of society, excluded from the official national image.

Creating an Icon: *Coraje/Courage* (Alberto Durant, 1998)

Coraje was one of only two national films released in 1998, after a barren year for national cinema production.[80] The initial optimism felt by some at the introduction of new cinema legislation in 1994 had quickly dissipated, and there was widespread disappointment at the delays in administering the proposed new funding competitions. The development and production of *Coraje* took seven years, during which time the political and cinematic landscape in Peru changed radically. The achievement of bringing a national film to the screen was widely acknowledged by critics such as Rafaela García de Pinilla, who pointed out at the time of *Coraje*'s release that 'to make cinema today in Peru is a titanic achievement that requires patience and commitment'.[81] This discussion explores the representation of a controversial woman whose real-life role as defiant community leader is presented in the film as an iconic figurehead for non-violent social change. (See Plate 13) It also probes further both the role of cinema as part of public debate on events of national concern, and its capacity to provoke alternative perspectives on the prevailing hegemonic discourse.

Production Contexts

Durant's film was profoundly affected not only by changes in the sociopolitical context that saw the demise of the Shining Path conflict and an increasingly repressive neoliberal regime, but also by reforms made to national cinema legislation. It therefore seems especially important to take account of the peripheral discussion about national cinema in 1998 before considering the approach taken in *Coraje* to the conflict. The legislative reforms resulted in increased production costs, a requirement to source finance from outside Peru amongst the highly competitive and increasingly demanding co-production market, and the involvement of several scriptwriters and funders with conflicting ideas and priorities.[82] The transnational complexity of the production arrangements had considerable bearing on the approach to representation of an important and controversial figure of recent Peruvian history, María Elena Moyano. The tendency of funders to prioritise images of the Peruvian nation that conform to essentialist stereotypes and myths about Latin American machismo and violence has to be borne in mind, especially since the main outlet for such a film would be the global film festival circuit.[83]

Despite its anti-authoritarian approach, the film's treatment by the state was ambivalent. On the one hand, its very existence depended at least in part upon the new cinema legislation introduced by the Fujimori regime: the project received government funding as one of the first feature script proposals to win an award from the newly established CONACINE. Placed second, it received a grant that amounted to almost 40% of a total budget of $1million, one of the largest to that date for any Peruvian film.[84] As such, it was regarded by critics as something of a landmark for national cinema at that time, even before it was released.[85] Not surprisingly, therefore, it generated a high level of expectation amongst domestic observers who wanted to believe that the new law would signal a change in fortunes for national cinema, but who acknowledged the constant struggles faced by Peruvian directors.[86] Veteran filmmaker Armando Robles Godoy proclaimed during an interview in which he discussed the state of national cinema at the time *Coraje* was released that, despite the welcome appearance of a new film, Peruvian cinema was in its death throes. He described it as an 'agony that began in 1992 when cinema was at the mercy of the Ministry of Economy and its sterile dogma of market theology'.[87] It was within this difficult economic climate that *Coraje* was brought to the screen, during a period that also witnessed the gradual stifling of debate across the national media on the 'dirty war'. Although cinema was not the target of direct censorship and fraudulent control in the same way that the national television and press were, it nevertheless suffered from economic pressures that led to the absence of home-grown product on domestic screens.

Framing Nation and Violence

Coraje is based directly on a specific episode of the Shining Path conflict and focuses on one extraordinary individual, María Elena Moyano (Olenka Cepeda), who was familiar to the Peruvian public since her exploits and eventual death were widely reported across the national media. This film depicts the final three months of her life as the vice-mayor of one of Lima's most important *barriadas*, Villa El Salvador, where she was an outspoken critic of both Shining Path and military violence. Shooting of the film began exactly six years after Moyano's assassination by Shining Path on 15 February 1992. It offers a largely sympathetic perspective, as one reviewer put it, of 'the colourful and polemical life of a woman of great virtue'.[88] It shows her in the roles of mother, wife, friend, colleague and community leader and presents her as a flawed but admirable fighter for community benefits at a time of heightened social crisis, soaring inflation and escalating guerrilla violence. At the beginning of the 1990s, Peru was 'on the edge of an abyss' and this film presents Moyano's story within that context of crisis.[89] Key features of her character and scenes from the last months of her life are selectively portrayed so as to emphasise the film's broader message that political alternatives to violence must be sought as the principal solution to the problems of Peru. Her story is used to insist on a rethinking of the outlook for a nation much troubled at that time by injustice, poverty and institutional corruption.

Moyano was one of the leaders of Villa El Salvador's Women's Federation, which was popularly regarded as one of the 'key pillars of the district's unique and much-heralded model of self-management' and which is depicted here as instrumental in the campaign to resist Shining Path violence.[90] The vital importance of this aspect of her work is stressed in the opening scene, which focuses on Moyano's return from a prize-giving ceremony in Madrid, where she received an award from the King of Spain for her work for women's rights. Indeed, many of the film's most compelling scenes thereafter show her battling to convince her frightened

Federation comrades that they should continue to provide the essential services of food and clothing despite the brutal intimidation tactics of armed Shining Path gangs. She is portrayed thus as the embodiment of the philosophy and ideology of non-violent protest as the only long-term solution to many of the problems faced by Peru, and in particular the immediate threat posed by Shining Path insurgents.

Christian Wiener draws attention to the notion that this film, ostensibly a straightforward reconstruction of one woman's remarkable life, might be interpreted more broadly as a discussion of the national political and economic crises and the various responses to them by both the state and the communities most affected.[91] Familiar key moments of Moyano's life are reconstructed partly so as to provide an insight into her heroic character, but also in order to prompt debate about the effect of the political violence on a community that had been severely affected by poverty resulting from the economic shock policies. Sumita Chakravarty argues in her discussion of film and terrorism that 'in narrative cinema a sense of collective identity can only be mediated and dramatised through the particular' and that would appear to be the approach in Durant's portrayal of the nation via Moyano.[92] As such, it is important to unravel the main points of this screen representation of one woman's life, and to get a sense of how the director attempts to encourage his audience to make the imaginative leap from the particular to the collective in an effort to ignite broader political debate.

In Wiener's description of Moyano's quest, he pinpoints, for example, the crucial aspect of her agenda that made this woman symbolic of those leaders and campaigners who regarded both government and Shining Path propositions as irrelevant to the needs of their community:

> Like other popular leaders who became victims of the indiscriminate terror of Sendero and the Armed and Police Forces, she fought to consolidate popular organisation, aiming thereby to improve the conditions for the poor of her district, and seeking a third way to resolve the dreadful conflict.[93]

Like several of the iconic protagonists in other films already discussed, Moyano stands out for placing herself firmly in the crossfire between insurgents and state. She assumes an important symbolic role that allows issues to be addressed pertaining to the complex and shifting relationships between national identity and violence in Peru. In this film, images of Moyano that depict her at the head of peace marches and taking a defiant stand in public against Shining Path demands for food and support demonstrate her refusal to accept their alternative vision for the nation based on a revolution defined primarily by destruction. The mediation of some of these episodes through reconstructed TV reports adds further weight to her perceived status as a key national figure whose political message as protagonist resonates beyond the borders of Villa El Salvador. At the same time, she is angered by the Fujimori government's failure to address urgently the problems of hunger and deprivation in such communities, and frustrated by the state's neglect in protecting its citizens from structural and political violence in the form of poverty and terrorism. Scenes that show her refusing to bow to convention when she goes to demand more food from the Minister reinforce this aspect of her character. *Coraje* thus embraces and embellishes Moyano's identity both as a symbol of resistance to Shining Path violence and as a female figurehead of peaceful struggle within Peruvian society more generally.

Moyano became famous nationally for confronting Shining Path at a time when the group's destructive strategies began to take their toll on the capital itself, and when the state response had mutated into one of intense brutality, with little or no concern for accompanying campaigns of social development. She was one of the few dissenters who dared to speak out against both insurgents and the state, and who at the same time attempted to offer an alternative solution based on human rights, especially those of Peruvian women. As one of the film's reviewers put it, her defiance was particularly notable because Shining Path was attempting to infiltrate key districts such as Villa El Salvador, by tempting its leaders with the offer of alliance and protection.[94]

Moyano was recognised as an articulate proponent of a non-violent path between state and guerrilla terrorism. She represented a new kind of leader emerging in the *barriadas*: 'young, feminist, nonwhite, progressive but not tied to any major political party'.[95] In *Coraje*, such features are emphasised and shown to contribute both to her triumph and to her downfall. While perceived by other community figures as brave in her determination to resist pressure, Moyano's position is shown as one of increasing isolation from the women's group she leads and in which she takes so much pride. This is in part due to her refusal to collaborate with Shining Path, which promises not to make them the target of future attacks if she will agree to provide them with the benefits of their achievements. Some of her oldest friends, more fearful of Shining Path reprisals than of state intervention, find it difficult to comprehend her decision instead to press ahead with negotiation with the government; indeed, they begin to suspect her of less altruistic motives than those she claims to have. Images show Shining Path propaganda leaflets that accuse Moyano of corruption and cronyism, appealing to the rivalries and divisions that are exposed through fear and poverty and further inflaming this criticism. So does a sequence that reveals a conversation with a taxi driver, who accuses her of collusion with the state for personal benefit. The film paints her as stubborn and strong-willed in the face of declining support, even ignoring the mayor's friendly warning not to speak out about Shining Path at the funeral of a neighbour's husband, who was a victim of guerrilla violence. Meanwhile, her best friend, Paulina (María Teresa Zúñiga), breaks off contact altogether with the Women's Federation, having witnessed the imprisonment of her husband as a Shining Path activist. Paulina is plunged even deeper into poverty and believes that only Shining Path will offer salvation. Such portrayals of intra-community fragmentation were indeed realistic; several studies attest to divisions in neighbourhoods like Villa that contradict more romantic claims about urban self-determination and popular unity.[96] However, in the context of this film they also serve to reinforce Moyano's status as a defiant leader who was willing to sacrifice everything she held dear in order to remain true to her principles. In this sense, then, they take the film beyond realism and elevate Moyano to the status of a symbolic national martyr for the cause of non-violent protest.

Moyano advocated social revolution and reform based on constructive strategies, and key scenes that depict her negotiations with both Shining Path cell leaders and state ministers emphasise this alternative ideological approach to the nation's problems. In life, she campaigned for a policy of grass-roots participation and solidarity, in opposition to both a reactionary government and the tyrannical insurrection of Shining Path.

In an interview in 1991, the 'real' Moyano spoke of her absolute faith in the power of strong community groups to combat terrorism: 'I believe that we women have a lot of strength. If we believe in what we are building, there's no reason to be afraid'.[97] Many of these words and sentiments make their way into the film's script. Given that the battle against Shining Path was worsening, many of those who did not consider her corrupt accused her instead of naivety. In *Coraje*, this is depicted sympathetically as devotion to her community, and as intense belief in the ethical superiority of her intentions. It is emphasised that she found it impossible to tear herself away from the people she loved so much and who helped to define and give her life purpose. Two key scenes highlight this urge as she insists on returning to Villa El Salvador from potential safe havens in Madrid and, later, in Miraflores, despite death threats and clear evidence of an assassination plot. She has adequate resources and support to transgress national borders, yet in her mind the local community, here signifying the 'nation-in-microcosm',[98] is the only meaningful entity.

To acknowledge and refute the accusations of naivety, there are moments in the film when Moyano is shown to be completely lucid about the danger to which she is exposing herself. She speaks to the Spanish doctor, Jimena (Rosana Pastor), about the sacrifices she is prepared to make rather than give in to Shining Path intimidation, and about how she feels torn between her responsibilities as mother and wife, and her duties as community leader. Nevertheless, the film is ambiguous in this respect, drawing attention to Moyano's egoism by tracking the development of her own awareness of her ability to overcome the invincible might of Sendero, as well as by her undoubted attraction to being in the media spotlight. In life, she appeared regularly in Lima's newspapers and weekly magazines as an example of how to combat terror and, as Jo-Marie Burt explains, she 'became something of a celebrity for her outspoken criticism of Shining Path'.[99] In the film, her fame within Villa El Salvador is emphasised; she appears to take pleasure in both the power that her fame brings and in the fame itself, neglecting her own family's need for her attention.

The final scene of the film, depicting her death, adds further weight to the criticisms of Moyano as egocentric and lacking in judgement. Her high public profile means that she is easily tracked by Shining Path spies and becomes a key target of aggression. While defiantly leading a peace march that most of the community ignores, she is handed an invitation to a community barbecue in an area of Villa El Salvador that she does not really know. She is reluctant to accept, but is persuaded to attend as guest of honour. The next scene shows her enjoying a day on the beach with her two sons, after which she goes to the community event, dragging the boys along with her. On the way, Paulina tries to warn her of the danger, but to no avail. She walks right into the trap: all around her are Shining Path sympathisers who regard her as being on the side of the enemy state. Not only is she shot dead at point blank range in front of her sons, but her body is blown up, destroying any physical trace of her existence and all she stood for.

In the end, however, the film appears to suggest that Moyano's belief in her role as community leader and her utter faith in the moral integrity of non-violent protest were more important than her own life and the needs of her family. Indeed, her death, as Skidmore and Smith remind us, 'made her a martyr for the cause of political reform, as distinct from revolution, and for the empowerment of women throughout Latin America'.[100] The film emphasises the notion of self-sacrifice by focusing, in the last moments, on her refusal to give in to the pressures of violence. The tragedy is further emphasised when Paulina, whose choice in committing herself to the Shining Path cause is presented as unfortunate but not without reason, is shown making efforts to save her friend despite their fundamental differences. Paradoxically, the film's own commitment to peaceful protest and social development as the only long-term strategy for resolving Peru's social and political issues of inequality is made absolutely clear by presenting Moyano's death in such a violent way.

Moyano is signalled as different not only by her gender and political beliefs, but also by her racial and ethnic identity. Referred to affectionately by friends as La Negra, she is racially and ethnically marked out as belonging to the minority Afro-Peruvian group. Her non-conformist nature and her different cultural roots are celebrated by the film. Her refusal to integrate, assimilate or to form politically expedient alliances is highlighted throughout, as is her pride in being part of and in part defined by a community that seems to value diversity. Nevertheless, she dies partly because she speaks and stands out, causing resentment, and partly because she is not totally aware of the danger her position of difference brings. She resists intimidation and makes choices that she did not even know she had. In real life this attitude of defiance went on record in a host of media interviews, while in the film she is shown broadcasting her views over national TV and local radio and discussing them privately with the fictional character Jimena.[101]

The final text that precedes the end credits implies that Moyano's assassination had the effect of galvanising broad national resistance to the conflict and to violence generally. However, Burt's extensive research on the infiltration of Shining Path into Villa El Salvador suggests that in reality the impact of her death was more complex. She writes that 'a massive funeral procession was held for Moyano, but numerous observers noted that local participation was minimal, and that Shining Path's intended objective – to inculcate fear and inhibit any further efforts at resistance in Villa El Salvador – had largely succeeded'.[102] After her death, Shining Path continued its campaign of intimidation of community leaders, infiltration of community groups, manipulation of internal rivalries, and further accusations of corruption that were 'undoubtedly exacerbated by the context of economic deprivation, which heightened suspicions of those with access to resources and power at all levels of society'.[103] Furthermore, the Peace and Development Group that Moyano had set up was disbanded, and new alliances were formed between Shining Path and various groups within Villa El Salvador that held grievances against the left-wing municipal leadership, with some even refusing to denounce Moyano's murder. Fujimori's *autogolpe* two months later did not help matters; instead, it heightened fears about the repressive nature of the state and the security forces. The film's attempt to position Moyano's death as marking 'the beginning of the end' of the conflict was an oversimplification of a very complex reality. For narrative impact, *Coraje* reifies her status as martyr, and emphasises the power of community solidarity, neatly avoiding many other factors that led to the end of the conflict, including the government's own success in capturing Shining Path's leader. This mismatch between reality and representation draws attention again to the problems raised by delays in producing and releasing national films. It also demonstrates the intention of the director to move away from documentary realism in his approach, and to use Moyano's story as a device with which to promote the wider issues of human rights as well as peaceful solutions to the political, economic and social problems that have become inextricably linked with a stereotypical view of Peru as violent and macho.

The film's protest against violence is further highlighted by its graphic portrayal of Shining Path characters and attacks. The terrorist presence in *Coraje* is first suggested with an image, shown from Moyano's horrified point of view, of a dead dog hanging from a lamp-post on the road from Lima to Villa El Salvador – the standard calling card of Shining Path intimidation. The audience is thus positioned from the outset to share the disgust of the protagonist at the guerrilla tactics of terror, and in fact at any form of violence. In one sense, the portrayal of these terrorists is sketchy and lacking in depth, with only fleeting images of hooded youths on motorbikes; a bespectacled cell leader who carries out negotiations and gives overall orders; the emotionless young women who spy on Moyano and perpetrate the final act of assassination. The hooded youths at first do little more than paint anti-state slogans, for which they become the target of police shooting. However, the sketchiness of this portrayal is in itself a device that serves to emphasise the film's broader political intentions. From this point on, the depiction of Shining Path violence focuses on attacks on specific community targets, thus exposing their intentions of destruction while also revealing factions within the neighbourhood self-help groups themselves. In one particularly dramatic scene, the soup kitchen is attacked and the main cook, a staunch supporter of Moyano, is badly injured and traumatised. As a result, she and other core members of the women's group are fearful of reprisals and reluctant to become more deeply involved. Their fear and desire to protect their families is shown in marked contrast with Moyano's strong sense of duty to the wider community. Later the town hall (symbolic of governmental authority and oppression) is burnt down. The slogans, graffiti and leaflets continue to spread propaganda, while activists chanting by night on the fringes of the suburb, where city meets Andean foothills, promote the chilling sense of an invisible, ubiquitous threat. Live TV and radio reports of violence are seen and heard at key moments in the film, and an image of a car bomb explosion on the front page of the Spanish daily *El País* prompts Moyano to return home from Madrid, despite the threats to her life.[104]

While Moyano's main anger is reserved for the brutality of the insurgent group, the government and its military force are portrayed as ineffective and neglectful in terms of their duty to protect the citizens of Peru. Some figures of authority, such as the local mayor, who is viewed more as a local resident than as a state representative, are treated sympathetically. National leaders, however, are depicted as remote and posturing, caught up in meetings to discuss the bigger picture rather than taking action to solve immediate, human concerns. Their position is undermined as they are shown as more involved with international relationships than with addressing local problems, as seen when Moyano barges in on a high-level meeting and demands more bags of rice for the soup kitchens. The critical thrust of the film is clear, emphasising the perception of state failure to provide peaceful long-term solutions to the nation's overall political, economic and social difficulties. Moreover, while Moyano is willing to make the journey from suburb to centre, the politicians are clearly unlikely to enter any shanty town in person. Meanwhile, the few interventions by the police or military are depicted as largely ineffectual. Their shooting at graffiti painters and the disappearing of suspected sympathisers without evidence serve mainly to deepen the rift between state and its people, pushing the latter towards retaliation and recrimination.[105]

The diversity of the marginalised of the Peruvian nation is conveyed by including the depiction of Villa inhabitants from a range of ethnic backgrounds. The positive aspects of such diversity are highlighted by drawing constant attention to Moyano's enjoyment of belonging to a culturally mixed, differentiated community. The joyful participation of a Spanish woman (Jimena) in community-building activities through her work as a doctor further underscores this point about tolerance. Jimena's cheerful response to the light teasing she receives from her brother for having picked up a local Villa accent emphasises the affection she feels for the community. Moyano acknowledges that the community has become united in large part due to their shared experience of poverty and hunger, which have resulted from the state's harsh economic policies, and she insists they take collective responsibility for improving the situation. However, some inhabitants of Villa El Salvador are clearly less deprived than others, and resentment builds up towards Moyano because of her overseas trips and comparative comfort. The location depicted by Durant becomes another example of a community caught in the crossfire, between state neglect and Shining Path violence, in which differences in response to such difficulties are exposed and exploited. Moyano is silenced for trying not only to defend her people but also to promote a more progressive model of participation and self-management, which was seen as a threat to Shining Path as an alternative framework for the renegotiation of the state's relationship with the citizens of Peru.

Shifting Landscapes

The fate of Durant's feature film was determined by shifts in the sociopolitical landscape in Peru during the film's seven-year period of development. I argue that this would have mattered less if the film had not been linked so directly to a complex national social-economic crisis. State oppression had replaced Shining Path barbarism, and open criticism of government authority was treated with suspicion. It is notable that the script went through 37 drafts, involving at least seven other writers, before being presented to CONACINE in 1998.[106] It is tempting to speculate that, in the process, some aspects of Durant's own political stance could have been tempered.

The complex funding arrangement noted earlier might also have affected the balance of representation of political conflict in *Coraje*. Due to the 1994 cinema legislation, much of the finance for feature projects had to come from non-state sources, and in the case of this film at least nine other supporters were involved, most based outside Peru and several of them outside Latin America. Many of these investors had motives beyond the desire to support national cinema that prompted their involvement in this production. Frecuencia Latina, for example, a private Peruvian TV channel, declared itself keen to use the film to promote itself outside

Peru, banking on the potential of guaranteed festival and TV screenings in Spain and Germany.[107] Moreover, while it is true that most of the main actors in *Coraje* are Peruvian, as were almost all of the scriptwriters, it is possible to detect more European influence in the content of *Coraje*, than, for example, in Lombardi's *La boca del lobo* in 1988. While co-production finance has been vital to support developing national cinema sectors, there are potential disadvantages relating to postcolonial power dynamics. As Wiener comments:

> In this context, it is often the case that projects are modified as a result of suggestions and pressure from the funders, who almost always have their own ideas, concepts and prejudices about third world and Latin American realities.[108]

He suggests that this might explain, for example, the slightly awkward long middle sequence, set in Madrid, and the inclusion of the doctor played by Spanish actress Rosana Pastor, both of which, he contends, do little more than detract from the core themes and events. In a similar vein, the heavy-handed musical soundtrack composed by the Spaniard Juan Bardem, which is heard whenever Moyano speaks of her love for her community, provides further evidence of sentimentality towards and simplification of a complex Peruvian reality, perhaps aimed at a European audience with less knowledge of the socio-political circumstances.[109] Moreover the framing of the drama in the publicity poster (see Plate 14) draws attention to the protagonist's emotional attachments and away from the harsh consequences of the decisions she made.

Despite its weaknesses, *Coraje* was regarded by many commentators as a necessary film that served a cathartic purpose for its Peruvian audiences. Salvador del Solar,[110] who plays Umberto, Moyano's political colleague and drinking partner, suggested in an interview that 'at a time when entertainment seems to be about what sells best, it's really important that past events such as these should be brought to us in this way'.[111] Film productions made as part of the national cinema sector offered reminders of an era of fear that had for the most part already been forgotten due to repression of critical discussion in the national mass media. Wiener suggests that the rather tepid domestic response to Durant's film could indeed relate to questions of cultural memory and collective trauma. Perhaps, he says, 'we should wait for time to pass and for wounds to heal, before we can speak openly about one of the most painful but important chapters of our contemporary history'.[112]

A study of the reviews that appeared at the time seems to show that most domestic critics were disappointed by the film's apparent lack of incisive critique of the role of the state in protecting communities such as Villa El Salvador. Others, meanwhile, suggested that it needed a clearer ideological message that would set itself more obviously against the violent message of Shining Path. These commentators complained that the image offered of the terrorists was too ambivalent, and that Shining Path activists were depicted more as delinquents than as a political threat to the stability of an entire nation.[113] However, the main dilemma of the film hinges not so much on Moyano's political affiliations as on her urgent need to decide whether or not to submit herself to exile from the community to which she is so profoundly attached. Understanding the bond she felt to her birthplace and her people is crucial to appreciating the drama behind her inevitable return, despite the certain danger that this act entailed. This element of thematic interest appears to have been overwhelmed by the topicality of the subject matter, by its ambivalent documentary form, and by the subsequent close attention paid by critics and audiences to the realism of the reconstruction of the last events in Moyano's life. The additional symbolic meaning with which the protagonist's quest is endowed and the transgressive aspects of her persona and behaviour suggested new ways of negotiating national identity, founded on feminism and political resistance, as opposed to patriarchy and violent repression.

4

Cinema, Memory and Truth, 2000–2004

The films examined in this chapter have succeeded in gaining international recognition, even while dealing with specific local and topical concerns, and which emphasise the way in which cinematic storytelling continues to be used as an expression of individual and collective reconciliation with traumas of the recent past. The work of those such as Mette Hjort and Susan Hayward on framing the nation and thematisation of the national, as well as by Deborah Shaw, Elizabeth Ezra and Rosalind Galt on questions of the 'transnational', are used to approach and understand the effective interweaving of topical and perennial concerns. The trope of the child is further located as a means of enabling audiences without specific knowledge of the local contexts portrayed nevertheless to access the meaning of the storylines; they are also enabled to ask to what extent the child's story serves as a 'metonym for wider suffering' and/or as a blank screen on which to 'project adult emotions and fears'.[1]

By the end of the 1990s and Fujimori's second term in office, dissatisfaction with the President's increasingly dictatorial style of government had spread and social unrest was on the rise. Despite winning a third term after a suspicious election in early 2000, he was forced to resign after the national media revealed a series of corruption scandals that implicated Fujimori and many of his senior ministers. An interim government oversaw fresh elections and established the Truth and Reconciliation Commission that had long been promised as a way of exposing some of the ugliest realities of the so-called 'dirty war'. While the Commission was welcomed by many, it was greeted with suspicion by others, who preferred, for a range of reasons, to forget the traumas of the past. Amongst other things, the Commission's final report, published in September 2003, argued that many of the acts of violence perpetrated by the military resulted from deep racial prejudice and lack of cultural understanding.

By 2003, the contentious cinema legislation established in 1994 was still in place, but only a small proportion of the intended funding had been made available during those first nine years of the new legal framework for supporting cinema production. It had proven difficult for the body established to oversee the administration of its activities to fulfil its mission in a way that would set the agenda and create the infrastructure for the development of a sustainable national film industry. Amongst the new generation of Peruvian filmmakers, there was increasing awareness and acceptance of the need to look beyond national borders for funding, an approach that represented a departure from the attitude of some of their predecessors, who had favoured the protectionist model of more vigorous state support.

Indeed, the funding histories of the films discussed in this chapter demonstrate both the possibilities and complexities of increasingly transnational co-production arrangements. These films turn towards a focus on the experience of young men whose childhoods were disrupted by traumas of domestic and political violence. *Paloma de papel/Paper Dove* (Aguilar, 2003) re-imagines its protagonist's childhood in a rural village and remembers his reluctant involvement with the insurgent campaign, while the eponymous protagonist of *Días de Santiago/Days of Santiago* (Méndez, 2004) struggles to cope with his return to civilian and family life in Lima after several years fighting as a member of the marines in remote parts of Peru. Each film exposes the persistence of prejudice rooted in cultural and economic difference.[2]

Shaping Memories of National Trauma: *Paloma de papel*/*Paper Dove* (Fabrizio Aguilar, 2003)

After a five-year hiatus during which national filmmakers struggled to find funding, and turned to popular genres such as comedy, historical epic and melodrama, the topical theme of social and political conflict returned to national screens in two of the most successful Peruvian feature films of recent years.[3] The first of these, *Paloma de papel*, by the *limeño* Fabrizio Aguilar, takes a child's point of view towards the trauma suffered by an Andean village caught in the crossfire of Shining Path violence. It became the third most popular film at the domestic box office in 2003, and was selected for screening at international events worldwide. A year later, *Días de Santiago*, the debut film from another young Lima-based director, Josué Méndez, appeared on cinema screens in Lima. This film, which depicts the difficult return of a young 'veteran' of armed conflict in the Peruvian jungle to civilian life in Lima, garnered awards at many international festivals, and enjoyed similar resounding success on domestic screens in 2004–2005. This and the following section of this study explore these two recent portrayals of political violence and national identity in feature filmmaking in Peru. They identify continuities with and breaks from their cinematic predecessors in terms of their approaches to representation of conflict and community. As before, the analyses emphasise the evolving role that national cinema seeks to play in reflecting and shaping the nation and national identity in times of uncertainty and social fragmentation. Given their temporal distance from actual events, the importance of memory, collective as well as individual, in both films is discussed. Finally, the cultural significance of acts and rituals of remembrance in dealing with traumatic episodes is explored.

Production Contexts

By the time the films by Aguilar and Méndez were released, some distance with their subject matter had been established, which allowed for a less divisive reception from authorities and at the box office. The political violence with Shining Path had officially ended over a decade before with the capture of Abimael Guzmán and the subsequent fragmentation of the insurgent cause. Yet during the intervening years, especially during the second term of the Fujimori regime (1995–2000), open debate about the effects and consequences of such a difficult and painful era in Peru's history was limited, and rumours of intimidation of those who persisted in trying to start such a debate were rife.[4] Instead of tackling themes of political violence, portrayals of other situations and issues of relevance to contemporary Peruvian society – such as delinquency, consumerism, the mass media and the role of women – were offered instead.[5] Several of these films, including those made outside Lima, where the horror genre was popular, also eschewed the more social realist approach to representation used by those covered in this study, and deployed historical myth, provocative satire or excessive melodrama instead.

The two films considered here offer an intimate view of contemporary events, and they focus on the 'intimate gaze' of their protagonists towards everyday life and immediate concerns.[6] *Paloma de papel* was the first national film since 1998 to focus on the specific political conflict between Shining Path and the military, and the first since 1993 to address the effect of that conflict on highland communities. It had won third prize in the feature project awards held by CONACINE in 2000, and eventually raised the remaining 60% of the $380,000 budget from the Hispanic film programme Ibermedia, the Cuban film institute ICAIC and the North American development agency USAID.[7] It became Peru's entry for the Academy Awards in 2004 and, as such, achieved a clear mark of approval from the administration under Alejandro Toledo (2001–2006), the first Peruvian president of indigenous identity. Aguilar also wrote the script, sourced the funds, identified locations and carried out casting trials with thousands of children; he thus continued the tradition set by several of his predecessors by taking lead responsibility for his film project and maintaining faith in it for half a decade. As Federico de Cárdenas points out, Aguilar's journey towards becoming a filmmaker is 'a story like many others with its mix of dream, reality and frustration when trying to make cinema in a poor country like ours'.[8]

Although the idea and script for *Paloma* were inspired by national TV reports watched by Aguilar, as a child, about the violent conflict raging in more remote areas of Peru, the film is not based on real events. Instead, it is a fictional account of what he imagines life might have been like for children growing up in the midst of violence. Born in Lima in 1973, Aguilar would have been the same age (12) as his protagonist, Juan, when Shining Path violence was reaching its peak in the Andean regions in the mid-1980s. The film thus appears to seek a connection between the director and his main character's experiences through his own memories of a childhood coloured by images of violence. During an interview given at the time of the film's screening at the Havana Festival of Latin American Cinema 2004, Aguilar admitted that he wanted to use cinema to focus on stories connected to his country.[9] In the same interview, he claims not consciously to have made a film that would become iconic for the suffering of millions of indigenous Peruvians, nor to be concerned with debates about violence and national identity. Nevertheless, the film was received as an effective invocation for human rights, in particular for those Peruvians caught up in the conflict whose story had yet to be told.

This broader understanding of the film arises in part as a result of the timing of its release, and its inevitable connection to events that affected the very fabric of Peruvian society and the way the nation imagined itself. By the time of the film's domestic release, Fujimori's regime had been denounced publicly as corrupt and oppressive, and an interim government attempted to stabilise the political situation until the elections in 2001, when Alejandro Toledo was appointed president.[10] Moreover, the Comisión de la Verdad y Reconciliación (CVR)/Truth and Reconciliation Commission had been in operation for over two years, and thousands of citizens from all over Peru had been offered the opportunity to give statements about what they had seen and suffered at the hands of both Shining Path and the armed forces.[11] The CVR's final report was published during the same month as the release of Aguilar's film, and both were interpreted as expressions of remembrance and acknowledgement of a traumatic national experience. At the same time, they both also drew attention to the deep cultural divides that persisted in Peruvian society. As Pilar Coll points out, the CVR's research highlighted 'the gravity of racial and cultural inequality that still prevails in our country';[12] meanwhile, *Paloma de papel* draws attention to some of the complexities of a conflict that killed many of the nation's most marginalised and impoverished people. In particular, as Eyde's *La vida es una sola* had attempted to do in 1993, it raises questions about the boundary between victim and villain and demonstrates the hazy nature of such a conceptual division at times of extreme social crisis.

This is a film that works on several levels, with a number of different approaches to the representation of conflict. While clearly concerned with the effects of political violence on an indigenous community in Peru in the 1980s, and on its children in particular, the film's broader concern is with the sudden coming of age and abrupt loss of innocence of a child caught unawares amidst the conflict of adults. His chief concern is with the survival of himself and of those he loves, but he is briefly seduced by the philosophy and the iconography of Shining Path. As such, Juan (Antonio Callirgos) is partly a cinematic relative of Florinda in Eyde's earlier film, who was also torn between her love for her family and her seduction by the Shining Path cause. In part, he is also connected to Vitín Luna in Lombardi's *La boca del lobo* (1988) in the way he engages in and then rejects violence as a meaningful, lasting solution. Juan's moral journey to iconic status will be traced here via a close address to his response to events around him and his eventual shift from a boy who responds passively to situations as they arise, to a young man who takes a proactive, defiant stance in the face of violence.

Framing Nation and Violence

The plot of *Paloma de papel* is told almost entirely from the point of view of its young protagonist, whose idyllic world is shattered by the sudden arrival of Shining Path forces. While battles are staged between Shining Path and the community (armed by the military), another, more intimate conflict is set up between the boy and the Shining Path leaders who try to indoctrinate him. He eventually resists these efforts but not before he has been forced to become embroiled in acts of violence himself. For many domestic critics, this concern with a kind of 'perverse apprenticeship' was the film's real achievement.[13] For them, this boy is also broadly representative of the many youngsters who were taken against their will by Shining

Path groups and forced or seduced into committing their lives to the revolutionary cause. However, although Juan crosses the line and becomes a reluctant killer, unlike most of those boys he purportedly represents, he survives and apparently atones for his guilt through the traumatic loss of his mother and his subsequent imprisonment as a traitor of the nation.

Set for the most part in a stereotypical village of the sierra, *Paloma de papel* follows Juan as he struggles to understand and deal with the violence that shatters his community and his own life in particular. (See Plate 15)

The first part of the film introduces, through flashback, Juan's hermetically sealed world, which is, on the whole, a peaceful one. He spends much of his time playing with his two best friends, Pancho (Angel Mojas) and Rosita (Anais Padilla), and helping out with agricultural tasks. Indeed, the first memory that the older Juan has of his childhood is its depiction as a timeless idyll, 'a kind of Andean arcade'.[14] He enjoys a strong, loving relationship with his mother, Domitila (Liliana Trujillo), who does her best to protect him from danger. His father is an absent figure and it is not until much later that we learn he is dead, probably as one of the earliest victims of Shining Path. The only person who disrupts this idyllic image for Juan is his drunkard stepfather, Fermín (Aristóteles Picho), who is later exposed as an unscrupulous Shining Path collaborator.

The younger children are vaguely aware of the threat of Shining Path but treat it lightly, without any notion of the brutal nature of the insurgent group. One evening, however, as they act out their own version of cops and robbers, they are stopped in their tracks by the horrifying sight of the body of Pancho's father, the mayor, hanging from the village hall and surrounded by pro-Shining Path slogans. It is at this point that the villagers organise a civil defence patrol to protect themselves, with basic weapons supplied by the military and warning bells erected around the village.[15] This is the first time that representatives of the state are portrayed. Their omission during the majority of the film serves to emphasise a failure on the part of the state to protect Peruvians located away from urban areas. Moreover, it highlights a failure to recognise such indigenous communities as national citizens that should be included in the remit of official state protection. The chief concern of the military is rather to ensure national security through the elimination of all threat of violence, and, as in *La boca*, little regard is shown towards the different cultural practices and beliefs they encounter in the highlands. Indeed, such communities are treated with suspicion and disdain based on ignorance and fear, and Juan's community suffers abuse at the hands of the military almost as much as it does at the hands of Shining Path.

The children witness Fermín talking to Shining Path rebels and discover guerrilla propaganda leaflets hidden in his room. Before they are able to denounce him to the community leader as a traitor, Juan is quickly delivered to the guerrillas and forced into a traumatic process of so-called re-education. He is renamed Cirilo by them, forced to learn how to set off bombs and use guns, and is taught the basics of Shining Path ideology. Juan, reluctant to submit to the authority of the party, is nevertheless forced to take goods from other poor *campesinos* and to kill a pleading soldier. Despite listening with some interest to the Shining Path ideology of radical social change and seeming to gain some pleasure from the sense of purpose generated by the group, he remains intent on escape and return to his mother. He might have been forced to kill, but he is shown to have developed a sense of humanity and morality that remain intact in the face of personal danger. When he finally breaks free, he is caught in the crossfire of a ferocious battle between Shining Path and the armed forces. His beloved mother is killed and he is taken away by the military as a presumed traitor to the nation. The film closes in the present as Juan returns to the village, having been released as part of an amnesty ordered by the interim government.[16] As he enters, he sees the visual signs of conflict that form the focus of memorial almost two decades later. Juan's story ends as he is embraced silently by Pancho and Rosita and thus welcomed back into the highland community, which appears to remain unchanged and remote from the rest of the nation. Although the narrative closure is more complete than that of *La boca* and *La vida*, a sense of isolation is suggested by Juan's long journey back from the prison in Lima to his village. The enduring remoteness of the place to which he returns is underscored by the tight framing of the final image of the three friends, which raises further questions about the arbitrary nature of national boundaries and the difficulty of identification with a nation that fails to recognise the diversity of its citizens.

The cinematic portrayal that Aguilar offers of violent conflict emphasises the suffering of indigenous Peruvians, excluded from political agency and protection, and at the same time highlights the dilemma for a child such as Juan, who becomes simultaneously victim and murderer. The audience is positioned from the beginning to share the older Juan's memory of his traumatic childhood experiences and is thus encouraged to feel a sense of injustice on his behalf and of that of his community, despite the fact that he also becomes a killer. Disadvantaged by their remoteness, the community seems especially vulnerable to attack from all sides. After a long, slow shot that pans across a wall of crumpled photographs and then draws back to reveal a community taking part in a memorial service, the film cuts to show a close-up of the hands of a young boy folding a white paper bird. The paper is clean, white and squared, like that used in school workbooks. The camera then moves back to reveal a young boy, a row of beds and a female guard, suggesting the location is some form of detention centre, before returning to the close-up of the hands and the paper. A graphic match cut takes us to the next close-up, which is almost identical to the first, but shows that the hands belong to an older boy, and the paper used to create the bird is from a greying newspaper. The camera then moves back again to reveal the same bed and the same detention centre. The cinematically contrived impression of a jump forward in time is confirmed by the subsequent shots and voice-over of a TV journalist reporting that 13 long-term political prisoners are being released as part of a government amnesty. The expression on the older boy's face suggests sadness and anxiety. He slowly leaves the safety of his prison environment with the sound of chanting supporters ringing in his ears, bids goodbye to a fellow inmate and steps outside to a very different world from the one he was forced to leave almost two decades before.

Unlike the others who leave with him, he has no welcome party of family and his isolation is emphasised by the long overhead shot that shows him walking away from the crowds towards the bus station. There is no one to greet him. As he travels back to the only place he knows, uncertain of how he will be received, Juan begins to remember the events that led to his imprisonment. This bus ride is not just a journey back to his roots, but also to his past, a voyage in space and in time, away from the modernity and emotional coldness of the city space and back to what he remembers as a supportive, protective community. The direction of the journey from Lima (centre) to Andes (periphery) is also significant, as is the metaphor created of the capital city as a prison from which he is now allowed to escape back to the comparative freedom of the Andes. The flashback thus begins, first in jarring fragments and then to a more discursive and linear form, that uses changes in colour and music to create a more sentimental tone befitting the world of a child.[17] Entering Juan's memory world in this way, the spectator is encouraged to identify and empathise with the plight of a boy who became an unwitting enemy of the state, struggling for political and social stability.

In terms of film form, there are some signs of the neorealist tendency that Aguilar has revealed as a key stylistic and philosophical influence and which pervades much of Latin American political cinema.[18] As well as the familiar devices of location shooting and the casting of a non-professional actor plucked from the highlands as protagonist, *Paloma* places the representation of a broad social reality at the core of its ethical concerns by retracing the boy's journey to adulthood as he gradually discovers the good and bad of the world around him.[19] However, while the first part of the film concentrates on the routine aspects of his life, as remembered by his older self, it does so by recalling this period in the style of a children's fairytale. Indeed, the memory of one specific tale about childhood, villains and doves, which is recounted within the diegesis by the old village magician and sage and later woven into the symbolic fabric of the film itself, draws attention to this stylistic approach, as do other recurring images of toys and games. As Federico de Cárdenas suggested, the mythic value of the film's narrative can be appreciated more fully by focusing on the memory as a nightmare, as Juan remembers being dragged away from his idyllic reality 'to be submerged in a nightmare full of monsters and violence'.[20] The boy is at first quite clear about who he perceives to be the heroes and villains of the village community. For him, the monstrous element to human life is represented by his alcoholic, treacherous stepfather, Fermín, whose portrayal is juxtaposed with that of the gentle character recalled only as The Old Man (Eduardo Cesti), presented here as the wise and kindly village blacksmith-cum-sage and magician, with whom Juan finds comfort and security.

For Juan, Fermín is the only recognisable villain in a community that appears, from the boy's point of view, to operate as a unified and supportive group in all areas of need. Two scenes emphasise this point, while drawing attention to Fermín's 'outsider' status, as well as to Juan's initial childhood battleground. In the first scene, Juan joins the village men as they prepare the ground for the construction of a community building. He and Pancho become covered in mud and inadvertently hit Fermín with clay as he passes. Pancho's father calms the enraged man and sends Juan to clean himself up. An idyllic memory of his beloved mother washing him down in the clear river water is evocatively framed by soft-focus lighting and sentimental music, whereas Fermín is remembered only as a violent man. On this occasion, he punishes the boy with a beating and sends him to sleep with the animals. As de Cárdenas further suggests, as far as Juan's idealised memory of traditional community life is concerned, the monsters only multiply when the Shining Path rebels arrive.[21] Although it is implied that Juan and his friends are vaguely aware of the guerrilla presence in the area, the youngsters' sudden awakening to the brutal reality of violence is imprinted on their minds when they discover the body of Pancho's murdered father.[22] Although this neat binary of good and bad is disrupted later by the Shining Path leaders who encourage Juan to reassess the mayor as a wrongful supporter of a corrupt state system, and thus as representative of a nation-state that Shining Path wishes to destroy, the boy continues to struggle to believe that his friend's father deserved his fate.

A further challenge to the crude juxtaposition of good versus bad is provoked by the depiction of key members of the Shining Path group as complex individuals whose motives, as Juan appears to recall, included a dangerous blend of altruism and faith in an absolute cause. This is particularly so in the case of cell leader Wilmer (Sergio Galliani), who, while brutal, is remembered by Juan as capable of compassion and humanity. The older man fulfils to some degree the paternal role that is missing from Juan's life by instructing and guiding him in his new environment, offering him a purpose in life that transcends individual concerns and freedoms. The viewer is invited, through the older Juan's memory of Wilmer's explanations of the Shining Path doctrine, to try to understand what leads this insurgent to act as he does. In so doing, the viewer is encouraged to appreciate why he, like so many other educated but disillusioned, socially impoverished and politically excluded young *mestizo* Peruvians at the time, might have been willing to deliver himself completely to the revolutionary cause.[23] The pivotal scene when Wilmer, framed evocatively by the mountains, attempts to explain the essential tenets of Shining Path ideology to Juan addresses the most fundamental aspects of Marxist/Maoist thought on which the Shining Path manifesto was based. The older boy remembers that he talked, for example, about the need to build a radically different social structure for Peru that would eliminate all injustice and poverty, and about the importance of violence not only as a means of destroying the old order but also, as Nelson Manrique explains, 'for its importance as a way of establishing the society of the future'.[24] This is a crucial turning point for the young Juan: violence is presented to him paradoxically as a creative as well as a destructive force and the film is at this point ambivalent in its position in this regard. Wilmer, assuming a mask of kindness and benevolence, makes his argument gently but unequivocally using language and examples that make the theory plausible and comprehensible to a child. Juan has difficulty understanding the abstract concepts of elitism, corruption, reactionary government and semi-feudal systems, but grasps the simple facts that people are hungry and that the existing conditions are unfair for many, and is seduced by the chance to participate in making life better for people like him and his community. Within this short scene, Wilmer explains that, according to Shining Path ideology, there would be no need for a capitalist system of monetary exchange leading to wealth for some and reliance on charity for others, if everyone had the right of access to all basic needs. Juan's confusion at the economic logic of this is matched by pleasure at the simplistic idea of having things without paying for them. He is also excited by the training games, the construction of a new familial structure, the admiration he gains from learning to use weapons, and the lighting of the torches across the mountainside in the shape of an enormous hammer-and-sickle symbol. The traumatic reality of the violence that was an inextricable part of the Shining Path campaign, and that took advantage of the dissatisfaction of the poor, had yet to be revealed.

This sequence of scenes is set amidst the impressive yet hostile Andean terrain, stripped of any manmade adornment. Through this succinct portrayal of the boy's memory of his indoctrination, the film reveals some of the basic tactics used to persuade susceptible young people living in impoverished areas to abandon their homes and engage in what was a class-based, ethnically inflected conflict. As Carlos Degregori explains, 'Sendero offered not only an intellectual explanation but also an organisation that welcomed these young people and gave them an identity'.[25] The insurgent group gave these youngsters a sense of purpose and hope, as well as a new sense of belonging, firstly to the Shining Path group and secondly to an imagined new national identity in which they would have a place.

It is precisely this sort of attempt at clarification, if not justification, of Shining Path ideology that led Aguilar's predecessor Marianne Eyde to experience such harsh public criticism for her depiction of the infiltration of Shining Path rebels into an Andean community one decade earlier with *La vida es una sola*. Aguilar admits that he was unsure about how best to present the Shining Path cause, and experienced similar, if less sustained, criticism for giving exposure, however limited, to its key tenets.

Aguilar acknowledged that it was difficult not to represent Shining Path only as a brutal organisation that, because of its radical ideology of social destruction, forced its militants to renounce all emotional ties with families, lovers and people they had cared about and who cared for them. The most common public perception of *senderistas* has been, after all, as '"flesh robots", radically dehumanised by dogmatism'.[26] As Víctor Vich further explains, militancy became, for Shining Path, 'the only important fact for the identity of its subjects',[27] and Wilmer, whose own background remains a mystery, tries to explain to Juan that he must renounce all affective bonds and commit himself entirely to the revolutionary cause. Yet the film includes amongst Juan's memories more complex relationships between some of the Shining Path characters that reveal some degree of compassion and humanity. Using facial close-ups, for example, it draws attention to the distress of Carmen (Tatiana Astengo) as she witnesses the shooting of her younger militant sister, Yeny (Melania Urbina), cross-cutting between her face and Juan's as he watches his own mother die in the crossfire, and thus linking momentarily the two family tragedies. A flicker of compassion is also seen on Wilmer's face when, as an apparent act of mercy, he is shown agonising as he is required to kill one of his most dedicated recruits who was seriously wounded after stepping onto a mine and begged to be shot dead so as not to become a burden to the party. While some critics accepted this approach as being entirely in line with the director's self-confessed 'humanitarian moral vision',[28] others were upset by what they perceived as an excessively generous portrayal of individuals behind the guerrilla cause. In particular, some were disturbed by the presentation of brutal death as 'heroic sacrifice and final victory over sadness', as an inevitable part of the campaign to change the social structure.[29] Admittedly, Shining Path is punished: Wilmer and Yeny are both killed in the final battle against the villagers, as is the collaborator Don Fermín, and grief-stricken Carmen disappears back into the mountains.

Meanwhile, Juan recalls that his only motivation was to ensure the survival of his community. Having crossed the line of morality by taking up arms and killing a soldier, he seems to accept that his own life is over. However, his redemption swiftly follows: rather than cave in to the vision and violence of the guerrilla group, he chooses to escape in a bid to warn his village of the impending Shining Path attack, which is motivated by suspicion of collaboration with the military unit located nearby. In so doing, he risks death at the hands of Shining Path and the armed forces, for he has become a traitor to both. The older boy remembers the distress he felt at having become complicit in the violence and the realisation that he too has become a killer. He appears to accept his guilt and makes no attempt to escape imprisonment for his crime. Despite his wrong-doing, he is presented as the true hero of the film, in that he is shown to have rejected violence, and to be willing to atone for his sins at a time when others remained silent.

By contrast, depiction of the state is perhaps best understood by its relative absence from the screen. The military, representing the state and hence the dominant national image, is shown entering in the village only twice; once to hand out arms to the community as part of the government strategy of defence, and once more at the end, to take Juan away. The remoteness of the regiment, and hence the state, is reinforced in two further scenes. On one occasion, the village leader risks his life by travelling to the regiment with intelligence on Shining Path's activities, as instructed by the ferocious military leader. He is brutally murdered by Shining Path shortly afterwards. On another occasion, the regiment is shown training in the hills, seeming to keep a wide berth from the village. Juan's memories of such neglectful behaviour echoes earlier representations of the state as ineffective in protecting all its citizens, leaving communities such as the one shown here to defend itself from insurgent attack.

The most overt criticism of state counter-insurgency policy is conveyed in the early sequence during which Juan is caught up in the television reporting on the release of political prisoners. Again inspired by real events, this cinematic representation serves to emphasise that the political conflict dealt perhaps the most severe blow to young men from the most impoverished indigenous communities of Peru. Boys such as Juan, seduced by Shining Path and excluded from the dominant national image, were imprisoned and convicted according to military court procedures, often without clear evidence of their crime or without right of appeal. During one brief exchange, a microphone is thrust before a weary ex-prisoner, who is asked to describe how he feels. The young man is speechless and it is left to his father to express his anger at having lost so many years with his son, thus reinforcing the frustration and resentment felt by a whole sector of Peruvian society at the time. Reference to the procedure of early release at the very start of the film raises uncomfortable questions about their detention, and the injustices of the conflict.

Negotiating Visions of Trauma

While Aguilar insisted that he strove for objectivity, several critics protested that his film had a similarly sentimental tone as 'those *indigenista* writers whose works recalled their summer travels in the mountains'.[30] Indeed, the evocation of an Andean idyll, suggested through heightened use of colour and dramatic musical score, seems to be the result of an admiring, deferential gaze that neglects to acknowledge the harshness of life in the Andes and fails to allow the marginalised to speak for themselves. The film even offended some for omitting use of the Quechua language, which would have been spoken by Juan's community, and for failing to acknowledge that such communities or their environment were rarely the idylls portrayed in this film. On the contrary, they were deeply impoverished, and rife with internal disagreement and conflicts of interest that were exploited by Shining Path leaders when recruiting *campesinos* to join their cause. Furthermore, the ambiguous status and sometimes dubious conduct of the civil defence patrol is not depicted; instead it is recalled by Juan as a heroic group of untrained amateurs who somehow defeat a fierce enemy without the backing of the military. Most critics seemed to prefer the film's focus on the emotional relationships among its characters rather than its efforts at intellectual abstraction. For them, the emphasis on the affective as opposed to the political enabled it to convey rather more effectively 'a vision of the Shining Path trauma in the Andes'.[31]

Above all, such concerns suggest that cinematic treatment of the Shining Path conflict and the behaviour of the military remained susceptible to criticism from those who were perhaps still wary of reopening barely healed wounds that threatened to disrupt a society still seething with unrest and to dismantle efforts to recreate a sense of national unity.[32] While one film cannot bear the responsibility of representing all the issues, the timing of the release of *Paloma de papel* bestowed upon it a more iconic status than its producers intended. The film forced viewers, and readers of reviews, to recall and debate an important period of national history that had such a dramatic effect on the way the Peruvian nation imagined itself. Its very existence acts as an uncomfortable reminder of the nation's recent past. Screenings in remote parts of the country, as well as amongst poorer communities in Lima inhabited by Andean migrants, gave those people who were caught up in the conflict an opportunity to see a small part of their experience dramatised on screen, even if a white urban Peruvian was telling their story for them. While some proponents of identity politics undoubtedly prefer to see the disempowered speaking for and representing themselves, the attempts made by Aguilar to represent the interests of his marginalised compatriots and to affiliate himself with their cause have been applauded by others.[33]

Through its many international screenings, this film familiarised a new generation with some of the socio-political realities of a part of the world which is rarely depicted within the global mass media. Of course, there are risks, some of which have been discussed, in terms of simplifying the complexities of certain situations for the sake of entertainment. On the one hand, a fictional portrayal such as the one offered by Aguilar runs the risk of 'exoticiz[ing] other cultures' and romanticising the struggle of indigenous Peruvians caught in a political conflict that, in the end, had little to do with improving their lives.[34] On the other hand, fiction cinema has the potential to lure, or interpolate, and suture the viewer into a certain ideological point of view through careful use of dramatic and affective devices. Hence, there is always the potential for 'a structuring of filmic identification across social, political and cultural situations', which can be dangerous (if the identification is uncritical) or enlightening, as some critics considered this one to be.[35]

While drawing attention to topics of great importance to Peruvian society and national identity, Aguilar created a film about the value of memory and the act of remembering. The flashback via which the older Juan recalls the key turning point in his life is framed by poignant signs of the memorial service held on the anniversary of the massacre in Juan's village. Burning candles, crumpled photographs of the deceased pinned to walls, mournful music and white flowers would be understood by audiences throughout the world. Juan's return in the middle of this service links past to present, while the flashback device confers upon the film its testimonial value. His story becomes thus symbolic of the thousands of witness statements collected by the CVR at the time the film was in production.

Whatever the director's intentions, the tone of the ending is ambivalent. On the one hand, Juan's guilt at having been a reluctant participant in Shining Path insurgency appears to have been redeemed. His crimes have been brutally punished not only by imprisonment but also by the death of his mother. His commitment to peace is reinforced by the handling of the paper dove, and a sense of his humanity is underscored by the focus on his childhood and on constant comparison with the apparent inhumanity of Shining Path and the armed forces. His reintegration into the community as signalled by his friends' welcoming embrace marks the closure of one chapter and the beginning of another. As the images fade to black, there appears a citation from Erich Fromm, reminding us of the director's intention to tell a story of love and life, of his desire to emphasise humanity over ideology.[36]

On the other hand, this ending is also troubling, for nothing appears to have changed and the possibility of a Peruvian national identity that celebrates diversity remains uncertain. The village church stands in ruins and the grief of its inhabitants is as acute as ever. Pancho and Rosita are standing in almost exactly the same spot from which Juan was taken away by the armed forces years before, and their final embrace closes them off from the rest of the world. The poverty and neglect that isolated such communities made them vulnerable to violent attack. In effect, despite its apparently hopeful point of closure, its recurrent motifs of peace, innocence and reconciliation, and the rejection of violence as solution by its charismatic protagonist, *Paloma de papel* offers an image of the nation that is as fragmented, divided and hierarchical as it was at the height of the political conflict. The next section explores further national cinema's concern with the disintegration of Peruvian society and identity as a result of violence via an analysis of a film that takes an intimate look at contemporary life in Lima.

Stasis, Dislocation and Open Wounds: *Días de Santiago/Days of Santiago* (Josué Méndez, 2004)

Released just one year after *Paloma de papel*, *Días de Santiago* takes quite a different approach to the recurrent and familiar themes of violent conflict and national identity. Set in the late 1990s, it follows the frustrated efforts made by Santiago (Pietro Sibille), its young working-class, mixed-race protagonist, to reinsert himself into family and civilian life after several years as a marine defending the integrity of his country in the remote Amazon and Andean areas of Peru. Particular sets of enemies mentioned in the film include the Ecuadorian army (engaged in border conflicts with Peru) and remnants of insurgent groups such as Shining Path, who had by this point become linked, according to official discourse, with traffickers of cocaine. Once home, Santiago tries hard to reintegrate into civilian life and to fulfil the expectations of others but is blocked at every turn. His relationship with his wife crumbles, his old army comrades try to draw him into a life of crime and he fails to develop any emotional tie with his family. His professional options are restricted and he becomes convinced that the only way to survive in the urban jungle of Lima is by applying tactics learnt as a marine, but ultimately he struggles to impose strict order on his life and on those around him. When this strategy fails, he tries instead to imitate the middle-class youngsters he meets who idle away their days by clubbing, drinking and shopping. Events spin wildly out of control when his violent brother's girlfriend begins to make seductive overtures and pleads with Santiago to kill her lover. In the end, Santiago cannot stop himself lashing out in frustration at those who confront and try to control him, and the narrative moves towards a disturbing and explosive ending. Although the film focuses on the troubled inner world of one traumatised individual who cannot escape the cycle of violence in which he has become entrapped, his story can also be taken metaphorically and symbolically as a painfully realistic vision of a generation in crisis within a specific national context. This analysis aims to untangle the key threads pertaining to identity and conflict as represented in the film, and to suggest ways in which they might help to elucidate issues of concern to young Peruvians at the turn of the twenty-first century.

Production Contexts

The drama of *Días de Santiago* is located in various districts of the capital city; the eponymous protagonist is a young man of *mestizo* working-class identity who has just returned to the capital city after a period of active service with the marines. Santiago's story begins with his return to a place that he no longer recognises and the narrative centres on the painful process of reintegration into a society that has moved on without him. Santiago's years in the armed forces obliged him to put certain ambitions on hold, only to have them cruelly dashed when he returns home. His world and his hopes crumble and disintegrate when he abandons the rigid structure of the armed forces; he faces an uncertain future without support and guidance from anyone who really understands what he has been through, or what he now lacks by way of psychological formation. His is an intensely personal struggle of reassimilation into civilian life that draws attention to 'the struggle against dissolution and fragmentation'.[37] (See Plate 16)

The formal quality of Méndez's film is raw, intense and fragmentary, reinforcing the psychological trauma of Santiago by the use of cinematic strategies of dislocation which provide a discomforting viewing experience and, in so doing, highlight the film's approach to identity as fractured, multi-layered, contradictory, complex and, to draw from Bauman, as fluid. It also focuses on the constant need to react and respond to changing social conditions and human emotions. *Santiago* strikes a pessimistic note about humanity, contemporary Peruvian reality and life for young people living in Lima by illustrating the tragic consequences of a society in meltdown. Moreover, although rejecting the traditional approach of flashback to depict directly Santiago's traumatic years in the jungle, the film nevertheless conveys a strong sense of an individual who cannot escape his past and who is paralysed by his own memories. As such, it deals more with the abstract concept of memory and the scars it can leave than with individual concrete memories. As one Peruvian critic pointed out, this film offers 'a painful exploration of the wounds left by war on human beings who return to their homes to battle for a "normality" that they will probably never have again'.[38]

Like Aguilar, Méndez scripted, directed and produced his first feature film while still in late 20s. His struggle to complete the production is again typical of Peruvian filmmakers generally, with increasing reliance on festival awards, television-based training and small but important amounts of government funding. On the strength of three award-winning short films, he was selected to participate in the prestigious Producer's Workshop run by the Festival des Trois Continents (Nantes, France) in 2000. The screenplay for *Santiago*, written over several years while he worked in TV and advertising, won a project development award from CONACINE. Meanwhile, the film's budget was kept extremely tight, partly by working on digital video throughout. Post-production funding was provided by the Hubert Bals Fund (Rotterdam, the Netherlands), while commercial distribution and promotional costs were largely covered by audience and critics awards at the Freiburg Festival in Switzerland. *Días de Santiago* was the surprise success for national cinema in 2004. It became the first Peruvian film to be selected for screening in the Official Competition of the highly regarded Rotterdam Festival. Méndez was also chosen to take part in the Cannes Film Festival residency programme for new writers and filmmakers from around the world. Perhaps the overwhelmingly positive reception by national critics as the best Peruvian film of recent years was even more surprising than the international success it enjoyed.[39] Furthermore, it remained on domestic screens in a competitive environment for an unprecedented six months from late 2004 to early 2005, and was shown in a variety of provincial cities as well as on the commercial Lima circuit.[40] Critics praised the way it drew upon a more experimental approach to the codes of film language and adapted them to the representation of a dystopian vision of urban Peru. Many were impressed by the director's use of a nervous, jump-cutting non-linear editing style, edgy hand-held cinematography, and unpredictable switches between black and white and colour, as well as the use of blue and orange tints – all serving to emphasise the inner turmoil of his main character, as well as the dislocation between past and present. They also applauded its impressionistic approach to the use of sound: the sparing use of lamenting tones in a zither-based soundtrack, and the experimentation with everyday sounds to evoke the tense, heightened reality of the moment. Moreover, tight composition and an intermittent voice-over further ensured that the audience was positioned to experience the world from inside the protagonist's tormented mind.[41] Most of all, they admired Méndez's obvious passion for cinema in general, and the implicit formal references in the film to the work of transnational filmmakers such as Krzysztof Kieslowski and Wong Kar-wai.

Framing Nation and Violence

The symbolic status of the film becomes clearer when the genesis of the script is taken into account, noting that a real Peruvian combat veteran inspired the story of *Santiago*. The initial idea came when Méndez saw a TV report on the difficult situation for ex-soldiers at the time of the signing of the controversial peace treaty with Ecuador in 1998, which itself provoked questions about the shifting nature of national identity and affiliation.[42] The young director, of a similar age to his potential subjects, was inspired to make a short documentary on their experiences after demobilisation. While conducting research he met Santiago, a former soldier who became involved as advisor on scripting, performances and locations, in a bid to ensure a high degree of authenticity. His experiences in the jungle were clearly shared by many young Peruvian men, mostly from impoverished social backgrounds, who had volunteered to fight on behalf of their nation-state.[43] In the jungle they became engaged in a series of violent battles far removed from and largely ignored by the urban population in Peru. They fought against the remnants of Shining Path and other insurgents; against drug-traffickers; and as part of a long-running border dispute with Ecuador, the outcome of which dealt a humiliating blow to the Peruvian army's macho and invincible sense of itself.[44] For some commentators, the film provides a critical view of the military and its responsibilities towards recruits, as well as of the general social, cultural and economic poverty of a nation that offered little hope to many of its young people.[45] For Méndez, protagonist Santiago represents 'a disappointed and betrayed generation that lost its youth and returned [from the jungle] to fight once again for survival against a society with no memory'.[46] But he achieves this by framing the subjective world of his protagonist over the national socio-political context, and by emphasising Santiago's increasing isolation from and frustration with all around him, even other former marines who find themselves in a similar predicament. (See Plate 17) While offering something of the overall social panorama, the director nevertheless focuses on the interior dilemma of a protagonist who thereby assumes a larger symbolic role that allows broader conclusions to be drawn about the ambivalent and shifting relationship between violence and national identity in Peru.

The symbolic value of Santiago's quest for peace is understood by interpreting it as an existential quest to find his place in an unfamiliar world. The film offers topical colour through its distinctive urban Peruvian background and by relating it to real events in the nation's recent past. The film's perennial concern, that of a soldier returning from conflict and struggling to adapt to civilian life, is one that has struck a chord with audiences from many different times and cultures and which has been the subject of many films made and seen throughout the world. Generally, such films depict characters faced with an unfamiliar social reality that is in some ways more frightening than the war situations they have just left behind. The rules of civilian society are different, often contradictory, and less clearly defined, with no one available to offer advice on how to cope with everyday life. As for the legal aspects that frame and affect human behaviour, Santiago soon realises that few people around him seem to pay much attention to laws that they consider to be largely irrelevant to their daily lives.[47]

Santiago appears to be haunted by the trauma of conflict and by guilt at the atrocities he took part in while serving in the army. Like many other soldiers in such a situation, he decides to leave the army, determined to clear his conscience and to change his life. However, the situation back at home is much more difficult than he could have imagined, especially as his experience of national service seems to be of little value or indeed relevance to the world to which he returns. He feels utterly alienated from and perplexed by a society that seems to be concerned more by the latest household products and hedonistic entertainment than with any sense of duty or social conscience, and with a kind of amnesia regarding recent and past political violence. Moreover, his dysfunctional family treats him like a stranger and his wife barely recognises him. As Ricardo Bula points out, connecting with others is impossible for him. 'His paranoia increases and tragedy threatens to strike at any moment'.[48] A war veteran aged just 23, Santiago can neither forget the conflicts he has participated in nor find adequate ways to deal with the sense of rejection he feels on returning from conflict. His wheelchair-bound former comrade Rata (Juan Gálvez) is so scarred physically and psychologically and consumed by the apparent impossibility of social reintegration that he kills himself.

Santiago's memories of conflict haunt him to such a degree that they restrict him from functioning normally in civilian life. As Kaja Silverman suggests in her study of cinema representations of servicemen returning from combat in World War II, such memories 'are like a psychic wound which marks him as somehow deficient'.[49] Using a psychoanalytical model to explore the various representations of lack found in such films, she explains that Freud's approach to war trauma 'encourages us to understand [it] as an *internal* response to an *external* danger', and that 'the subject suffering from a war neurosis constantly relives his traumatic experiences as a way of binding those experiences, and so of integrating them harmoniously into his psychic organization'.⁵⁰ In this film Santiago constantly relives, reimagines and re-enacts his days in the jungle. His compulsive obsession repeatedly to recall as well as to re-enact incidents and responses from his past is conveyed to the spectator without the need to resort to flashbacks since they accompany him in the present. He imagines fighting off delinquent assailants as he walks through the potentially hazardous streets of Lima; he is shown lying in full combat gear in his bedroom after particularly stressful encounters with his family; and he retreats at night to the beach or the hills, well away from the city, where he puts himself through rigorous army exercises. He clearly does not achieve the harmonious integration that Freud suggests is necessary for psychic stability. In fact he is, like the characters from one of the films discussed in Silverman's analysis, 'so scarred by lack that [he is] incapable of effecting a re-entry into the dominant fiction'.⁵¹

According to Margarita Saona, Santiago's failure is due to the disappearance of the patriarchal hierarchical order with which he was familiar.⁵² His deficiencies manifest themselves externally in numerous ways, each of which contributes to his psychological decline. In general, he lacks both the material and emotional resources to deal adequately with the past and is constantly reminded that he is now socially inferior and worthless. In the army he at least assumed a clearly defined role within a recognisable structure, and gave himself – proudly at first – to the cause of fighting for his country. Back home, stripped of the uniform that was supposed to symbolise achievement and self-respect, he is reduced to nothing. The nebulous pride of being an ex-soldier is undermined by the guilt of having participated in a series of largely pointless conflicts that are in any case perceived as irrelevant and meaningless to those he encounters in the city, as well as to his wife and his brother. Even the department store manager tells him his military identity card is worthless now that he has 'retired'. His inability to control the way others perceive him causes him enormous pain and distress. Having trained for and survived unspeakable events in the jungle, Santiago lacks the skills to cope with everyday situations in the city. He desperately wants to integrate and learn, and is shown signing up for a computer course as well as imitating the young people at the discotheque, but nothing compensates for the gaps in his social development that make him feel excluded, nor for the torment he carries from his military life. His desperate quest thus becomes a metaphor for the fragmentation and exclusion that occurs along class, ethnic and gender lines in terms of national identity.

The sense of dislocation from society is emphasised in the opening sequence, which first offers an intense and ambivalent close-up of a woman's face (later revealed as his wife) staring with resentment towards the camera. In a reverse shot, the protagonist is shown struggling to return the gaze and anxiously looks around him as they both wait for the bus to arrive. This sequence is shot in black and white. There is an abrupt cut to a different location, possibly a different day, and then a short sequence in colour during which he arrives home alone only to find nothing but leftover rice for him to eat. Finally, another close-up shot shows him eating elsewhere; the voice of another woman is heard urging him to apologise, and her arm is shown caressing his face. In a reversal of the classical cause-and-effect structure, it is unclear at this stage who either of these women are, or for what he is being required to apologise. The film continues in this provocative vein, without ever providing comfortable answers or a satisfying closure.

The tension is compounded by his encounters with others throughout the film, each instance reinforcing his sense of difference, inferiority and marginalisation. In the next sequence, Santiago walks nervously but purposefully through the busy streets of Lima until he finally stops at a college in Miraflores, the most affluent area of the city. The receptionist is dismissive when he enquires about available courses. His shabby appearance in a non-designer T-shirt and jeans is an obvious visual marker of his difference; his very short haircut is another. Without the uniform that would anchor the social meaning of the haircut as a signifier of his military background, it simply makes him appear a threatening and aggressive *mestizo*. His undisguised reaction of shock at the information about how long it will take and how much it will cost to retrain for civilian professional employment provokes a further disdainful response from the young woman, who turns her attention back to her telephone conversation. In this encounter, his low economic status combined with his mixed-race background cause him to be rejected and infantilised,[53] and his self-confidence is further eroded by this encounter.

This scene also highlights the contrast between Miraflores and other districts of the capital which draws further attention to fragmentation of the national image. The work by Alberto Flores Galindo on violence in Peru considers the impact of the way Lima is divided on the impossible struggle to create a cohesive sense of national identity with such an enormous city (Lima has one-third of the national population).[54] He laments the lack of public spaces where people of different ethnic and social backgrounds might come together, holding this responsible in part for the lack of tolerance and rise in antagonism between different social groups. Indeed, as Santiago transgresses these imagined boundaries and crosses over into a more obviously middle-class space, he encounters both elitism and racism, which shock him. His confused reaction provides a rare moment of humour that draws attention to the absurdity of an impossible situation, one where he is rejected, to follow Maria Chiara D'Argenio's analysis, for representing the 'monstrous'.[55]

After this abrupt rebuttal, Santiago heads back to the hustle and bustle of central Lima, the heart of the urban jungle. He pauses at the bus stop to tell a young woman that her skirt zip is undone, thus setting himself apart from the youths who were mocking and enjoying her state of undress. He is then annoyed by the same young men who enter the bus in a rowdy fashion and has to restrain himself from reacting aggressively. Walking along the crowded main shopping street of central Lima, Santiago appears edgy and nervous; one critic compares him to 'a hunted animal which is unfamiliar with this urban jungle where social peace is simply a continuation of war in another form'.[56] He struggles to deal with what he regards as the disorder and chaos all around him, presenting an almost overwhelming threat to the unity and cohesion he desires and requires. By alternating between colour and black and white, often within the same scene, to coincide with dislocating jump cuts, the film offers a growing sense of Santiago's isolation and impending subjective collapse. He repeats his motto, 'without order, nothing exists', over and over, as if the words themselves might help him to construct an imagined sense of the order that he believes will prevent his inner world from total disintegration and 'radical unbinding'.[57] But, as Nicholas Azalbert points out, 'his obsession with order and logic provides no help in the face of the chaos that surrounds him'.[58] Silverman further argues that:

> The male subject's aspirations to mastery and sufficiency are undermined from many directions – by the Law of Language, which founds subjectivity on a void; by the castration crisis; by sexual, economic, and racial oppression; and by the traumatically unassimilable nature of certain historical events.[59]

Santiago's own efforts at mastery and sufficiency are indeed undermined from every direction, and especially by the female characters in the film, who provoke uncertainty about his macho sense of self, thus reinforcing the broader symbolic value of aggression as an integral part of Peruvian national identity. His growing social impotence suggests that his training as a fighter has left him ill-equipped for life outside the marines, where violent conflict is increasingly regarded as ineffective and counter-productive.

For a while, Santiago manages to suppress his own violent instincts. He realises that he can afford neither the time nor the money to register for the electronics course he would have preferred; he opts for shorter and cheaper computer training instead. He raises the money for this by working informally as a taxi driver, using the car of his deceased friend, Rata. While earning his living, he is thus constantly reminded of the physical and psychological suffering of his former comrade-in-arms, as well as of the potential futility of his efforts at reintegration. He is also reminded of his own failure to recognise and respond to Rata's desperation, of the wider lack of state support for veterans of the armed services, and of the awful moment of discovery of Rata's dead body. Just as the gravity of Rata's situation was ignored, so too is Santiago's fate; the suicide of the former signals one possible way out for the latter.

Even his wife, Marí (Alheli Castillo), is unable or unwilling to understand the reasons for his aggressive behaviour, and the breakdown of their relationship is in part due to Santiago's failure to articulate his feelings. This problem of communication, a metaphor perhaps for a larger social failure to connect and interact, is most effectively conveyed during the scene when he waits for Marí to return from work. Already undermined by her position as the main breadwinner of the household, and by the seeming reversal of traditional gender roles, he is frustrated by the lack of order in the house, by her absence and by her failure to prepare meals and to replenish the cupboards with food. Alone in the kitchen, he rehearses out loud the speech he has prepared which outlines the way he would like the house to be run, including a daily schedule of tasks that he hopes will restore a more traditional order to the household. But such a flawed attempt at reclaiming authority fails to take account of Marí's reaction, of the way she has had to change while he has been away, and of the way social developments have given rise to a generation of more economically independent young women. When Marí does return with only bread for their lunch, she derides and thus infantilises him further by urging him to eat and by taking charge of the conversation by telling him they need a refrigerator. Language deserts him and he slams his fist on the table in frustration. Having lost control of his marital relationship and unable to assume the traditional masculine position of command, he symbolically represents the failure of the dominant to deal with a situation in which vulnerability has been exposed other than with violence. His identity as former serviceman, representative of the state, suggests that the point should be more broadly interpreted as a critique of past failed attempts to deal with national problems through violence as opposed to negotiation or social investment.

Días de Santiago draws attention to marginal male subjectivity in the contemporary Peruvian context by tracing the path of a figure who is not 'equal to the phallic legacy'.[60] Santiago's crisis of masculinity is compounded further during an encounter in a department store. Already exposed as over-sensitive towards those in positions of authority who treat him as inferior, he becomes infuriated by the department manager's reluctance to help him make his purchase. The protagonist's downgraded social status leaves him without cash or a profession that would in effect guarantee credit to buy a consumer item that would in itself signal a slight but significant movement up the social ladder. The painful realisation that the identity of *ex*-veteran is meaningless comes as a severe blow and results in Santiago threatening the manager with violence. The subsequent reminder from his wife that she could act as credit guarantor due to her own respectable career as a nurse only makes his sense of worthlessness more acute, and their subsequent row ends with him lashing out at her. His pent-up inner rage thus exposed, he is paralysed by remorse, guilt and shame. She has by this time lost all respect for him and their relationship effectively ends at that point. Once again, the harmful consequences of violence are emphasised, and the inadequacy of it as solution is reinforced.

Instead of returning home to Marí, Santiago retreats to the house of his parents but, unable to connect with them either, he sleeps outside, in the car. This car gains in symbolic capital as the film progresses, just as Travis Bickle's did in Scorcese's *Taxi Driver* (1976), with which *Santiago* has been favourably compared. On the one hand, it is the source of much-needed income, as well as a comforting reminder of his deceased friend. It also represents a safe social haven in which he relearns simple and unthreatening interaction with others. It provides him momentarily with status and focus as he progresses from errant pedestrian to purposeful motor driver, and thus enables him to regain some control and self-respect as a taxi driver, taking others around the city. Moreover, the inside of the car becomes the only space in which Santiago feels sufficiently comfortable to attempt to talk about his feelings to others.

On the other hand, he is anxious about the informal and inferior status of a taxi driver in the eyes of both state and society. He is further alarmed by the apparently irrational and unpredictable behaviour of those fares he picks up, from the seemingly demure young woman who loses all inhibitions on the back seat with her boyfriend, to the priest who takes a crafty swig of brandy when he thinks no one is looking. Like Bickle, he becomes the 'cabbie-cum-voyeur observing the decadent sights he does not want at first to see, but then watching them compulsively'.[61] He cannot control what goes on behind him and cannot help but take a peek from time to time. Moreover, it should be remembered that this car is not really his: he did not buy it and does not officially own it. Rata left it to him, and this position, according to John Orr, is a 'degraded, inauthentic form of automotive being'.[62] The car reminds him again of his impotence and identifies him with a generation of young Peruvian men for whom labour options were restricted to construction work or taxi driving.[63] As a signifier of everyday life in the Peruvian context, it symbolises low social status and it further unravels the traditional dominant image of machismo.

For a while, however, this car provides the illusion that he might rediscover a sense of self-worth and regain control over his destiny. Thanks to the vehicle and the social interaction it provides, Santiago encounters and strikes up a friendship of sorts with four young women from middle-class families who recognise him from their computer course. Andrea (Milagros Vidal), Rita (Giselle Bidón), Jimena (Ana María Roca Rey) and Sandra (Sandra Vergara) treat him as their strange little 'pet', while he is bewildered by their decadent approach to life. His seriousness contrasts sharply with their hedonistic lifestyle and their apparent disregard for money. Aged 16, they are about to enter a very different growing-up period compared with the one he experienced in the jungle. While he was committed to fighting for his country and getting himself out of poverty, they are dedicated to having as much fun as possible, with little care for others beyond their immediate social circle. Despite feeling alienated, Santiago is intrigued and spends more and more time with these girls, whose apparently carefree attitude helps him to forget his responsibilities elsewhere and allows him to pretend he is recapturing the youth he never experienced. However, he fails to realise that their social differences cannot easily be erased. The first time Andrea climbs confidently into the front passenger seat, she teases Santiago light-heartedly, and in fact takes control of both the car and him. Any status he had gained as driver of the car is thus erased by becoming their driver, always at their beck and call.

Although Andrea is a young woman barely older than his sister, and therefore ought not to pose any serious or immediate threat to Santiago's sense of self, her family's economic status and social aspirations make her socially superior. Wealthier, whiter and six years younger than him, she has been brought up to affiliate herself more with the modern lifestyle and attitudes of an imagined West than with the heterogeneous culture of her own country. Her clothes, make-up, accent and behaviour towards others all confirm her aspirations. Her skin colour may not look that different from Santiago's but the two characters are nevertheless ethnically and socially divided by their backgrounds, their families and their connection with (or disconnection from) the national situation. He has been shaped in part by an era of violence and economic difficulty that threatened to destroy his country and left him with neither opportunity nor political agency.

Andrea, on the other hand, is representative of a wealthier social class and a neoliberal generation driven more by consumerist self-interest than co-ordinated social responsibility.[64] She may like him, flirt with him and claim to want to be his girlfriend, but she has no real intention of getting to know him or his past. She is using him in the short term as part of her growing up, perceiving and fetishising him as an exotic and virile ex-marine who flatters her own sense of self. She does not understand his profound need to talk through his problems. When he tells her about his habit of taking a different route to the college each day for fear of being followed, she laughs in a way that further undermines his masculine self. As he tries to explain the feelings of paranoia, anger and guilt that are mounting within him, he may as well be speaking another language. She looks confused, teases him, goes to kiss him and grabs his gun, provoking a violent outburst that ends their fragile friendship forever.

Santiago's failed relationships with women are the most obvious sign of his impotent self. His economically independent wife tires of his violent outbursts; his brother's manipulative wife uses him for her own sexual gratification; and the girls from college treat him as their plaything. His machismo is undone as he is subjected to different types of control by three different sets of female characters, and his friendship with Andrea turns sour partly as a result of his inability to keep his volatile emotions in check. Despite such aggression and apparent physical strength, he is unable to protect his mother, his younger sister or his brother's wife from domestic abuse, and the status of violence as destructive and ineffective is illustrated yet again. While his brother's wife, Elisa (Marisela Puicón), appears to be the helpless victim of Coco's (Erick García) temper, and receives regular beatings while Papá (Ricardo Mejía) turns a blind eye, she compensates for this by taking advantage of Santiago's vulnerability and actively manipulates the situation herself. Her flirting is more sexually provocative and deliberately manipulative than Andrea's, and she persuades Santiago to help her dispatch his drunken older brother for good by appealing knowingly to his sense of duty and promising him affection in return. However, she has no intention of leaving Coco and, in the end, the revelation of her apparent acceptance of their violent relationship sets Santiago off on his final rage. He brutally drags her across to his car, and then suffers the final humiliation of being beaten by his less robust brother. The film seems to suggest finally that there is no way out for Santiago, especially given the shocking exposure of his father's sexual abuse of his younger sister in the film's most explicit and traumatic scene. His family, his social class, his gender and his generation are steeped in a history that seems to consider violence as the only possible response to crisis and attack. And yet the film clearly intends the viewer to reject such a response, rooted in a patriarchal and macho nationalism, and to look instead for alternative strategies.

Cinema as Social Testimony

Santiago acts as a powerful social testimony, a statement on life for many poor young male Peruvians at the end of the 1990s, and as an indictment of a system that prepares boys for war only to abandon them once 'peace' is attained. It offers a dystopian vision of the 'disconnected fragments' of contemporary urban reality that lead in some instances to intense feelings of isolation and alienation from society.[65] Méndez emphasises this cinematically by creating an insurmountable distance between Santiago and the society he no longer recognises. The orange-toned sequences of the protagonist, dressed in full combat gear, practising his army training alone in the middle of the night high above Lima with the lights of the city clearly visible in the background, emphasise his compulsive need to retreat far from the alienating urban environment of the capital. There is no rational purpose to this mock training other than to remind himself 'enactively' that he once meant something to society.[66] He has become the typical war neurotic who suffers 'from the compulsion to repeat traumatic experiences',[67] as if hoping that by taking himself back to the original scene of trauma, he will overcome and be rid of the memories that plague and paralyse him. The blue-toned, tilted close-up shots of Santiago's empty face, with the waves of the sea crashing behind him, offer further evidence that he is out of kilter with both society and himself. His violent impulses are, it seems, inescapable and uncontrollable, yet ineffective and counterproductive, suggesting more broadly that while violence might be perceived as endemic to the national image, its emphasis on destruction is no longer relevant to the contemporary situation. He stands out anachronistically, as at odds with an emerging desire for a new national image that embraces different approaches to crises beyond the violent.

While maintaining its primary focus on the traumatised individual, Méndez's film demonstrates that its chief protagonist is not the only one to experience difficulty with a return to civilian life. Nevertheless, the secondary characters who were his comrades in battle serve mainly to reinforce Santiago's sense that there is no hope for ex-soldiers in Peru. The tragic demise of Rata, already recounted, shows Santiago one possible way out of his predicament. He meets his former comrades on two further occasions, on a desolate hilltop that overlooks, but is remote from, the city centre. Here they plot their assault on civilian life as if preparing a battlefield mission, and it is in these scenes that Méndez differentiates Santiago from the other veterans of conflict. Leader Sandro (Sandro Calderón) mocks Santiago on their first meeting because he does not own a mobile phone, the primary consumer trapping and first sign of integration into a modern, technologised society. On the second meeting, after Rata's death, Sandro is less concerned with integration and, disillusioned with the lack of support from the state and lack of recognition from society, he tries to persuade Santiago to join him in a bank robbery. Santiago refuses to take part in such a declared battle with legitimate society and, by taking a determined step towards a rejection of violence, he thus sets himself apart from his friends and never sees them again. As Silverman points out, once away from the battlefield, 'the traumatized veteran no longer enjoys the support of his comrades-in-arms'.[68] Santiago finds that his former fighting partners do not all appreciate the turmoil he experiences, and do not comprehend his need to forsake violence. Even watching TV news of their arrest after the botched robbery attempt some days later offers him no satisfaction, reminding him instead of their shared desperation and his own isolation.

As Sandro discovers, and as the film in general emphasises, the figure of the soldier no longer holds much prestige in Peruvian society. Until 1992, with the capture of Guzmán, members of the military were treated with some respect but even before then, with the transition to democracy, the public image of the armed forces had altered. As Portocarrero suggests, the military lost much of its honourable character of self-sacrifice and social duty during the 1990s, when the ultimate failure of the military government of 1968–1980 was recognised.[69] By the time the corruption of the Fujimori–Montesinos regime was exposed in 2001, the social influence of the armed forces had been much reduced. In any case, after nearly two decades of Shining Path conflict, many Peruvians did not wish to be reminded of their nation's recent violent past, nor of the ongoing social inequalities that the veteran soldiers' situation represented. Sandro and his team are depicted as feared delinquents rather than as heroes of battle, and their efforts to defend the nation-state as soldiers are erased from collective memory.

Santiago's solitude and sense of exclusion from the mainstream throw into sharp relief the pessimistic vision offered by Méndez of a dislocated and fragmented society in a world of competing individuals. His doomed story seems to confirm Portocarrero's idea that in contemporary Peru, 'respect is only held for people like me, for someone familiar or known. The rights of people who are different or unfamiliar tend to be ignored.'[70]

Santiago is different, monstrous even in the eyes of many who find him grossly unfamiliar, but he is not a delinquent. For all his compulsive aggression, he wants to live a quiet life away from the killing fields. Méndez presents a complex, traumatised individual who wants to help others and lead a decent life, but who cannot comprehend the reluctance of society to accept him and who finds it impossible to control the violent urges that were honed by years of combat. He seems now to desire social integration more than anything else, but fails to understand how to achieve it in a world that has started to regard violence and machismo as futile. The wedding photographs that his wife leaves behind merely reinforce the distance he feels from a memory of himself as respected husband and admired soldier, more suited to a strictly patriarchal world that has been exposed as brutal and ugly. As his inner world threatens to collapse, so too does his relationship with the exterior world. Memories of conflict have invaded his psyche, trapping him in a perpetual present, and preventing him from moving forward peacefully. There is no hopeful resolution or satisfying closure to Santiago's tale. He may not have loaded the gun to kill himself on this occasion but there is no suggestion that he will be able to stop himself doing so in the future.

Alone, and apparently unable to shake off his violent impulses, he does not know how to negotiate his way through a reconfigured nation. Violence is depicted critically as central to Santiago's understanding of his own identity, as well as of the dominant image of the nation-state. While his experiences as a marine involved the use of aggressive military action in defence of the integrity and unity of the nation, violence is exposed here as demeaning, socially destructive and ineffective on an individual and on a national scale. Regarding the latter, while the signing of the peace treaty with Ecuador was welcomed by some, it was regarded by many others as a failure on the part of the military to defeat the enemy and defend Peruvian national borders.

Finally, then, this film offers a savage critique of state and public indifference in Peru at the turn of the millennium. It provides a vision of a fragmented society divided in many ways, including by experience of and response to political conflict. It exposes the fragility of democracy in a nation-state that has failed to protect its citizens from violence, and puts forward a plea for the reconstruction of social responsibility. It raises many difficult questions about the development of a coherent and cohesive national identity that might embrace and tolerate difference. However, the ambiguity of the ending of this forceful film, and the much more active role played by the three main female characters, mark a break with other recent Peruvian films that deal with social and political conflict. Through drawing attention to the social redundancy of the military man, and the blurring of traditionally defined gender roles, the film seems to suggest that the dominance of patriarchal culture is questionable, and that the role played by violence in defining masculine identity in Peru is open to debate.

5

New Generations and Open Wounds, 2005–2016

Seeking Closure

When Lombardi returned from the gala screening of *La boca del lobo* at Havana Film Festival in 1988, he was anxious that Peruvian national cinema might soon lose the support of flawed but invaluable protectionist legislation. He hoped, however, that the success of his film and the debate it generated would highlight the need for the government to allow this cultural activity to develop, as a sign of the nation's own political and economic maturity if nothing else. This study has demonstrated the extent to which individual feature films play a role in provoking controversy and concern amongst politicians, the film industry and audiences alike. In so doing, it has also attempted to draw attention to the ways in which political conflict and social crisis affect the logistical, legislative and aesthetic development of an intermittent national film industry.

Issues of violence and identity have continued to be concerns of many of those films made after 2000 by a 'new' generation of filmmakers who had grown up with the impact and consequences of Shining Path themselves either directly or via media reports. This period also witnessed the emergence of the transnational star auteur Claudia Llosa, whose work (most notably in the context of this study given their themes of conflict and self-discovery *Madeinusa*, 2006, and *Milk of Sorrow*, 2009) has excited global audiences, critics, scholars and educators in a way that had not happened for Peruvian cinema before. Other feature fiction films addressed in this final chapter include festival successes *Las malas intenciones* by Rosario García-Montero (2011), *NN: sin identidad* (Héctor Gálvez, 2014), *Magallanes* (Salvador del Solar, 2015) and *La última tarde* (Joel Calero, 2016), each of which has added to the post-memory bank of cultural production surrounding Peru's worst civil conflict in contemporary times.

By 2016, despite many positive developments and successes, much of Latin American cinema remains largely atomised and personalised, and Peruvian cinema is no exception; moreover, characterising a media industry, even a small-scale sector like Peruvian cinema, is a complex undertaking. I hope I have shown that all of the films considered here, despite their different formal qualities and ideological approaches, are nevertheless united in their common concern for the effect of political violence on the various communities of Peru. They examine the tension between these groups, antagonism rooted in the nation's history of cultural dualism that was exploited to a certain extent by the insurgency. Furthermore, they reveal some of the events, characters and policies that emerged from the conflict between state and Shining Path and that contributed to the reshaping of personal and collective identities. Most of them have attracted controversy by focusing on those minority sectors of Peruvian society – migrants, *campesinos* and neglected provincial citizens – that had been excluded from dominant national discourse and identity and use cinema to voice the concerns of the disadvantaged and impoverished of Peru. As Francisca da Gama has argued, 'the different status accorded to each of these films as representations of Peru's war with Sendero … centers on the competing conceptions of national identity they present'.[1]

The mixture of approaches to the representation of the Shining Path insurgency tells us something important as to the relationship between politics and culture at a time of threat to national security. It also prompts discussion about the nature and effects of developments in legislation relating specifically to cinema and more generally to acts of terrorism. The period under scrutiny here began with the controversial release of

Lombardi's seminal *La boca del lobo*, which portrayed the arrival of a defence force in a suspicious Andean community, raised pertinent questions about cultural difference and misunderstanding between the different social groups of Peru, and showed how conflict could arise out of ignorance. Because Shining Path remained an invisible but palpable threat, symbolised to a certain extent by the hostile landscape, and because the focus of the drama shifts to the tense relationship between the lieutenant and the novice, the film's topicality was downplayed at the time by most commentators and the director himself. The removal of any explicit reference to the slaughter of citizens at Soccos, despite a scene that appears to restage that exact event, led to its interpretation instead as a metaphoric meditation on masculinity and violence as intertwined features of Peruvian identity. Nevertheless, the many newspaper articles that explored the message of the film at the time, and the recurrent screenings and academic discussions of it since, attest to its immediate and enduring role as an important agent of debate at a time of crisis.

Not until the release, over a decade later, of *Paloma de papel* and *Días de Santiago* did national cinema receive such critical acclaim. As has been noted, not all those films made during the intervening years were concerned with the Shining Path conflict, nor with violence in other forms, and yet both remained ongoing points of interest for several of Peru's most prominent and outspoken filmmakers. Pereira del Mar, whose controversial speech at the first CONACINE awards revealed his mistrust of the Fujimori regime, was the first after Lombardi to offer a film that contributed to the debate about political violence and personal suffering as consequence of social difference and economic injustice. A number of reasons, aesthetic and political, have been suggested to explain the film's poor reception at the domestic box office, but it nevertheless survives as evidence of a continuing cinematic preoccupation with immediate social themes. Three years later, in early 1993, Marianne Eyde gave numerous forthright interviews in defence of her film, *La vida es una sola*, the release of which was stifled by political paranoia in the wake of Fujimori's aggressive *autogolpe* and the triumphant capture of Abimael Guzmán. Veteran leftist filmmaker Alberto Durant, a staunch proponent of human rights, produced two films during the decade that dealt with the conflict, *Alias la gringa* (1991) and *Coraje* (1998), the latter of which in particular suffered from a long gestation period caused by funding concerns resulting at least in part from the new market requirements of revised cinema legislation. Lombardi's own struggles to find funding, despite his indisputable reputation, led him to work more closely with Spanish producers, whose ideas about appealing to international audiences impacted on the treatment of topical and national themes. In addition to such issues, increasing restrictions to freedom of expression imposed by Fujimori's regime, through the tightening of anti-terrorist legislation, created the need for more suggestive approaches to issues of social concern. The return to an explicit cinematic treatment of Shining Path in Aguilar's *Paloma de papel* (2003) and to themes of political violence, identity and contemporary social crisis in Méndez's *Días de Santiago* (2004) suggest not only that such topics continued to be important to the new generation, but also that the freedom to explore them critically had been restored. The largely positive response to both films by domestic audiences and the debates that they provoked in the national media were testament to that. Collectively, these films affirm the role of cinema as mediator of collective memory, marker of social histories and instrument of political debate.

Fractured Continuities

'A country that forgets its history is condemned to repeat it', became the motto of the Truth and Reconciliation Committee, whose final report was published in 2003.

The traces of the Shining Path era, the *manchay tiempo* as referred to by Quechua speakers from Peruvian Andean regions, live on in Peru's fiction cinema, with post-conflict projects released almost every year that are funded by state-supported schemes and normally selected as the country's nomination for the Academy Awards.[2] While there is now a much greater diversity of topics and genres than ever before, those films that somehow connect to the nation's recent civil war are still the ones that are most likely to travel the global festival circuit and return with armfuls of awards. Moreover, these are the films that have resonated most with funders, critics and the general public through their constant reminders about issues of nationwide concern, and which have succeeded in keeping Peruvian cinema alive during some very dark years, culturally, socially and politically. This final section draws attention to the key features and recurring themes of some of the more well-known films, and seeks to bring this study to a close.

These films include acclaimed features by Claudia Llosa, *Madeinusa* (2006) and *La teta asustada/Milk of Sorrow* (2009), the latter of which presents an infantilised Quechua-speaking protagonist, Fausta (Magaly Solier), who is scarred by the conflict in both physical and psychological ways in the sense that Hodgin and Thakkar discuss as being representative of ongoing trauma, in that she was conceived when her mother was raped by Shining Path guerrilla fighters and is fearful of everything. As Leslie Marsh notes, Llosa's second feature addresses the lingering effects of violence committed at the hands of the state and insurgent groups in Peru during the 1980s and 1990s and is notable for being one of few films to develop its narrative around a female protagonist of indigenous descent and her relationship to the past.[3] It is revealed that her response to this trauma was to place a potato inside her own vagina in order to protect herself from attack, serving as a physical reminder of the very intimate horrors of the past. However, as Deborah Shaw has noted, 'rather than focusing on the violence of former times, the film sets up a series of encounters between urban and rural Peru, and between white, wealthy middle-class criollos (Peruvians of Spanish ancestry), and those of poor Andean origins, and is thus more interested in ideas of identity in contemporary Peruvian society ... [than in] the more recent period of conflict of the 1980s and 1990s'.[4] I argue thus that Shining Path is used here as a springboard for an intimate exploration of Peruvian identity in the twenty-first century. Moreover, Llosa offers through Fausta a new vision of the urban Indian, one who is not yet comfortable with modernity but interacts with it. Unlike Jeremías of *Ni con dios* (Pereira del Mar, 1989), the outcome of her struggle against all sorts of external and intern demons is to find a resolution that brings her into the modern world without losing her sense of self.[5]

That same year, Fabrizio Aguilar released his second feature after *Paloma de papel*, titled *Tarata* after the street in the residential Lima district of Miraflores in which one of the final Shining Path terror attacks took place in 1992. It tells the story of a middle-class family who live in that district struggling to come to terms with the loss of their comfortable way of life as well as to communicate with each other about the various personal dilemmas they are suffering. Amongst other things, it shows how Lima society was unable for a long while to acknowledge the civil conflict that the rest of the country was undergoing until the very moment when the violence hit them most personally. The film shows scenes of 'curfew parties' and make-up lessons interspersed with images of Shining Path slogans on walls and news headlines of car bombs in the city centre. Above all what the film portrays is the complete incapability of many Lima citizens to deal with the Shining Path violence even though it had already reached the capital, embodied in particular by the protagonist Claudia (Gisela Valcarcel) who cannot comprehend the suffering of her bereaved housekeeper. As such it re-exposes all the wounds of class and ethnic division that had been revealed in all the films analysed in detail in this study.

Other films made during first decade of the new millennium that further reiterate the desire to keep trying to make sense of the past through reopening the wounds and scars left by the period of violence include *El rincón de los inocentes/Where the Innocent People Live* (Palito Ortega Matute, 2005), *Vidas paralelas/Parallel Lives* (Rocío Lladó, 2008), *Illary* (Nilo Pereira del Mar, 2009) and *Paraíso/Paradise* (Héctor Gálvez Campos, 2010). All of these use cinema to explore events of the recent past that affected the emotional and personal lives of their main characters who are portrayed as confronting, as Bedoya notes 'the traumas suffered by their parents'.[6]

El rincón de los inocentes was made by one of Peru's most prolific directors who represents a different perspective on cinema, as an anthropologist, as well as on Peruvian society, as an indigenous man. His first feature was *Dios tarda, pero no olvida/God Might Be Late but Does Not Forget* (1997) which told the story of Cirilo (Edwin Bejar Ochante), an indigenous boy who sees his parents die at the hands of the Shining Path, is then exploited by his surviving relatives, and ends up on the streets until he migrates to Lima, where he finally finds refuge when he becomes an altar boy for a local church. Ortega Matute's later post-memory film takes the form of a witness statement narrated by a victim of the subversive violence which began in Ayacucho. Manuel (Fabio Jeri) is a young boy from that region who is visited by reporters who want to know how he lost his family during the dark years of terrorism. In similar stylistic mode to *Paloma de papel*, a flashback technique is used to take the spectator back to those chaotic times when Manuel, as a child, witnessed the brutal murder of his older brother. More broadly it also tracks the unsuccessful struggle by Manuel and scores of other bereaved families to reclaim their rights.

Vidas paralelas, the first feature by Rocio Lladó, is also set in Ayacucho, and – like Lombardi's landmark film of 1988 – has a sympathetic protagonist in the form of a brave solider who neither abuses the enemy nor disrespects the local population. Unlike Lombardi's film however, there is no sense of any of the abusive behaviour that it is believed took place within the military and against the local communities. As such, the film seems to suggest – controversially in light of the reports from the Truth and Reconciliation Committee published in 2003 – that the actions of the Armed Forces and the State in the counter-subversive struggle are largely blameless. Moreover, they are portrayed as embodied within one psychologically scarred officer who also experienced in his adolescence the pain of losing his father in a Shining Path attack on the mountain town where he grew up. Abductions, killings, extrajudicial operations, amnesties, and the full range of human rights violations that often put the State on the level of its alleged aggressors are absent.

Meanwhile *Illary*, by Pereira del Mar, takes the perspective of looking back on the childhood and adolescent lives of two young women, Ana (Jackelyn Vásquez) and Eva (Urpi Gibbons), who were born in a small village in the Andes and who, despite being close childhood friends, never knew they shared the same father. The political crisis of the 1980s forces both families to migrate to the capital where each woman chooses a different path in life. While Ana becomes an Intelligence official, Eva takes the path of political activist, which – in Peru at that time, shaken by terrorism – implies that they came to represent apparently irreconcilable political positions.

In Héctor Gálvez Campos' *Paraíso*, five teenagers – three boys and two girls – live in a refugee neighborhood south of Lima known as the gardens of paradise. Together with their parents, they share memories of wartime massacres between the army and the Shining Path. Despite their trauma, they yearn to move on with their life. But in an isolated world without opportunities, they have little hope of succeeding.

At the start of the next decade, *Las malas intenciones/Bad Intentions* (Rosario García-Montero, 2011) was released across global festival circuits; set in 1983, it features a child protagonist, Cayetana (Fatima Buntinx), whose daily life is surrounded by signs of Shining Path insurgency. As Sarah Thomas has highlighted, the 'political instability has clearly infiltrated the child protagonist's consciousness despite adults' efforts to keep it from her' and provides a useful backdrop to this 'complex and nuanced representation of child subjectivity', which stands in stark contrast to the external events that surround Cayetana in real life.[7] As with Claudio Llosa's *La teta asustada*, García-Montero's debut focuses on revealing intimate moments of a young person's world amidst middle-class family turmoil, rather than provide any detailed exposition of the external conflict. The film deploys the Shining Path conflict largely as the backdrop for a dark portrait of Cayetana's morbid childhood, and of her abrupt and early transformation to adolescence, in line with the experience of so many young people in urban and rural Peru at that time and as had been portrayed more directly in Marianne Eyde's landmark film of the 1990s, *La vida es una sola*. The violence and its aftermath are part of the backdrop to the diegesis, helping to link the narrative and its characters with the national experience without explaining those events precisely. For Cayetana, the need for household adjustments such as strengthened windows, heightened walls, candles to cope with the electricity blackouts becomes part of her everyday life: she is annoyed that she can no longer peer over the garden wall to chat with the neighbours who live in far more impoverished circumstances, but she is unable to appreciate the broader significance of the social divisions that are thereby indicated. The young protagonist might not be aware of the politically motivated events around her, but her coming-of-age story provides a politicised message by demonstrating in her film that the cost of sustaining the privileges of the upper classes is the state of constant fear in which they live. The film thus renders private citizens as political subjects and centres the political within intimate spaces. The core message of the film appears to be therefore that active participation and agency are essential, whether in family life or more broadly; passive spectatorship and denial are not acceptable ways of being beyond childhood. As her grandmother tells Cayetana on the way to visit her newborn brother in the hospital: "You can't act as if nothing is happening." (See Plates 18 and 19)[8]

NN: sin identidad/NN: Without Identity (Héctor Gálvez, 2014) takes a more direct approach to the Shining Path past, with a sombre crime drama that focuses on the professionals who are tasked with exhuming and attempting to identify the victims of conflict found in mass graves. Their aim is to deliver long-delayed justice and to bring closure to families. The film does not lay blame at the door of any specific groups or individuals, but offers a critique of the apparent indifference of politicians and judiciary to the atrocities of a previous generation. (See Plate 20) Based on an actual discovery of an unidentified body with only a photograph in his shirt, the film and this image emphasise the stubborn refusal on the part of those who suffered to let the past fall into oblivion. With this intimate focus on the people who suffered, the film transcends crime drama conventions and becomes a more fundamental tale about mourning and seeking closure.[9]

Fidel (Paul Vega) is the senior staff member of a team whose job is to use forensic science and basic detective work to identify the corpses of people who "disappeared" during the Peruvian government's campaign against the Shining Path. As they are excavating a site in a remote mountain region, they find nine bodies, one of which appears to have been much more brutalised than the others, and with a small photo of a young woman attached to it.

From these remains Fidel and his co-workers must try to piece together an individual identity, with the hopes of delivering long-delayed justice and bringing closure to families who have spent long years without knowing what happened to their relatives. News of this latest discovery reaches Senora Graciela (Antonieta Pari), who desperately hopes one of the bodies might be her husband, Pedro, who was pulled off a bus by military police in 1988 and never heard from again.

The year 2014 also saw the release of *Viaje a Timbuctú/ Trip to Timbuktu* (Rossana Diaz Costa) which tells the story of two middle-class teenagers

Ana (Andrea Patriau) and Lucho (Jair García) who fall in love as they grow up just outside Lima (La Punta, Callao) during the 1980s. The film – which won the award for Best Festure Film at the Peruvian Film Festival in Paris 2015 – shows that for young people such as this couple, the only way to cope amidst violence, poverty and lack of opportunities is through finding refuge in their love and companionship. A little like Cayetana in *Las malas intenciones*, they also invent an imaginary country called Timbuktu as their escape zone. However, the harsh reality of the violence reaches La Punta, destroying their utopian adolescent world.

One year later saw the festival release of *La hora azul/Before Dawn* (2015), the first feature film by Evelyne Pegot-Ogier which tells the story of Adrián Ormache (Giovanni Ciccia), a successful, respected lawyer for whom keeping up appearances is more important than all else. But his apparently tranquil life is disturbed when he finds out about the dark past of his father, the Comandante Ormache, who with his troops tortured those suspected of terrorism and raped women during with conflict with Shining Path. He learns that his father met and fell in love with Miriam (Jackie Vásquez) during this time while holding her captive until she escaped. Adrián defies his wife's advice and goes in search of Miriam with the aim of silencing her and preserving his reputation, and yet finds his life changed by the quest and the encounter.

The sins of the past also come back to haunt the protagonist of *Magallanes* (2015), made by actor-turned-director-turned Minister of Culture Salvador del Solar. Inspired by Alonso Cueto's contemporary novel *La pasajera* (2015), this political thriller follows one man's attempt to right a past injustice through desperate criminal acts. The eponymous Magallanes (Damien Alcazar) is an ageing Lima cab driver whose dark history as a military aide is ever present. He is framed intermittently as staring with sunken eyes into the rear-view mirror of his cab, as if always looking back with fear and regret. He was at once victim and perpetrator of the 1980s military crackdown on the Shining Path insurgency, an era he cannot forget, in part because the old man who is one of his daily customers was once his boss, the feared Colonel Rivero (Federico Luppi). (See Plate 21) A chance encounter with Celina (Magaly Solier), whom he helped kidnap at age 14 so she could be kept as the Colonel's sex slave, leads him to a quest for redemption. Celina's victimisation is portrayed as a broad indictment of Peru's abusive treatment of its indigenous population: in one crucial scene, she reverts to her native Quechua and while her unsubtitled speech may not be understood by very many of those listening – whether in the frame or in the cinema – their impact is clear. The tearing open of old wounds holds resonance on a personal and a political level through this intimate narrative that stands for a country still coming to terms with its fight against Shining Path and its troubled relationship to indigenous people. The Peru-Argentina-Colombia-Spain co-production was a resounding success across the global festival circuits as well as on domestic screens, winning awards and nominations at many of the major Hispanic events. Its subject matter point to the continuity of structural violence in Peru. Despite being a genre film, it is also deeply political: as Cynthia Vich notes, 'it attacks any effort to wipe out the memory of the conflict' and proposes a need for ongoing critical reflection on the violent nature of inequality as experienced by many citizens in Peru.[10]

Finally for this study, *La última tarde/One Last Afternoon* (Joel Calero, 2016) tackles the topic of the Shining Path conflict by keeping it in the background and centring on the conflict between its protagonists, former lovers and militants Laura (Katherina D'Onofrio) and Ramón (Lucho Cáceres). They are brought back together for one afternoon, 20 years after their affair and the conflict formally ended, and reminisce as they wander the streets of Barranco while waiting for their divorce papers to be signed. (See Plate 22) The leftist tendencies they shared as young people brought them together ideologically and romantically, despite differences of class and race, but while one character seems to have suppressed memories of that era and created a new life, the wounds and scars of the other remain raw and tensions rise quickly to the surface. The city spaces they occupy during their encounter take on an expressive symbolism, with signs of the past serving as signifiers of the broader conflict that frames their own turmoil, as etched on their faces throughout. (See Plates 23 and 24) Just as the protagonists need closure on this turbulent chapter of their lives, it is suggested that so too does the population of Peru more broadly.

Conclusion

As Peruvian commentator Jorge Zavaleta noted in a recent presentation on cinema, literature and society in Peru, filmmaking in this nation continues to be extremely challenging despite the digital revolution and the gradual increase of state support.[11] Moreover, the relationship between cinema and the Peruvian state remains complex. While most of the films discussed in this study received some support from the government via its legislative structures for cinema, it should be remembered that cinematic expression of a political crisis that threatened to destabilise the nation flew in the face of prevailing discourse that preferred to limit critical debate throughout much of that time. Even *La boca del lobo*, although cautiously applauded by President García at the time of its release in 1988 and an enormous hit domestically and internationally, was condemned by the Peruvian authorities more generally. They were concerned that the film criticised the brutality of counter-insurgency tactics at a time when the construction of a sense of national unity, homogeneous identity and uncritical support for the state's mission to overcome the enemy were crucial. Throughout the 1990s, during the increasingly repressive regime of Alberto Fujimori, it became more and more difficult to challenge state strategy, even though the conflict had officially ended. Fujimori's desire to maintain tight control led to the dismantling of democratic structures and practices, and ever tighter restrictions on freedom of expression. In fact, the state of emergency linked to the Shining Path conflict was not repealed in several key rural areas until 2000, when the Fujimori government had crumbled amidst revelations of corruption.

On the relationship between national cinema and national identity, Emma Wilson makes the observation that 'cinema may provide us with identity images, yet it can also remind us that identities are unstable, change through time, location and encounters, have many facets and are inherently unknowable'.[12] Susan Hayward goes further in arguing that national cinemas 'should function as a *mise-en-scène* of scattered and dissembling identities'.[13] The films discussed in this study seem to go some way towards fulfilling this brief. The potential for commercial fiction cinema to draw attention, dramatically and compellingly, to those deep-rooted ethnic and class-based divisions that were part of the source of social tension in Peru would perhaps help explain why direct cinematic representations of the conflict in rural areas became fewer in number throughout the 1990s. Uncomfortable questions were inevitably raised about the historical domination and colonisation of Peruvian 'national' identity by Lima (the centre), and its problematic relationship with Andean communities (marginalised, on the periphery), with its origins in the Spanish conquest of Peru in the sixteenth century, and perpetuated by a Lima-based Hispanic ruling elite (whether military or civilian) since the country gained independence in 1821.

Such considerations might also have sparked a concern on the part of individual filmmakers not to be seen to set up challenges to the political status quo, nor to be labelled as a threat to national security. A situation of self-imposed censorship is likely to have sprung from a desire not to risk losing financial, political and popular support for future national film projects. This fear of restrictions on freedom of expression gained new credence in the light of the details that emerged of the manipulation of the mass media by Fujimori's own head of intelligence, Vladimiro Montesinos, through substantial payments to those they needed to control.[14]

One of the features of any cinema supported by national structures is to express and explore some aspect or aspects of national identity, an identity built in large part 'on shared memories of some past or pasts'.[15] All the films in this study achieve this to varying degrees through their exploration of the motives and consequences of Peru's recent political violence. However, Hayward also states that while memory as treated by much national cinema 'stands for collective memory, a shared culture, shared memories of a collective past ... memory also means amnesia'.[16] Citing Anthony Smith's work on nationalism, she further notes that 'the importance of national amnesia and getting one's own history *wrong* [is essential] for the maintenance of national solidarity'.[17] Smith's assertion on amnesia and culture is particularly helpful when trying to understand the differing reception to the films under discussion in this project. By 1988, the year of the release of *La boca del lobo*, the political violence had spread to Lima and affected the daily lives of all its inhabitants, regardless of class or ethnic background. A film that debated such violence may not have been warmly welcomed by all, but the topic it portrayed was at the heart of public opinion, and freedom of expression was in any case largely supported by García's relatively liberal government. By 1993, however, there had been a change of regime, of political structures and of national constitution following Fujimori's *autogolpe*, and with that a move to an increasingly centralised and repressive mindset that brought the benefit of capturing a terrorist leader, but the disadvantage of restraints on civil liberties. Indeed, the Fujimori-led campaign of post-conflict regeneration aimed above all to wipe from the nation's minds all memory of the increasingly 'dirty' aspects of the political violence in Peru, in particular the military's counter-insurgency tactics, which betrayed a frequent disregard for basic human rights and democratic freedoms. Nevertheless, neglected economically by the state, national cinema seems to have enjoyed greater freedom to keep the memory of the conflict alive than most other mass media forms, which were restricted from doing so by Fujimori's repressive, fraudulent and corrupt regime. 'National amnesia' regarding the chaotic and brutal role of the military in much of the violence since 1980 was strongly encouraged, for the sake of national solidarity and social stability. In such a political context, which also involved a change to the country's economic systems and an abolition of the very law established to promote national cinema, it is hardly surprising that films such as Eyde's *La vida es una sola*, which explicitly exposed the 'masquerade of unity'[18] of Peruvian society, and drew attention to structures of power and knowledge that appeared to position the indigenous communities as inferior victims, would undergo such a rough ride from audiences and authorities. This episode in turn provoked anxiety amongst fellow filmmakers, who continued to rely on both for their professional survival. Nevertheless, the desire to explore an issue of major national concern on cinema screens did not diminish and, as has been shown throughout this project, national filmmakers have returned to it in different ways ever since.

Above all, the films addressed in this study share an overriding concern to look back at a recent and very painful period of the nation's history, and to shape narratives that provoke uncomfortable questions about, for example: the relationship between state and society; the apparently integral role played by violence and a distinctive macho masculinity in the national image; the subordination of certain cultural groups; and the divided nature of Peruvian society. These are questions which remain pertinent to the contemporary Peruvian situation and which cannot themselves be consigned to history. Indeed, the blurring of fact and fiction in many of the films, so often questioned by critics and audiences, seems to reinforce the notion that we ought to move beyond consideration of these films as relatively straightforward works of social realism, and instead view their protagonists as more broadly symbolic of a general and ongoing desire for change in the face of social, political and cultural crisis. Thus, actual massacres, such as the ones implicitly depicted in *La boca del lobo* (1988) or remembered in *NN* (2014), become reference points within narratives that have more to say about the experiencing and contemporary acts of memorialising of violence. Moreover, central characters, whether fictional or based on real people, have become icons for resistance to violence and a desire for social change. The protagonist of *Días de Santiago*, for example, drew attention in 2004 to the breakdown of traditional patriarchal order, a certain crisis of masculinity and a perception of the military as ineffective in protecting its citizens, maintaining social order and ensuring equality of opportunity for all. That the endings of most of the films are ambiguous in tone suggests that the journey towards change is far from over, but the rejection of violence as a viable and effective instrument for reshaping national identity is satisfying nonetheless. Peru's national cinema seems thus to have played an important role in recuperating, revisiting and rewriting events from the nation's past. Indeed, while struggling to contend with its own identity crisis, national cinema seems to have had a significant impact on the shaping of a new sense of national identity/ies, in which difference is at least acknowledged if not officially challenged and critiqued, and violence as a strategy for change is at least debated if not effaced entirely.

Despite the gradual shift towards a more diverse, heterogeneous and inclusive national image, it must be acknowledged that most national cinema production remains in the hands of the white Lima-based elite; most of the nation's commercial cinemas are based in affluent areas of Lima; and most spectators hail from the more economically secure sectors of urban society.[19] Nevertheless, audiences at the important network of cine-clubs and cultural centres that exist in most of the country's larger towns, where prices are usually lower, are often more mixed. Moreover, some directors, such as Aguilar with *Paloma de papel* and Llosa with *Madeinusa*, have made important efforts to take their films around the country, thus increasing access to them, stimulating debate about the issues depicted with their audiences, and encouraging interest in film as a cultural activity for all. Meanwhile, the regional cinema movement has gained substantial visibility in Peru and elsewhere, drawing on its own global influences and networks.[20] The task of critically debating the specific trauma of the Shining Path conflict on cinema screens has been a heavy burden for those filmmakers who have somehow defied the logistical and ideological odds to do so. Some may qualify such activity, in a nation with more pressing economic concerns, as a pointless indulgence that achieves little of great consequence. Meanwhile, others (such as the late Robles Godoy) celebrate the very existence of a diverse, critically engaged and politically committed national cinema, however fragile its legislative and economic structures, as a symbol of democracy and enlightened modernity.

> When a Peruvian film is released, it is cause for celebration, not for the film in itself, but because where there is cinema, there is freedom of expression.[21]

In spite of the counter-hegemonic intentions of the films discussed here, and the impact they have had in terms of provoking public debate, overall it would appear that together they reinforce the notion that violence and Peruvian national identity are inescapably and inevitably connected. Although the message from *Alias la gringa* and *Anda, corre, vuela …* appears to be that peaceful change and harmonious relationships based on tolerance and understanding should be possible, in fact their characters achieve this only by operating outside the conventions of authority. Meanwhile, the more widely travelled productions of *La boca del lobo*, *Días de Santiago*, *La teta asustada*, *Magallanes* and *La última tarde*, whose protagonists are failed by those around them, leave the overriding impression of a society scarred by conflict, of a divided and fragmented population, and of a nation still struggling with its own complex processes of mourning, healing and identity formation.

Notes

Introduction: Peruvian Cinema and Culture

1. Walter Salles, 'Preface', in Elena and Díaz López, p. xv.
2. In September 2017, the government finally approved a new Cinema and Audiovisual Law which, it was hoped, would triple the resources dedicated to this sector.
3. The Shining Path insurgency began in 1980 with the symbolic burning of ballot boxes during the presidential elections. Dismissed at first by the authorities as delinquents, the rebels swiftly made their presence felt in the remote highland villages of Ayacucho and Junín, provoking a 'dirty war' against state forces, during which crimes were committed on both sides and in which the line between victim and assailant was frequently blurred. The group's authoritarian leader, Abimael Guzmán, was captured in 1992 and, while the violence seemed to end, debate about who was to blame was suppressed by President Alberto Fujimori's regime using whatever means were deemed necessary.
4. Two examples of the preoccupation with lurid accounts of archaeological discoveries that would appear to provide evidence of the deep-rooted place of violence in Peruvian culture include: 'Warrior queen or ritual sacrifice: The amazing secret unearthed in Peru', *Daily Mail*, 18 May 2015, p. 11; and 'City where sacrificial slaughter was way of life', *Daily Telegraph*, 2 September 2015, p. 3.
5. For example, via the #NiUnaMenos/#NotOneLess campaign against sexual violence that began in Peru with a demonstration in central Lima in August 2016 that brought together women from many different class, racial and ethnic groups.
6. León Frías et al., 'Diccionario temático del cine peruano'.
7. Turner, *Film as Social Practice*, p. 152.
8. Monaco, *How to Read a Film*, pp. 127–130.
9. Turner, p. 134.
10. Anderson, *Imagined Communities*, p. 6.
11. Hayward, 'Framing national cinemas', p. 90.
12. Higson, *Waving the Flag*, p. 5.
13. Higson, *Waving the Flag*, p. 6.

14. Higson, 'The limiting imagination of national cinema', p. 35.
15. Higson, 'The limiting imagination of national cinema', p. 35.
16. Hayward, p. 89.
17. Hayward, p. 93. Original emphasis.
18. Mike Wayne, *Political Film: The Dialectics of Third Cinema*, p. 6.
19. Hayward, p. 95.
20. Norma Fuller in Castro and Paredes, 'La Peruanidad', p. 8.
21. Carlos Contreras in Castro and Paredes, p. 9.
22. *Mestizaje*, as discussed by Amaryll Chanady, is primarily a racial marker of hybridity. See Chanady, 'Identity, politics and *mestizaje*', p. 192. It is positioned as subordinate to the creole (*criollo*) elite defined as the Spaniard native to America. As Chanady points out, 'official discourses of *mestizaje* ... stress assimilation, Europeanization and whitening' (p. 192), and thus emphasise the hierarchy of ethnicity, with white perceived as being the most socially acceptable. Philip Swanson also stresses that early *mestizos* were largely 'the product of the continual rape of indigenous women by common Spanish soldiers and parvenus [and that] given these origins, *mestizos* were often looked down upon as subhuman'. Swanson, *Companion to Latin American Studies*, p. 28.
23. Velarde in Cárdenas, 'Ser Peruano (I)', p. 16.
24. Ojeda, 'Nicomedes Santa Cruz and the vindication of Afro-Peruvian culture', p. 241.
25. Wood, *De sabor nacional*, p. 21.
26. Wade, *Race and Ethnicity in Latin America*, p. 108.
27. Wood, *De sabor nacional*, p. 256.
28. Hodgin and Thakkar, *Scars and Wounds*, p. 3.
29. Enrique Silva reported that after a period in the early 1990s during which many cinemas closed down, by 1997 the growth in number of cinema screens in Lima seemed unstoppable. He wrote that the first main cinema to restructure its architecture so as to offer greater comfort and increased choice was El Pacífico in Miraflores, which divided its enormous screen into six separate ones in 1995. Throughout the last half of the 1990s, luxurious malls were constructed in various parts of Lima that included multiplex cinemas, most of which were financed by distributors such as the transnational company Continental Films. It should be noted, however, that this development resulted in greater opportunities for more affluent urban citizens to view studio films from the US rather than support for an emergent diversity of film culture in Peru generally. It also led to a sharp increase in cinema ticket prices, from 6 to 14 soles in 1997. Silva, 'Nuevos cines en Lima', p. 18.
30. Lombardi in Bedoya, *Entre fauces y colmillos*, p. 201.
31. Wiener, 'Miedos de guerra', p. 18.

32. An account of the journal's inception was given in Bedoya's 1995 text *Cien años de cine en el Perú* and also appeared on Bedoya's blog as part of the fiftieth anniversary celebrations: http://www.paginasdeldiariodesatan.com/pdds/?p=1242, 14 February 2015.
33. For example, Núñez Gorritti, *Pitas y alambre: la época de oro del cine peruano, 1936–1950* (Lima: Editorial Colmillo Blanco, 1990).
34. King, 'Andean images'.
35. Bedoya, *Cien años de cine en el Perú: una historia crítica*; *Entre fauces y colmillos: las películas de Francisco Lombardi*; *Un cine reencontrado: diccionario ilustrado de las películas Peruanas*; *Imágenes del cine en el Perú*. All were produced to commemorate the centenary of cinema in Peru.
36. Bedoya, '*La boca del lobo/The Lion's Den*'; Bedoya, 'Peru: Films for after a war', '*El cine peruano en tiempos digitales*.
37. www.paginasdeldiariodesatan.com/pdds/
38. For example: Galleno, 'El ataque sexual y canibalismo de la bestia en *La boca del lobo*'; Palaversich, 'Cultural dyslexia and the politics of cross cultural excursion in Claudia Llosa's *Madeinusa*'; Maseda, 'Songs of pain: female active survivors in Claudia Llosa's *The Milk of Sorrow*'; D'Argenio, 'A contemporary Andean type: the representation of the indigenous world in Claudia Llosa's films' and 'Monstrosity and war memories in Latin American post-conflict cinema'; Shaw, 'European co-production funds and Latin American cinema; and Vich, 'De desadaptaciones y reiteradas violencias: la distancia entre el film *Magallanes* y la novela *La pasajera*'.
39. Middents, *Writing National Cinema*, p. 25
40. The most important of these were produced by lawyer José Perla Anaya. See for instance Perla Anaya, *Censura y promoción en el cine* and *Los tres primeros años*.
41. Rosen, 'History, textuality, nation', p. 18.
42. Chanan, 'The economic condition of cinema in Latin America', p. 196.

1 Cinema, State and National Identity

1. Kern cited by Singer, *Melodrama and Modernity*, p. 19.
2. López cited by Schelling, *Through the Kaleidoscope*, p. 149.
3. Schelling, *Through the Kaleidoscope*, p. 149.
4. Bedoya, *Cien años de cine en el Perú*, pp. 23–6.
5. Elmore, *Los muros invisibles*, gives a rich account of the development and display of modernity in Lima during the twentieth century.
6. Larrain, *Identity and Modernity in Latin America*, p. 103.
7. Bedoya, *Cien años de cine en el Perú*, p. 43.

8. Elmore, p. 11.
9. Anderson, p. 7.
10. Larrain, p. 40.
11. Starn, Degregori and Kirk, eds, *The Peru Reader*, pp. 215–218.
12. Many cultural producers during the 1920s and 1930s were linked to *indigenismo* and opposed Leguía's regime, so it was perhaps to be expected that they focused on the rural and indigenous dimensions of Peruvian identity. Note that the making of Ugarte and Rada's film in the early 1920s coincided with the formal legal recognition of the indigenous population of Peru and the initiation of official discussions on their situation.
13. During this period, a new political party emerged that signalled the entry of the lower and middle classes into national politics. The ideology of APRA (Alianza Popular Revolucionaria Americana), led by Víctor Raúl Haya de la Torre, was based on anti-imperialism and pan-Latin Americanism and a bringing together of all those who had been marginalised and excluded by the ruling elite. It should be noted, however, that APRA focused more on supporting the urban and coastal working class than the highland indigenous populations foregrounded by Mariátegui, and that Haya and Mariátegui went their separate ways after profound political disagreements in the 1920s.
14. Bedoya, *Cien años de cine en el Perú*, p. 68.
15. Eight feature-length films were made in Peru during the 1940s, one of which, *Alerta en la frontera/Alert at the Border* (Kurt Hermann, 1941), a documentary about the war with Ecuador, was withdrawn from exhibition and 'lost' until 2014, when it was screened at Lima Film Festival. Only two were made in the 1950s. Exceptional in terms of their portrayal of Peruvian cultural diversity are the remarkable *Kukuli* (Figueroa, 1961) and *Jarawi* (Villanueva and Nishiyama, 1966), both made under the auspices of the Cuzco Cinema Club and filmed in the Andean highlands.
16. King, 'Andean images', p. 200.
17. Bedoya, *Cien años de cine en el Perú*, p. 305.
18. Anaya, *Censura y promoción en el cine*, p. 115.
19. de Lucio cited by Bedoya, *Cien años de cine en el Perú*, p. 189.
20. Wiener, 'Tan duro de vivir, tan duro de morir', p. 22.
21. Gellner, *Nations and Nationalism*, pp. 24–29.
22. Bedoya, *Cien años de cine en el Perú*, p. 188.
23. King, 'Andean images, pp. 201–202.
24. See Anaya, pp. 115–136, and Bedoya, Cien años de cine en el Perú, pp. 185–196, for full details of these incentives.
25. See Perla Anaya, pp. 126–127, for a full explanation of these criteria.
26. See Bedoya, *Cien años de cine en el Perú*, p. 191, for details of the composition of COPROCI.

27. Johnson, 'Film policy in Latin America', p. 133.
28. Schnitman, *Film Industries in Latin America*, p. 45.
29. As will be seen in the analyses that follow, apart from Lombardi's *La boca del lobo/The lion's den* (1988), made when the Cinema Law remained buoyant, almost all of the national films that dealt with the Shining Path conflict and its social consequences received mixed critical reviews, partly due to their perceived technical deficiencies but also due to their content and approach.
30. Bedoya and León Frías, 'Volver a vivir', p. 110. See also Martínez, Gabriela, 'Cinema law in Latin America', www.ejumpcut.org
31. Bedoya and León Frías, 'Volver a vivir', p. 110.
32. Cited by Wiener, 'Tan duro de vivir, tan duro de morir', p. 24.
33. Cited by Leira, 'Entrevista con Robles Godoy', p. 16.
34. Cited by Leira, p. 17. Throughout the second half of the 1990s, critics and filmmakers debated the value of the competitions that were at the heart of the second Cinema Law, mainly via the pages of the journal *La Gran Ilusión*. Perhaps the most provocative article appeared in 1998, in the form of a lively conversation among filmmakers such as Emilio Salomón, who declared themselves 'in disagreement with the results of the competitions', and critics Bedoya and León Frías, who had been members of the jury that made those decisions. Salomón et al., 'Premios y desencuentros'.
35. Between 1994 and 1997, just four films were made and released in Peru: *Sin compasión* (1994) and *Bajo la piel* (1996) by Francisco Lombardi; *Anda, corre, vuela …* (Augusto Tamayo, 1995) and *Asia, el culo del mundo* (Juan Carlos Torrico, 1996). No Peruvian films were released in 1997.
36. The releases were: in 1998, *Coraje* (Alberto Durant), *La carnada* (Marianne Eyde) and *No se lo digas a nadie* (Lombardi); in 1999, *La yunta brava* (Federico García) and *Pantaleón y las visitadoras* (Lombardi); in 2000, *Ciudad de M* (Felipe Degregori) and *A la media noche y media* (Marité Ugaz and Mariana Rondón); and in 2001, *Tinta roja* (Lombardi), *El bien esquivo* (Tamayo) and *Bala perdida* (Aldo Salvini).
37. León Frías, 'Peru' (2003), p. 266.
38. León Frías, 'Peru' (2004), p. 235.
39. Ibermedia is a Hispanic co-production venture, established in 1997 in Venezuela, which focuses its efforts and resources on four support programmes for cinema: development; co-production; distribution and promotion; and training. For the first three years, benefits for Peru's filmmakers were hampered both by a lack of state funds to match those offered by Ibermedia, and also by the failure of Fujimori's government to fulfil its own annual contribution of $100,000 to the overall pot of around $4million. See studies by scholars such as Nuria Triana Toribio (2013) and Tamara Falicov

(2017) for discussions of the challenges and benefits of these and other co-production schemes.
40. Stock, 'Migrancy and the Latin American cinemascape', p. 157.
41. Moreover, the emerging filmmakers of that time felt that the legislation set up in 1994 excluded them from developing their skills, and they would have liked to see a return to the more supportive infrastructure for short filmmaking that guaranteed screening and a portion of the box office return for every short film made by a Peruvian director. See Pérez Torres, 'La década del silencio'. Indeed, León Frías reports that, while an unprecedented 30 feature film scripts were submitted to the CONACINE competition in early 2005, only three were selected to receive a sum that was just a part of the production budget. He lamented also that few of the other entries would ever find the funding required to get produced. See León Frías, 'Peru' (2006), p. 223.
42. Robles Godoy cited by Bedoya and León Frías, 'Entrevista con Armando Robles Godoy', p. 104.
43. Deutsch cited by Schlesinger, 'The sociological scope of "national cinema"', p. 20.
44. Higson, *Waving the Flag*, p. 7.
45. Jarvie, 'National cinema', p. 81.
46. Hayward, p. 101.
47. Hayward, p. 95.

2 Cinema, Transition and Turmoil

1. The anti-terrorism legislation, introduced in 1981 and enhanced twice in 1987, made it much easier for the government to imprison anyone suspected of promoting a point of view that was deemed to be sympathetic towards the Shining Path cause.
2. Jelin, *State Repression and the Struggle for Memory*, p. xvii.
3. De Guzmán, '*La boca del lobo*: máximo galardón en el festival de La Habana', p. 8.
4. Lombardi's earlier films all portrayed acts of violent crime and provoked debate about issues of identity and violence. They explored the socio-political and psychological motivations for such actions, and considered varying responses to them. These films are: *Muerte al amanecer/Death at Sunrise* (1977), about the last hours of a violent criminal condemned to death by firing squad; *Los amigos/The Friends* (1978), about the reunion of four childhood friends who become violent when one finds out that another is homosexual; *Muerte de un magnate/Death of a Tycoon* (1980), a fictional reconstruction of the 1972 assassination of a fraudulent businessman; *Maruja en el infierno/Maruja in*

Hell (1983), about a young woman who dreams of escaping the violence and squalor of her life in Lima; and *La ciudad y los perros/The City and the Dogs* (1985), an adaptation of Mario Vargas Llosa's novel about the harshness of life in a military training camp. See Bedoya, *Un cine reencontrado*, pp. 218–220, 232–235, 250–253, 257–261.

5. Each of the films mentioned in the last footnote is set in Lima. Between 1988 (the year that saw the making of *La boca del lobo*) and 2004, Lombardi made seven films, of which only two are located outside the capital, Lima. *Bajo la piel/Under the Skin* (1996) is set in a fictional town in the northern coastal region of Peru, while *Pantaleón y las visitadoras/Pantaleon and the Visitors* (1999), another adaptation from the work of Vargas Llosa, was set in the Amazon jungle. Both focus on the response of their young male protagonists to violence around them, and continue Lombardi's exploration of the relationship between violence and national identity. Both also utilise the nature of the respective landscapes in illustrating and emphasising the underlying tension and oppression felt by each main character.
6. Skidmore and Smith, 'Peru: Soldiers, oligarchs and Indians', p. 216.
7. See Peralta Ruiz, *Sendero Luminoso y la prensa, 1980–1994*, p. 145. Headlines that appeared at about the same time as the film's release in the influential US newspaper the *New York Times* included, for example: 'Peru urged to curb abuses in fighting rebels', 20 December 1987; 'Peru's disappearing democracy', 29 December 1988; and 'Peruvian guerrillas emerge as an urban political force', 17 July 1988. See Peralta Ruiz, pp. 159–163.
8. In Cuba, for example, where guerrilla-like civil war is also an important part of the nation's history and collective memory, the film was criticised by some for offering a vision of the battle between military and insurgents that was perhaps too sympathetic towards the former, despite the portrayal of abuses committed by both sides. See, for example, the interview with Lombardi recorded on his arrival back in Lima after the festival screening of *La boca* in Havana: 'Entrevista con Francisco Lombardi', *La República*, 19 December 1988, p. 9.
9. Lombardi cited by Bedoya, *Un cine reencontrado*, p. 179.
10. Lombardi cited by Bedoya, *Entre fauces y colmillos*, p. 180.
11. Balbi, 'Entrevista con Francisco Lombardi', *La República*, 27 November 1988, p. 8.
12. Lombardi points out in the same interview that one politician even claimed at the time that the film presented a danger to state security, and suggested that national cinema should wait at least 15 years before tackling such a sensitive topic. This chimes with Jelin's view that since political authorities are 'concerned primarily with the stability of democratic institutions', they will thus prefer the policies of oblivion, or at least deferral. See Jelin, p. xvii.
13. Mauceri, pp. 116–117.

14. See Peralta Ruiz, p. 131. Note that in May 1988, a military patrol based in Ayacucho had executed 28 peasants whom they accused of collaborating with Shining Path. According to Peralta, this new massacre 'reopened press debates about the upsurge of the "dirty war", alongside the inability of García to control the excesses committed by the military and the police'. See Peralta Ruiz, p. 136.
15. De Guzmán, p. 8.
16. The film, which was shown at festivals around the world, won many awards for both the quality of its production as well as its impact on human rights. It is still screened at events today. Indeed, in Cannes 2005, it was one of four films selected for the special section devoted to Peruvian cinema as part of that festival's 'Cinéma du Monde' strand. Further, it should be noted that the success of this film came at a time when national cinema was on the verge of possibly its worst crisis. Lombardi was applauded and rewarded for his tenacity and achievement in the face of a continued lack of formal infrastructure for national cinema, as well as for the general high quality and social commitment of the film. Even so, despite the record number of spectators, the film did not recoup any more than 50% of its costs because the ticket revenue had decreased in value at least fourfold due to hyperinflation, which peaked at 2000% in 1988. Nevertheless, the critical acclaim ensured that Lombardi remained attractive to international investors during most of the 1990s, one of the few Peruvian directors to enjoy such a position of independence from state finance and interference. See León Frías, 'Peru' (2005), pp. 234–235.
17. This text in itself, although apparently objective and focusing mainly on the background of the Shining Path campaign prior to 1983, angered some critics for drawing attention to the notion of a 'dirty war', which implies a certain lack of regard for human rights, and for informing audiences that the main victims of that battle for control of Peru's central sierra were villagers of the Andes. As a final appeal to authenticity, the text ends by asserting that: 'This film is inspired by events that took place between 1980 and 1983'.
18. Soon after his arrival, Roca puts his men through their paces by making them run through the mountains, making their mark on the terrain that has thus far been the domain of the 'enemy'. They chant an aggressive war cry in unison, thus igniting the hatred towards the enemy that Roca felt was required in order to overcome Shining Path. Moreover, the leader's own derogatory view of the local community is clear: while beating the villagers during interrogation, Roca refers to them as 'fucking Indians' and 'trash'.
19. De Guzmán, p. 8.
20. Manrique, 'The war for the central sierra', p. 193.
21. Manrique, 'The war for the central sierra', p. 193.

22. This conclusion is based on Manrique's study of statistics relating to deaths of villagers and attacks on Andean villages between 1980 until 1991, and analysis of the different strategies deployed by both Shining Path and the military. See Manrique, 'The war for the central sierra', pp. 193-223.
23. This concept of 'wilful forgetting' is taken from Susan Hayward's account of national cinemas and draws on Anthony Smith's assertion that 'the importance of national amnesia and getting one's own history *wrong* [is essential] for the maintenance of national solidarity'. See Hayward, p. 90.
24. Mauceri, *State under Siege*, p. 137.
25. Muñoz reports that 'the number of disappeared persons increased from 125 in 1987 to 410 in 1989, and then declined to 230 in 1992', and that in 1992 'the Human Rights Sub-Commission of the United Nations noted Peru as the country with the most disappearances of that year'. See Muñoz, 'Human rights and social referents', p. 467.
26. Muñoz, p. 459.
27. Bedoya, '*La boca del lobo/The Lion's Den*', p. 185.
28. Huayhuaca cited by Bedoya, '*La boca del lobo/The Lion's Den*', p. 189.
29. Cavallo and Martínez cited by Bedoya, *Un cine reencontrado*, p. 279.
30. Although one Shining Path suspect is captured, questioned and taken away for interrogation, his identity and status within the village remain unclear, and no further Shining Path individual is shown. This would appear to add further credence to the view that the film asks us to focus more on the soldiers and their behaviour. Moreover, as Crabtree points out, 'Shining Path proved impossible to penetrate and infiltrate ... in great measure due to [its] tight clandestine organization, but [also by] the lack of confidence of local peasant authorities in the military authorities'. See Crabtree, *Peru under García*, p. 106.
31. De Guzmán, p. 12.
32. Freud, *Civilization, Society and Religion*, p. 313. Freud proposes that aggression in so-called civilised society is restrained by external authority (such as parents, school, church, institutions of law and order) and by an internal authority that is associated with the development of a sense of moral conscience and guilt. Both these aspects of authority are stripped away in the case of these soldiers, under attack and abandoned by the state, and both are replaced by the new 'father figure' of Roca, who does all he can to reignite the repressed aggressive instinct of his men. Freud further points the blame at a failure to establish, or to prevent the collapse of, emotional ties between different sectors of society, suggesting that the strengthening of such ties and the encouragement of shared interests might help to prevent war by replacing one instinct with another (pp. 251-362). This is also echoed in the complete lack of cultural and social bonds between villagers and soldiers in *La boca*.

33. Mauceri, p. 136.
34. Bedoya, 'La boca del lobo/The lion's den', p. 186.
35. Flores Galindo, *Los rostros de la plebe*, p. 174. In an interview at the time of the film's release, screenwriter Giovanna Pollarolo also pointed out that increasing numbers of Peruvians were convinced that indiscriminate violence was perhaps the only response to Shining Path, despite earlier sentiments to the contrary. See Miguel Díaz Reyes, 'Entrevista con Giovanna Pollarolo', *La República*, 18 December 1988, p. 10.
36. Flores Galindo, p. 172.
37. Connell, *Masculinities*, p. 83.
38. Bedoya, *Entre fauces y colmillos*, p. 93.
39. Gellner, p. 7.
40. Hayward, p. 101.
41. Bedoya, 'La boca del lobo/The Lion's Den', p. 187.
42. Crabtree, *Peru under García*, p. 202.
43. Bedoya, *Entre fauces y colmillos*, p. 105.
44. The psychological consequences of this experience of excessive violence on the young men involved was explored 16 years later in Josué Méndez's *Días de Santiago* (2004).
45. Billig, *Banal Nationalism*, p. 85.
46. Lombardi cited by Bedoya, *Entre fauces y colmillos*, p. 180.
47. Billig, p. 86.
48. The national anthem is discussed by Billig as one of the other main markers of nationhood. Indeed, Peru's anthem, *Marcha Nacional*, was chosen in 1822, just one year after the battle for independence had ended in victory, at which point Peru began to reconstruct itself as a nation in its own right. The lyrics celebrate freedom of oppression and the end of slavery under the Spaniards, and speak of all Peruvians as if they are united and equal in their joy at being liberated, but omit to acknowledge the diversity of experience within the borders of the nation and fail to take account of the new structures of oppression that developed since 1821.
49. Bedoya, *Entre fauces y colmillos*, pp. 86–9.
50. Bedoya, *Entre fauces y colmillos*, p. 87.
51. De Guzmán, p. 8.
52. This film does not fall into the trap of glorifying the indigenous way of life. It concentrates instead on highlighting the difficulty of overcoming internal conflict when there is no sense of unified national identity, or indeed one that allows recognition of all the differing cultural identities of Peru, and that embraces the richness of multiplicity rather than fears the complexities of fragmentation. It blames this as much as economic inequality for the crisis of Shining Path.

53. Bedoya, 'La boca del lobo/The Lion's Den', p. 186.
54. Lombardi cited by Bedoya, *Entre fauces y colmillos*, p. 180.
55. Bueno cited by De Guzmán, p. 8.
56. De Guzmán, p. 8.
57. Lombardi cited by Bedoya, *Entre fauces y colmillos*, p. 92.
58. Lombardi cited by Bedoya, *Entre fauces y colmillos*, pp. 108–109.
59. de Cárdenas, *El cine de Francisco Lombardi*, p. 77.
60. Poole and Rénique, *Peru*, p. 102.
61. Wade, *Race and Ethnicity in Latin America*, p. 64.
62. Pereira del Mar cited by Perla Anaya, *Los tres primeros años*, p. 20.
63. Bedoya, *Cien años de cine en el Perú*, p. 289.
64. Wood, *De sabor nacional*, p. 28.
65. Aliaga, *Terrorism in Peru*, pp. 36–37.
66. Peralta Ruiz, p. 64.
67. Aliaga, p. 41.
68. Flindell Klarén, *Peru*, p. 397.
69. Amnesty International 1987–1989 in Aliaga, p. 42.
70. Crabtree, *Peru under García*, pp. 108–118.
71. Peralta Ruiz, p. 31.
72. Wiener, 'Miedos de guerra', p. 19.
73. Snead, *White Screens, Black Images*, p. 5.
74. Radcliffe in Wade, *Race and Ethnicity in Latin America*, p. 38.
75. Chanady, pp. 196–199.
76. Hunefeldt, *A Brief History of Peru*, pp. 104–105.
77. Radcliffe, 'Ethnicity, patriarchy, and incorporation into the nation', p. 379.
78. Cordero, 'Women in war', p. 349.
79. Gorriti, *The Shining Path*, p. 119.
80. Scott Palmer, *Shining Path of Peru*, p. 8.
81. Anderson, p. 6.
82. Shohat and Stam, *Unthinking Eurocentrism*, pp. 116–117.
83. Shohat and Stam, *Unthinking Eurocentrism*, p. 116.
84. Silverman, *Male subjectivity at the margins*, p. 141.
85. Bedoya, *Cien años de cine en el Perú*, pp. 288–9.
86. Higson, *Waving the flag*, p. 5.
87. Mette Hjort draws on Michael Billig's (1995) notion of banal nationalism to discuss recognisably national material elements such as locations, language, actors and props that 'provide the basis for a given film's national quality' without constituting a theme of nation in themselves. Hjort, 'Themes of nation', p. 108. As she further explains, 'banal nationalism involves the ongoing circulation and utilisation of the symbols of the nation, but in a manner that is so deeply ingrained and habitual as to involve no focal awareness'. Hjort, p. 108.

88. Hjort, p. 113.
89. Scott Palmer, p. 4.
90. As Peter Wade argues, '*mestizaje* as an ideology of national formation is far from benevolent, as it commonly combines with a powerful ideology of whitening ... in which mixture ... is a value-loaded process of the elimination of blackness and indigenousness from the national body politic in favour of whiter types of mestizos'. See Wade, 'Images of Latin American *mestizaje* and the politics of comparison', p. 357.
91. Four other films were made but none of these achieved commercial release in Peru. Instead they went straight to video release in the US as part of a low-budget production project sponsored by Roger Corman and produced by Luis (Lucho) Llosa of Iguana Films. See Bedoya, *Un cine reencontrado*, pp. 294–301.
92. According to Bedoya and Wiener, the film attracted over 400,000 spectators during its commercial release, making it the third most successful film screened in Peru in 1991. See Bedoya, *Un cine reencontrado*, p. 298; Wiener, 'El cine peruano en los noventa', p. 103. Released at 12 cinemas in Lima, it remained on screens for four weeks, even though the guaranteed screening benefit of the 1972 Cinema Law had been abandoned by exhibitors, on commercial grounds. Unusually, it was also screened in the provincial towns of Arequipa and Trujillo and the film's stars travelled to those cities for promotional reasons.
93. Gringo/a is a Latin American term that refers to a white person of European or North American origin. It can be used in a friendly or pejorative way, depending on the context. 'La Gringa' as a nickname in the specific context of this film is based on the protagonist's successful escape attempts when disguised as a white woman and, thus, removed from all suspicion. These attempts are not seen in the film, since they took place before the plot begins, but are referred to in dialogue and emphasise the hierarchical superiority of whiteness (even female), over *mestizo* identity.
94. John Crabtree notes that although the brutality of the intervention might not have been intended by President García, he was 'at the very least seen as guilty of major political misjudgement in his handling of the issue'. See Crabtree, *Peru under García*, p. 81.
95. Núñez del Pozo cited by Bedoya, *Un cine reencontrado*, p. 296.
96. During one promotional interview at the time of the film's release, Durant stressed that, for him, 'individualism can turn into our worst enemy', and that his film was one way to show the need for social responsibility in Peru. See León Frías, '*Alias la gringa*', p. 15.
97. Crabtree, *Peru under García*, p. 184.
98. Christine Hunefeldt points out, for example, that Belaúnde (1980–1985) 'did little to reverse the reforms implemented by the military, nor did he move them much further along. He began urban building projects in a lukewarm

fashion, but he had no funds to do more because interest on Peru's huge external debt was eating up revenues'. See Hunefeldt, p. 237.
99. Cotler and Grompone, *El fujimorismo*, p. 17.
100. Crabtree, *Peru under García*, p. 150.
101. Bedoya, *Un cine reencontrado*, p. 296.
102. Bedoya, *Cien años de cine en el Perú*, p. 269.
103. Peralta Ruiz, p. 112.
104. Gorriti, *The Shining Path*, pp. 244–245.
105. Professor Montes is loosely based on Pastor Anaya, the priest accused by the Peruvian state of being a Sendero sympathiser and who was adopted by Amnesty International as a prisoner of conscience. See Gorriti, *The Shining Path*, p. 248.
106. Gorriti, *The Shining Path*, p. 248.
107. Bustamente, 'Diccionario temático del cine peruano: violencia', p. 70.
108. Bedoya, *Un cine reencontrado*, p. 298.
109. Bedoya, *Cien años de cine en el Perú*, p. 269.
110. Bustamente, p. 70.
111. Mulvey, 'Visual pleasure and narrative cinema', pp. 833–844.
112. Hayward, p. 99.
113. Crabtree, *Peru under García*, p. 184.
114. de Cárdenas, '*Alias la gringa*', p. 4.
115. This process is known as whitening, or *blanqueamiento* – a psychological and cultural changing of one's self along with a rejection of ethnic origin associated with a darker skin colour that has connotations of barbarism and backwardness.
116. Hjort, p. 115.
117. During an interview with Isaac León Frías, Durant further protested that 'the long crisis endured by the country is endangering the continuity of cinematic production in Peru which has given the world names such as Francisco Lombardi'. León Frías, '*Alias la gringa*', *El Peruano*, 7 December 1991, p. 15.
118. Note that Durant started out as a documentary filmmaker, and shifted from making political documentaries to feature films with a political backdrop, with human relationships as the central focus.

3 Cinema, Oppression and Ideology, 1992–2000

1. Eyde was born in Norway and retains close links with her country of birth, although she was brought up in Peru and took Peruvian citizenship at an early age. She was best known before this film as a documentary filmmaker who worked mainly with indigenous subjects. Her medium-length feature *Los ronderos*, released in 1987, was also set in an Andean community and revealed her sympathy for their marginalised social status.

2. Peralta Ruiz, p. 61.
3. Hanley, 'La vida es una sola', p. 595.
4. This drive to promote national amnesia was hampered in the short term by the discovery, in early 1993, of the bodies of a professor and eight students from La Cantuta University, apparently killed by the military command that had abducted them a year earlier. However, headlines that appeared in the most influential national daily newspaper, *El Comercio*, continued to offer support and high praise for the success in capturing Guzmán. See Peralta Ruiz, pp. 230–237.
5. Hayward, p. 90.
6. Starn, 'Villager at arms', p. 225.
7. As an addendum to his review of this film, Fernando Vivas was moved to publish the following statement: 'in defence not of Marianne Eyde's film but of the wellbeing of Peruvian cinema, I must express my discomfort at reading the declarations of colleagues who accuse the film of being an apology for terrorism and demand that cinemas that screen it be burned down'. Vivas, '*La vida es una sola*: un filme de una presencia contundente', *El Suplemento*, 31 October 1993, p. 16.
8. de Cárdenas cited by Bedoya, *Un cine reencontrado*, p. 307.
9. Del Pino H., 'Family, culture and "revolution"', p. 163.
10. Stern, *Shining and Other Paths*, pp. 14–15.
11. Cordero, p. 353.
12. See Mariátegui, *Seven Interpretative Essays on Peruvian Reality*.
13. Del Pino, p. 163.
14. Del Pino reveals that Shining Path in fact had a 'hidden script that [eventually] surfaced to reveal repugnance, intolerance, and racism'. Del Pino, p. 163.
15. Connell, p. 83.
16. Whittaker, *The Terrorism Reader*, p. 159.
17. Cordero, p. 349.
18. Cordero, p. 351.
19. Cordero, p. 349.
20. Vivas, p. 16.
21. This notion of self-sacrifice was labelled 'the quota', which is described by Gustavo Gorriti as 'the willingness, indeed the expectation, of offering one's life when the party asked for it'. Gorriti, 'The quota', p. 324.
22. Hayward, p. 90.
23. Cordero, pp. 349–350. Rosa María Olórtegui reported in an interview with Fernando Vivas that she based her character on university peers whom she suspected were Sendero members because of their behaviour and opinions. See Vivas, p. 16.
24. Vivas, p. 16.

25. Manrique, 'The war for the central sierra', p. 193. Indeed, the scale and consequences of such a strategy were not publicly acknowledged until the revelations of the report of the Truth and Reconciliation Committee in 2003, and even then were greeted with further denial by some former members of the military.
26. Wood, *De sabor nacional*, p. 21.
27. Cordero, p. 354.
28. Ponciano del Pino notes that many communities organised civil defence patrols, but also that these did not really start to take effect until the second half of the 1980s. Del Pino, p. 163. Hence, at the time when this film's narrative events take place (1983), the notion of organised self-defence against a terrorist enemy was relatively unknown in Peru's rural communities. Eyde thus appears to conflate aspects of history so as to emphasise even more strongly the vulnerability of the abandoned community of Rayopampa and others like it.
29. Vivas cited by Bedoya, *Un cine reencontrado*, p. 307.
30. Bedoya, *Un cine reencontrado* p. 308.
31. Cordero, p. 350.
32. Vivas, p. 16.
33. Flores Galindo, p. 189.
34. Eyde cited in 'Entrevista con Marianne Eyde', *La República*, 9 November 1992, p. 11.
35. These included Armando Robles Godoy, José Carlos Huayhuaca, Juan Carlos Torrico, Federico García, Fernando Espinoza and María Ruiz.
36. Stock, p. 157.
37. Stock's article draws on the work of Néstor García Canclini, who, writing at the same time as this film was being made, raised questions about the relevance of national identities in a time of globalisation and interculturalism and the complications that arise when artists cross borders. See Canclini, '¿Habrá cine latinoamericano en el año 2000?'.
38. Bedoya, *Cine*, 8 November 1993, p. 11; and León Frías, *Caretas*, 28 October 1993, p. 15.
39. Vivas, p. 16.
40. Vivas, p. 16.
41. Muñoz, p. 463.
42. Crabtree and Thomas, *Fujimori's Peru*, p. 18.
43. Bedoya notes that this combination of popular characters was often a winning combination: *Gregorio* (1984), which tells the story of one indigenous boy's adventures and difficulties when he is forced to leave his community for Lima, was seen by a million spectators in Peru. *Juliana* (1989), about a

young girl who dresses as a boy so as to join a group who earn a living in the capital by singing and pick-pocketing on the buses, was the fourth most successful film in 1989, with 630,000 spectators. See Bedoya, *Un cine reencontrado*, p. 317.

44. In addition to Kaspar, the Grupo Chaski in the 1990s consisted of Fernando Espinoza, Alejandro Legaspi, Rene Weber, Oswaldo Carpio, Susana Pastor and María Barea. They made various shorts (fiction and documentary) and a medium-length documentary, *Miss Universo en el Perú* (1982). They also concentrated on distributing independent films around Peru. Their work continues to draw on Italian neorealist principles in terms of style and philosophy, using non-professional actors from the *barrios* and a range of familiar locations to demonstrate compassion for the plight of their marginalised characters and aiming to provoke the social conscience of spectators.
45. McClennen, 'The theory and practice of the Peruvian Grupo Chaski'.
46. Before this film, Tamayo had directed numerous shorts, one part of the episodic feature *Cuentos inmorales* (1979) and a feature of his own, *La fuga del chacal* (1987), that was described by critic de Cárdenas as an 'attempt to translate to a national level the all-Amnerican genre of the action move'. Federico de Cárdenas, 'Demasiados desencuentros: *Anda, corre, vuela ...*', p. 93.
47. Beasley-Murray, 'Disneyfication', https://posthegemony.wordpress.com/2007/11/16.
48. Crabtree, *Peru under García*, p. 185.
49. Durkheim, *The Division of Labour in Society*, pp. 70–110.
50. Kaspar in Bedoya, *Un cine reencontrado*, p. 317.
51. de Soto cited by Skidmore and Smith, p. 215.
52. Skidmore and Smith report that 'as of the mid-1980s, it was estimated that 48% of Peru's economically active population and 61.2% of the total work hours were devoted to informal activities which contributed nearly 40% of the gross domestic product recorded in national accounts'. p. 215.
53. Cotler and Grompone describe how the divisions within Peruvian society have restricted the chances of universal application of a single legal framework, suggesting that many citizens 'feel that they exist in a legal vacuum'. p. 89.
54. Peralta Ruiz, p. 207.
55. This was, as mentioned briefly in the introduction to this analysis, the year of Fujimori's infamous *autogolpe*, when, irritated by parliamentary opposition to the extreme nature of his economic and anti-terrorist plans, he aligned himself with the military, 'suspended the constitution and shut down congress, the judiciary, and regional governments'. Hunefeldt, p. 258.
56. Skidmore and Smith, p. 217.

57. Flores Galindo, p. 189.
58. Vich, *El caníbal es el otro*, p. 36.
59. Vich, p. 41.
60. See, for example, Rowe's discussion of the work of José María Arguedas in various sections of Rowe and Schelling, *Memory and Modernity: Popular Culture in Latin America*. In this he applauds Arguedas for shedding light on the creative potential of Andean culture to direct 'the transformative power of twentieth century technology towards the making of a new civilization, a task in which the various national governments have spectacularly failed'. p. 60. In a later discussion of the importance of magic to Andean culture, he further suggests that 'to legitimate magic can be a vindication of pre-capitalist culture, against the logic of capitalist accumulation and positivist social engineering'. Rowe and Schelling, p. 214. Such an understanding helps to explain the persistence of 'antagonism of colonial and republican society in Peru'. p. 215.
61. Rowe and Schelling, p. 213, explaining Arguedas's vision.
62. Hjort, p. 108.
63. Bedoya, *Cien años de cine en el Perú*, p. 278.
64. Bedoya, *Cien años de cine en el Perú*, p. 279.
65. Ribeyro, *Ribeyro*.
66. Starn et al., p. 466.
67. Bedoya, *Cien años de cine en el Perú*, p. 278.
68. A website devoted to Peruvian rock describes the music of Los Mojarras as '"hard chicha" with authentic Peruvian sounds'. It further informs us that their original compositions 'are akin to ethnographic recordings of the Peruvian metropolis'. www.chicama.com/mojarras.htm. Theirs was also the first CD soundtrack to be released with a national film.
69. Bedoya, *Un cine reencontrado*, p. 257.
70. Frith, 'Music and identity', pp. 109–110.
71. Frith, p. 125.
72. Zweiten Deutschen Fernsehen, the major German TV network, is credited in the opening titles as the main co-production partner, while several German church and human rights organisations are acknowledged as supporters in the closing credit sequence.
73. Bedoya, *Un cine reencontrado*, p. 317.
74. Bedoya, *Un cine reencontrado*, p. 317.
75. For example, both León Frías and García de Pinilla argued that the style of social protest characteristic of the Chaski Group projects of the 1980s, that drew on Italian neorealism and Peru's own Cusco School of the 1950s, is not apparent in this film which, for them, is little more than an unconvincing love

story set amidst violence and persecution. León Frías, 1995, p. 3; García de Pinilla, 1995, p. 16.
76. For example, it was screened at festivals in Biarritz, Uruguay, Huelva, Havana, Berlin (children's section) and Montreal, where it won the best film award.
77. Wiener, 'Miedos de guerra', p. 20.
78. Bedoya, *Un cine reencontrado*, p. 318.
79. Wood, *De sabor nacional*, p. 33.
80. The other was Lombardi's *No se lo digas a nadie*, adapted from Jaime Bayly's novel about sexual identity.
81. García de Pinilla, '*Coraje*'.
82. Funders and supporters additional to CONACINE included: the European Script Fund; Guggenheim Memorial Foundation; Instituto de Cooperación Iberoamericana; TVE; Hubert Bals Fund; Frecuencia Latina; ICAIC; Centro Cultural de la Pontificia Universidad Católica del Perú; Morgane Productions; and a number of private individuals.
83. These debates about the transnational have been developed by Shaw, Dennison, Falicov, Middents and Barrow in 'Latin American Cinemas Today: Reframing the National', *Transnational Cinemas* (special issue), 2013.
84. In fact, it was the first to be released. The winner of the first prize, *Guaman Poma*, submitted by Del Pino, was not completed, and third place went to the proposal for *Ciudad de M*, an adaptation based on the novel *Al final de la calle*, by Oscar Malca, submitted by Felipe Degregori and released in 2000.
85. Wiener, 'Una Moyano demasiado lejos: *Coraje*', p. 105.
86. Marcelo Robles, '*Coraje*', 1998.
87. Bedoya and León Frías, 'Entrevista con Armando Robles Godoy', p. 94. It should be recalled that Robles Godoy was directly involved in the establishment of the first cinema law, in 1972, and was, at first, supportive of the new legislation introduced during Fujimori's first term. He was pleased at the creation of CONACINE, which he was optimistic would campaign on behalf of national filmmakers. By 1998, however, he and many like him were already deeply disillusioned by the decisions made by that institution and by the lack of funds made available to it.
88. León Frías, '*Coraje*', p. 11.
89. Hunefeldt, p. 242.
90. Burt, 'Shining Path and the "decisive battle" in Lima's *barriadas*: The case of Villa El Salvador', p. 279.
91. Wiener, 'Una Moyano demasiado lejos', p. 106. He compares it, for example, to the Argentinian film *Yo, la peor de todas* by María Luisa Bemberg (1990), which drew on the story of its protagonist to draw broader conclusions about the contemporary situation for women in Argentina.

92. Chakravarty, 'Fragmenting the nation', p. 226.
93. Wiener, 'Una Moyano demasiado lejos', p. 106.
94. León Frías, 'Coraje', p. 7.
95. Starn et al., p. 371.
96. Starn et al., pp. 371–376; Burt, pp. 267–306.
97. Moyano, '"There Have Been Threats"', p. 374.
98. Chakravarty, p. 228.
99. Burt, p. 289.
100. Skidmore and Smith, p. 216.
101. These include the extensive interview conducted by Mariella Balbi that was published three months before Moyano's death, 'Entrevista con Moyano', p. 17.
102. Burt, pp. 291–292.
103. Burt, pp. 292.
104. It is interesting to note that, as Peralta Ruiz argues, the assassination of Moyano represented a turning point in the way *El País* reported the violence of Shining Path. Moyano's murder represented an 'irreconcilable rupture between the Shining Path project and the popular project'. Cited by Peralta Ruiz, p. 187.
105. Villa El Salvador was of strategic importance to Shining Path due to its location bordering the Pan-American highway and close to other *barriadas* in the foothills of the Andes. Capture and control of this 'iron ring' around Lima provided Shining Path with the possibility of strangling the capital.
106. Wiener, p. 105; Perla Anaya, *Los tres primeros años*, p. 54.
107. Robles, *El Comercio*, p. 16. Note that Frecuencia Latina was set up in 1983 as the popular alternative to traditional channels, with a particular interest in broadcasting high-quality programmes from overseas. The channel uses a product placement tactic to promote itself within the film's diegesis; for example, when Moyano speaks out against Shining Path to the media, she is shown to do so via this channel.
108. Wiener, p. 105.
109. *Coraje* was screened at several international festivals before it was released in Peru, including events in Colombia, Cuba, Chile, Biarritz, Berlin and Spain, and at Sundance (US). It won an award for humanitarian content at Viña del Mar (Chile), and best actress and audience awards at Huelva (Spain).
110. Del Solar has become a notable figure in Peruvian cinema of this period. He was appointed Minister of Culture in the new Peruvian government in December 2016. Prior to that he directed/starred in two other films mention in the final chapter of this study, *Magallanes* and *El elefante desaparecido*.
111. Milagros Leira, 'Entrevista con Robles Godoy', p. 17.
112. Wiener, p. 107.
113. Servat, 'Coraje', p. 15.

4 Cinema, Memory and Truth, 2000–2004

1. Lury, *The Child in Film*, pp. 106–107.
2. Some aspects of the analyses of the following two films appeared in a journal article: 'Out of the Shadows: "New" Peruvian Cinema, National Identity and Political Violence', Modern Languages Open, Liverpool University Press, Dec 2014, 1–17.
3. From the release of *Coraje* in 1998 to the appearance of *Paloma de papel* in 2003, CONACINE was weakened by a lack of resources needed to fulfil its obligations. The few films that were made during this period had to rely more heavily on external sources of funding and support, and most chose – or were encouraged – to develop less political themes. Meanwhile, overseas investors became less and less interested in supporting risky film projects that had no domestic backing. Hardly any of them performed well enough at the box office (domestic and/or international) to recoup their costs, and only a handful enjoyed critical acclaim and festival screenings and awards. The main exception to this was Lombardi's *Pantaleón y las visitadoras* (1999), adapted from the Vargas Llosa novel of the same title, with the aid of Spanish co-production funds.
4. During his second term, Fujimori's economic policy started to falter and his popularity declined. The President's response was 'to tighten his control of the country, acting in tandem with the military to consolidate power.... [He] also moved to silence his political opposition and exerted an increased control on mass media', making use of the Grupo Colina, a death squad attached to the Intelligence Services, in the most urgent and severe cases of repression. Hunfeldt, p. 262.
5. The most notable of these films were: Marianne Eyde's *La carnada* (1999), which tells a story based on the life of women in a traditional fishing community; Lombardi's *Tinta roja* (2001), about a rookie journalist's initiation into the world of crime-reporting in Lima; Felipe Degregori's *Ciudad de M* (2000), about life in Lima for disaffected young people; Aldo Salvini's *Bala perdida* (2001), which recounts the adventures of a group of middle-class youths from Lima who travel to the ancient city of Cuzco and discover a violent underworld; and Velarde's *El destino no tiene favoritos* (2003), a parody of class and popular culture. All but the last title have violent conflict at their core, but none makes direct or indirect reference to the Sendero struggle. Instead they depict different aspects of Peru's fragmented society and, in most cases, give an impression of a nation coming to terms with change with some difficulty.
6. Bedoya, 'Un aprendizaje perverso: *Paloma de papel*', p. 4.

7. USAID is an independent federal government agency that receives overall foreign policy guidance from the Secretary of State. It gave a grant to support the filming of *Paloma* as part of its programme of conflict management and transition initiatives in 2000. See the website 'OTI highlights: Truth Commission', *USAID/OTI Peru Field Report*, June 2002, www.usaid.gov/our_work/crosscutting_¬programs/ transition_initiatives/country/peru/rpt0602.html.
8. de Cárdenas, '*Paloma de papel*', p. 30.
9. 'No es tan fragil la paloma', *Diario del Festival*, p. 7.
10. Skidmore and Smith summarise the collapse of Fujimori's regime as follows: 'In mid-September 2000 a tape was released to the public showing Vladimiro Montesinos, Fujimori's top advisor and intelligence official, bribing an opposition congressman to join the Fujimori coalition. The public outcry was deafening. Montesinos and Fujimori were hopelessly exposed.', p. 219. This was the first of many revelations that led to Fujimori's eventual resignation by the end of that year.
11. The final report of the 12-member CVR, published in September 2003, gave details of investigations into acts of political violence that took place in Peru between 1980 and 2000. It concluded that nearly 70,000 people had been killed, half by Shining Path insurgents and half by security forces and government-backed peasant militias. Most were poor and suffered social exclusion; more than 40% were from the region of Ayacucho; 79% lived in the most remote areas of the Andean highlands; and 75% spoke Quechua or another indigenous language.
12. Pilar Coll, *Informe final CVR*, p. 14.
13. Bedoya, 'Un aprendizaje perverso', p. 4.
14. Bedoya, p. 4.
15. These civil defence patrols, sanctioned by the central government in Lima, began to be established properly throughout the emergency zones from 1983. In many instances, the villagers had no choice but to arm themselves: reluctance to form a patrol was interpreted by the military as implicit support for Shining Path. 'Neutrality was permitted neither by the military nor by Sendero'. Fumerton and Remijense, 'Civil defence forces', p. 54.
16. Note also that the state of emergency in the region of Ayacucho ended officially only in 2000. The same year, interim President Valentín Paniagua announced new elections for 2001 and sanctioned the establishment of the CVR, which gathered thousands of testimonials from Peruvians nationwide.
17. Such sentimentality may result from the director's identity as *limeño* and hence a certain romanticism of life in the Andes that chooses to ignore the harsh realities of everyday life in the highlands. He also omits any recognition of the restrictive, oppressive nature of strong traditional values that

bind those communities, and that privilege collective will over individual freedom.
18. Aguilar spoke about this during a conversation with this author in Lima, August 2004, and also in press interviews at the time of his film's release.
19. Monticelli, 'Italian post-war cinema and neorealism', p. 458.
20. de Cárdenas, '*Paloma de papel*', p. 42.
21. de Cárdenas, '*Paloma de papel*', 42.
22. Note that the camera fixes on the traumatised faces of the children at the sight of their gruesome discovery, rather than on the dead man, emphasising the significance of this moment as marking a sudden break with childhood innocence.
23. Portocarrero, 'Nuevos modelos de identidad en la sociedad peruana', p. 22.
24. Manrique, *El tiempo del miedo*, p. 22.
25. Degregori, *El surgimiento de Sendero Luminoso*, p. 193.
26. Manrique, *Razones de sangre*, p. 19.
27. Vich, pp. 27–28.
28. Madedo and Fanelli, 'Por un cine humanista'.
29. Manrique, *Razones de sangre*, p. 29.
30. Rojas, 'Urpillay: *Paloma de papel*', p. 9.
31. de Cárdenas, '*Paloma de papel*', 2003, p. 31.
32. For example, Fujimori's attempts, in 2000, to win election for an unprecedented third term led to protest on the streets of Lima, resulting in the deaths of six people. Some protestors were led by the man who later became President, Alejandro Toledo, while others were part of an uprising organised by the relatively new Movimiento Etnocacerista, a left-leaning nationalist group whose leaders included retired military officer Ollanta Humala. Humala, who had fought against Shining Path and in the brief conflict against Ecuador in 1995, came second to Alan García in the 2006 presidential elections.
33. In August 2004, Aguilar was presented with a special commendation from the Peruvian section of Amnesty International for bringing violations against human rights in Peru to the attention of cinema audiences worldwide, and for reopening the debate about war crimes internally.
34. Shohat and Stam, p. 347.
35. Shohat and Stam, p. 351.
36. The final citation is from the work of Fromm, the German-born social philosopher and psychoanalyst and member of the Frankfurt School of critical theory who was a key proponent of the idea that most human behaviour is a learned response to social conditions.
37. Bauman, p. 77.

38. Cachay, 'Un francotirador en Lima', p. c8.
39. The film won the critics award, as well as the best actor award, at the Lima Festival of Latin American Film, August 2004.
40. By 2004, cinemas in Peru were run mainly by multinational companies and screened Hollywood blockbusters almost exclusively. It was difficult even for a successful European film to gain an exhibition slot, and almost impossible for a Peruvian feature to do so given the poor performance of earlier national releases.
41. Cynthia Tompkins writes about the formal qualities of this film in a chapter entitled 'The past engulfs the present', in her *Experimental Latin American Cinema*. Tompkins, pp. 146–156, arguing that they offer something very distinctive in stylistic terms.
42. On 26 October 1998, the Presidents of Peru (Fujimori) and Ecuador (Jamil Mahuad) signed a peace agreement to formalise acceptance of a clearly defined border between their two countries after three wars and the death of hundreds of soldiers and civilians. In addition to clear historical, strategic and economic reasons for the long-running land dispute, fears regarding loss of national self-esteem and – for those who lived along the disputed border – loss of national identity, were clearly at the heart of the conflict. According to one press release issued at the time of the signing of the peace treaty, many young men died as a result of the long-running dispute.
43. On reaching 18 years of age, Peruvian men were, until 2002, required to carry out a two-year period of military service, after which they were considered to be available for military action for a further 10 years. Many were in fact economic conscripts, forced into the army as a way out of poverty. As Santiago tells Andrea at one point in the film, his options were severely limited and a career in the marines offered a way out of poverty and a move away from a likely life of delinquency.
44. Obando reports that the conflict with Ecuador exposed a critical weakness in the Peruvian armed forces and intelligence services, since humiliating military losses were suffered despite a much smaller Ecuadorian opposition force. See Crabtree and Thomas, p. 204.
45. In a report of Freiburg Film Festival in southern Germany in 2004, at which *Santiago* won four out of five of the awards, the various juries recognised the 'universal' appeal of the film, praising it for drawing attention to an important issue of social concern for Peru and elsewhere in the world. They also praised its emphasis on the story of a few days in the life of one young man.
46. 'Interview with Josué Méndez', 51st Sydney Film Festival, June–July 2004, www.sydneyfilmfestival.org.

47. As Gonzalo Portocarrero observed in his study of everyday behaviour of urban-dwelling Peruvians, the problem of contemplating a homogeneous society was that many citizens felt excluded by the legislation that framed and guided it and tended therefore to ignore the rules that are supposed to determine the legal framework of everyday life. Portocarrero, 'Nuevos modelos de identidad en la sociedad peruana', pp. 82–83. Note, for example, that out of 26 million inhabitants in Lima in the late 1990s, only 140,000 paid taxes and thus contributed formally to the economy of the state. This has since been tightened in recent years, but the shift to a perception of inclusion via social contribution remains slow.
48. Bula, 'Poderoso testimonio social', p. 1.
49. Silverman, p. 53.
50. Silverman, pp. 56–57.
51. Silverman, p. 53.
52. Saona, 'Cuando la guerra sigue por dentro', p. 168.
53. Portocarrero, *Razones de sangre*, p. 282.
54. Flores Galindo, p. 189.
55. D'Argenio, p. 86.
56. Azalbert, 'Equateur', p. 49.
57. Silverman, p. 58.
58. Azalbert, p. 49.
59. Silverman, p. 52.
60. Silverman, p. 65.
61. Orr, *Cinema and Modernity*, p. 132.
62. Orr, p. 130.
63. Manrique, 'The war for the central sierra', p. 198.
64. Gonzalo Portocarrero, in his 2001 study of shifting identities in contemporary Peruvian society, discusses the relationship between market economics and the rise of individualism. He further argues that neoliberalism has been a controversial achievement for Peru, that politics has been almost totally discredited by the chaos and corruption of most of the presidential regimes since the transition to democracy, and that since the free market model is regarded as the only civilised option, alternatives are rarely discussed.
65. Portocarrero, 'Nuevos modelos de identidad en la sociedad peruana', p. 12.
66. MacDougall, *Transcultural Cinema*, p. 238.
67. Silverman, p. 60.
68. Silverman, p. 63.
69. Portocarrero, p. 22. It was during the 1970s that Shining Path leader Abimael Guzmán developed his deadly strategy, taking advantage of the social rifts and racial prejudices that were not adequately addressed by the military regimes of

Velasco (1968–1975) and Morales Bermúdez (1975–1980), both of whom had come to power via a coup d'état.
70. Portocarrero, p. 83.

5 New Generations and Open Wounds, 2005–2016

1. da Gama, 'Filming the war with Sendero'.
2. The period of 1980 to 2000 was known to many Peruvians as *manchay tiempo*, meaning 'time of fear' in a hybrid of Quechua and Spanish. Communities in the Andes refer to it as *Sasachakuy tiempo* ('difficult time').
3. Marsh, 'Memory, youth, and regimes of violence', p. 304.
4. Shaw, pp. 1–12.
5. Here I refer in part to Anne Lambright's analysis of *La Teta Asustada*, but refute the suggestion she makes that the Andean immigrant in Lima had not yet been touched by Peruvian cinema. Llosa moves this on, but the topic had already been addressed by such films as those by the Grupo Chaski (*Gregorio, Juliana* and *Anda, Corre, Vuela*. of the 1980s and 1990s) and other such as *El Rincón de los Inocentes* (2005), *Vidas Paralelas* (2008) and *Ilary* (2009). Lambright, *Andean Truths*, p. 73.
6. Bedoya, *El Cine Peruano en Tiempos Digitales*, p. 77.
7. Thomas, '"Yo no soy invisible"', p. 54.
8. See Barrow, 'Through female eyes', pp. 48–69, for a fuller discussion of this film.
9. *NN* (*Non Nomine*) was typical of this new generation of films in terms of its mosaic of international funding, in this case from the Hubert Bals Development Fund, the Cinémas du Monde Fund, the World Cinema Fund and the Ibermedia Fund. It won the Best Unproduced Script at the 2011 Havana Film Festival and was Peru's entry to the Academy Awards.
10. Vich, 'De desadaptaciones y reiteradas violencias', p. 3.
11. 'Cinema and society in contemporary Peru', PUCP, Lima, 1 December 2016.
12. Wilson, *Personal Histories*, p. 20.
13. Hayward, p. 101.
14. For further details of this phenomenon, see Bowen and Holligan, *The Imperfect Spy*.
15. Hayward, p. 90.
16. Hayward, p. 90.
17. Smith cited by Hayward, p. 90.
18. Hayward, p. 101.
19. Middents noted in 2009 that most of Peruvian filmmaking until 1996 (the year when so-called 'regional cinema' emerged) was limited to Lima and Cuzco

Notes to Pages 187–188

and their surrounding areas, the former standing for the 'urban' and the latter, problematically for Peru's second largest city, as the 'rural'.
20. See Emilio Bustamente and Jaime Luna Victoria's two volumes (2017) on this important area of filmmaking in Peru.
21. Bedoya and León Frías, 'Entrevista con Armando Robles Godoy', p. 104.

Bibliography

Books

Aliaga, Jorge, *Terrorism in Peru* (Edinburgh: Jananti, 1995)
Anderson, Benedict, *Imagined Communities* (London: Verso, 1983)
Arguedas, José María, *Formación de una cultura nacional indoamericana* (Mexico City: Siglo XXI, 1975)
Arguedas, José María, *Los ríos profundos* (Buenos Aires: Losada, 2004)
Ashby, Justine and Andrew Higson, eds, *British Cinema Past and Present* (London: Routledge, 2000)
Azalbert, Nicholas, 'Equateur: latitude "zéro"', *Cahiers du Cinéma*, 598 (2005), 48–49
Barnard, Timothy and Peter Rist, eds, *South American Cinema: A Critical Filmography, 1915–1994* (Austin: University of Texas Press, 1996)
Barrow, Sarah and Tamara L. Falicov, 'Latin American cinemas today: Reframing the national', *Transnational Cinemas* (special issue), 4:2 (2013)
Barrow, Sarah, 'Out of the Shadows: "New" Peruvian Cinema, National Identity and Political Violence', Modern Languages Open, Liverpool University Press, Dec 2014, 1–17.
Barrow, Sarah, 'Through female eyes: Reframing Peru on screen', in *Latin American Women Filmmakers: Production, Politics, Poetics*, ed. by Deborah Martin and Deborah Shaw (London: I.B. Tauris, 2017)
Bauman, Zygmunt, *Identity* (Cambridge: Polity, 2004)
Bayly, Jaime, *No se lo digas a nadie* (Barcelona: Seix-Barral, 1994)
Beasley-Murray, Jon, 'Disneyfication', https://posthegemony.wordpress.com/2007/11/16/
Bedoya, Ricardo, *Cien años de cine en el Perú: una historia crítica* (Lima: Universidad de Lima, Fondo de Desarrollo Editorial, 1995)
Bedoya, Ricardo, *El cine peruano en tiempos digitales* (Lima: Universidad de Lima/Fondo de Desarrollo Editorial, 2015)
Bedoya, Ricardo, *Entre fauces y colmillos: las películas de Francisco Lombardi* (Huesca: Festival de Cine de Huesca, 1997)
Bedoya, Ricardo, *Imágenes del cine en el Perú* (Lima: Banco Central de Reserva del Perú, CONACINE, 1999)

Bibliography

Bedoya, Ricardo, 'La boca del lobo/The Lion's Den', in *The Cinema of Latin America*, ed. by Alberto Elena and Marina Díaz López (London: Wallflower Press, 2003), pp. 185–192

Bedoya, Ricardo, 'Las tumbas removidas', *La Gran Ilusión*, 6 (1996), 110–113

Bedoya, Ricardo, 'Peru: films for after a war', in *The Film Edge: Contemporary Filmmaking in Latin America*, ed. by Eduardo Angel Russo (Buenos Aires: Teseo, 2010), pp. 145–158.

Bedoya, Ricardo, *Un cine reencontrado: diccionario ilustrado de las películas peruanas* (Lima: Universidad de Lima/Fondo de Desarrollo Editorial, 1997)

Bedoya, Ricardo and Isaac León Frías, 'Entrevista con Armando Robles Godoy', *La Gran Ilusión*, 6 (1996), 94–106

Bedoya, Ricardo and Isaac León Frías, 'Volver a vivir: cronología (accidentada) de la ley de cine', *La Gran Ilusión*, 3 (1994), 108–110.

Berger, James, *After the End: Representation of Post-Apocalypse* (Minneapolis: University of Minnesota, 1999)

Bhabha, Homi, *The Location of Culture* (London: Routledge, 1990)

Billig, Michael, *Banal Nationalism* (London: Sage, 1995)

Bowen, Sally and Jane Holligan, *The Imperfect Spy: The Many Lives of Vladimiro Montesinos* (Lima: Peisa, 2003)

Braudy, Leo and Marshall Cohen, eds, *Film Theory and Criticism: Introductory Readings*, 5th edn (Oxford: Oxford University Press, 1999)

Burt, Jo-Marie, 'Shining Path and the "decisive battle" in Lima's *barriadas*: The case of Villa El Salvador', in *Shining and Other Paths: War and Society in Peru, 1980–1995*, ed. by Steve J. Stern (London: Duke University Press, 1998), pp. 267–306

Bustamente, Emilio and Jaime Luna Victoria, 'El cine regional en el Perú', *Contratexto*, 22 (2014), 189–212

Bustamente, Emilio and Jaime Luna Victoria, *Las miradas múltiples. El cine regional peruano. Tomos I y II* (Lima: Universidad de Lima/ Fondo de Desarrollo Editorial, 2007).

Bustamente, Emilio, 'Diccionario temático del cine peruano: violencia', *La Gran Ilusión*, 6 (1996), 70

Canclini, Nestor García, '¿Habrá cine latinoamericano en el año 2000? La cultura visual en la época del postnacionalismo', *Jornada Semanal*, 193 (1993), 27–33

Canclini, Nestor García, 'Remaking passports: Visual thought in the debate on multiculturalism', in *Visual Culture Reader*, ed. by Nicholas Mirzoeff (London: Routledge, 1998), pp. 372–381

Canclini, Nestor García, *Hybrid Cultures: Strategies for Entering and Leaving Modernity*, trans. by C.L. Chiappari and S.L. Lupez (Minneapolis: University of Minnesota Press, 1995)

Carbone, Giancarlo, *El cine en el Perú, 1897–1950: testimonios* (Lima: Universidad de Lima, 1991)

Bibliography

Carbone, Giancarlo, *El cine en el Perú, 1950-1972: testimonios* (Lima: Universidad de Lima, 1991)

Chakravarty, Sumita S., 'Fragmenting the nation: Images of terrorism in Indian popular cinema', in *Cinema and Nation*, ed. by Mette Hjort and Scott Mackenzie (London: Routledge, 2000), pp. 222-238

Chanady, Amaryll, 'Identity, politics and *mestizaje*', in *Contemporary Latin American Cultural Studies*, ed. by Stephen Hart and Richard Young (London: Arnold, 2003), pp. 192-202

Chanan, Michael, 'The economic condition of cinema in Latin America', in *New Latin American Cinema, Volume I: Theory, Practices and Transcontinental Articulations*, ed. by Michael T. Martin (Detroit: Wayne State University Press, 1997), pp. 185-200

Church Gibson, Pamela and John Hill, eds, *Oxford Guide to Film Studies* (Oxford: Oxford University Press, 1998)

Coll, Pilar, *Informe final CVR: ejes temáticos de las conclusiones* (Lima: Instituto Bartolomé de las Casas, 2003)

Connell, R. W., *Masculinities* (Cambridge: Polity, 2005)

Cordero, Isabel Coral, 'Women in war: Impact and responses', in *Shining and Other Paths: War and Society in Peru, 1980-1995*, ed. by Steve J. Stern (Durham: Duke University Press, 1998), pp. 345-374

Cotler, Julio and Romeo Grompone, *El fujimorismo: ascenso y caída de un régimen autoritario* (Lima: Instituto de Estudios Peruanos, 2000)

Crabtree, John, 'Neo-populism and the Fujimori phenomenon', in *Fujimori's Peru: The Political Economy*, ed. by John Crabtree and Jim Thomas (London: Institute of Latin American Studies, 1998), pp. 7-23

Crabtree, John, *Peru under García: An Opportunity Lost* (London/Oxford: Macmillan/St Anthony's College, 1992)

Crabtree, John and Jim Thomas, eds, *Fujimori's Peru: The Political Economy* (London: University of London, Institute of Latin American Studies, 1998)

Crofts, Stephen, 'Reconceptualising national cinema/s', in *Theorising National Cinema*, ed. by Valentina Vitali and Paul Willemen (London: British Film Institute, 2006), pp. 44-60

da Gama, Francisca, 'Filming the war with Sendero', *Jump Cut: A Review of Contemporary Media*, 49 (2007), www.ejumpcut.org

D'Allemand, Patricia, 'Of silences and exclusions: Nation and culture in nineteenth-century Colombia', in *Contemporary Latin American Cultural Studies*, ed. by Stephen Hart and Richard Young (London: Arnold, 2003), pp. 215-227

D'Argenio, Maria Chiara, 'Monstrosity and war memories in Latin American post-conflict cinema', *Cinej: Cinema Journal*, 5:1 (2015), pp. 85-113

Bibliography

D'Argenio, Maria Chiara, 'A contemporary Andean type: The representation of the indigenous world in Claudia Llosa's films', *Latin American and Caribbean Ethnic Studies*, 8:1 (2013), pp. 20-42

Davies, Nigel, *The Ancient Kingdoms of Peru* (London: Penguin, 1997)

de Cárdenas, Federico, 'Demasiados desencuentros: *Anda, corre, vuela* ...', *La Gran Ilusión*, 5 (1995), 93-95

de Cárdenas, Federico, *El cine de Francisco Lombardi: una vision crítica del Perú* (Santiago de Chile: Uqbar Editores, 2014)

de Cárdenas, Federico, '*Paloma de papel*', *Tren de Sombras*, 1 (2004), 42

de Soto, Humberto, *The Other Path: The Invisible Revolution in the Third World* (New York: Harper and Row, 1989)

Degregori, Carlos Iván, *El surgimiento de Sendero Luminoso* (Lima: IEP, 1990)

Degregori, Carlos Iván, José Coronel and Ponciano del Pino H., 'Government, citizenship and democracy: A regional perspective', in *Fujimori's Peru: The Political Economy*, ed. by John Crabtree and Jim Thomas (London: ILAS, 1998), pp. 243-264

Del Pino H., Ponciano, 'Family, culture and "revolution": Everyday life with Sendero Luminoso', in *Shining and Other Paths: War and Society in Peru, 1980-1995*, ed. by Steve J. Stern (Durham: Duke University Press, 1998), pp. 158-192

Dostoyevsky, Fyodor, *Crime and Punishment*, trans. by David McDuff (London: Penguin, 1991)

Durkheim, Emile, *The Division of Labour in Society*, trans. by George Simpson (New York: Free Press, 1960)

Durkheim, Emile, *Suicide: A Study in Sociology*, trans. by John A. Spaulding and George Simpson (London: Routledge, 1952)

Elena, Alberto and Marina Díaz López, eds, *The Cinema of Latin America* (London: Wallflower, 2003)

Elmore, Peter, *Los muros invisibles: Lima y la modernidad en la novela del siglo XX* (Lima: Mosca Azul Editores, 1993)

Ezra, Elizabeth and Terry Rowden, eds, *Transnational Cinema: The Film Reader* (London: Routledge, 2006)

Falicov, Tamara L. 'Film Funding Opportunities for Latin American Filmmakers: A Case for Further North-South Collaboration in Training and Film Festival Initiatives', in *A Companion to Latin American Cinema*, ed. by Stephen Hart, Maria Delgado, Randal Johnson (New York: Blackwell-Wiley, 2017)

Faubion, James D., ed., *Power: Essential Works of Michel Foucault, 1954-1984* (London: Penguin, 2000)

Flindell Klarén, Peter, *Peru: Society and Nationhood in the Andes* (New York: Oxford University Press, 2000)

Flores Galindo, Alberto, *Los rostros de la plebe* (Barcelona: Crítica, 2001)

Bibliography

Freud, Sigmund, 'The uncanny', in *The Collected Psychoanalytical Works of Sigmund Freud, Vol. XXVII (1917-1919): An Infantile Neurosis and Other Works* (London: Hogarth Press, 1964), pp. 218-252

Freud, Sigmund, *Civilization, Society and Religion: Group Psychology, Civilization and its Discontents and Other Works* (London: Penguin, 1985)

Frith, Simon, 'Music and identity', in *Questions of Cultural Identity*, ed. by Stuart Hall and Paul Du Gay (London: Sage, 1996), pp. 108-127

Fumerton, Mario and Simone Remijense, 'Civil defence forces: Peru's Comités de Autodefensa Civil and Guatemala's Patrullas de Autodefensa Civil in comparative perspective', in *Armed Actors: Organised Violence and State Failure in Latin America*, ed. by Kees Kooning and Dirk Krujit (London: Zed Books, 2004), pp. 52-72

Galleno, Lucía, 'El ataque sexual y canibalismo de la bestia en *La boca del lobo*', in *Pachaticray (El mundo al revés): testimonios y ensayos sobre la violencia política y la cultura peruana desde 1980*, ed. by Mark R. Cox (Lima: San Marcos, 2004), pp. 139-147

Gellner, Ernest, *Nations and Nationalism* (Oxford: Blackwell, 1983)

Getino, Octavio and Fernando Solanas, 'Towards a third cinema', in *Movies and Methods: An Anthology*, ed. by Bill Nichols (Tucson: University of Arizona Press, 1976), pp. 44-64

Gorriti, Gustavo, 'The quota', in *The Peru Reader: History, Culture, Politics*, ed. by Orin Starn, Carlos Iván Degregori and Robin Kirk (Durham: Duke University Press, 1995), pp. 316-327

Gorriti, Gustavo, *The Shining Path: A History of Millenarian War in Peru*, trans. by Robin Kirk (Chapel Hill: University of North Carolina, 1999)

Hanley, David, '*La vida es una sola*', in *Historical Dictionary of South American Cinema*, ed. by Peter H. Rist (New York: Rowman and Littlefield, 2014), pp. 593-595

Hart, Stephen, ' "Slick grit": Auteurship versus mimicry in three films by Francisco Lombardi', *New Cinemas*, 3:3 (2006), 159-167

Hayward, Susan, 'Framing national cinemas', in *Cinema and Nation*, ed. by Mette Hjort and Scott Mackenzie (London: Routledge, 2000), pp. 88-102

Higson, Andrew, 'The limiting imagination of national cinema', in *Cinema and Nation*, ed. by Mette Hjort and Scott Mackenzie (London: Routledge, 2000), pp. 63-74

Higson, Andrew, *Waving the Flag: Constructing a National Cinema in Britain* (Oxford: Clarendon Press, 1995)

Hjort, Mette, 'Themes of nation,' in *Cinema and Nation*, ed. by Mette Hjort and Scott Mackenzie (London: Routledge, 2000), pp. 103-118

Hjort, Mette and Scott Mackenzie, eds, *Cinema and Nation* (London: Routledge, 2000)

Bibliography

Hodgin, Nick and Amt Thakkar, eds, *Scars and Wounds: Film and Legacies of Trauma* (Basingstoke: Palgrave Macmillan, 2017)

Hunefeldt, Christine, *A Brief History of Peru* (New York: Checkmark Books, 2004)

Jarvie, Ian, 'National cinema: A theoretical assessment', in *Cinema and Nation*, ed. by Mette Hjort and Scott Mackenzie (London: Routledge, 2000), pp. 75–87

Jelin, Elizabeth, *State Repression and the Struggle for Memory* (London: Latin America Bureau, 2003)

Johnson, Randal, 'Film policy in Latin America', in *Film Policy: International, National and Regional Perspectives*, ed. by Albert Moran (London: Routledge, 1996), pp. 128–147

King, John, 'Andean images: Bolivia, Ecuador and Peru', in *Magical Reels: A History of Cinema in Latin America* (London: Verso, 2000), pp. 189–206

King, John, ed., *The Cambridge Companion to Modern Latin American Culture* (London: Cambridge University Press, 2004)

Kooning, Kees and Dirk Krujit, eds, *Armed Actors: Organised Violence and State Failure in Latin America* (London: Zed Books, 2004)

Kristeva, Julia, *Powers of Horror: An Essay on Abjection* (New York: Columbia University Press, 1982)

Lambright, Anne *Andean Truths: Transitional Justice, Ethnicity, and Cultural Production in Post-Shining Path Peru* (Liverpool: Liverpool University Press, 2015)

Larrain, Jorge, *Identity and Modernity in Latin America* (Cambridge: Polity, 2000)

León Frías, Isaac, 'Peru', in *Variety International Film Guide 2003: The Ultimate Annual Review of World Cinema*, ed. by Peter Cowie (London: Faber and Faber, 2003), pp. 266–267

León Frías, Isaac, 'Peru', in *Variety International Film Guide 2004: The Ultimate Annual Review of World Cinema*, ed. by Peter Cowie (London: Faber and Faber, 2004), pp. 234–235

León Frías, Isaac, 'Peru', in *The Guardian International Film Guide 2005: The Ultimate Annual Review of World Cinema*, ed. by Daniel Rosenthal (London: Button Publishing, 2005), pp. 234–235

León Frías, Isaac, 'Peru', in *The Guardian International Film Guide 2006: The Definitive Annual Review of World Cinema*, ed. by Daniel Rosenthal (London: Button Publishing, 2006), pp. 223–224

León Frías, Isaac, 'Peru', in *International Film Guide 2008: The Definitive Annual Review of World Cinema*, ed. by Ian Haydn Smith (London: Wallflower Press, 2008), pp. 242–243

León Frías, Isaac, 'Peru', in *International Film Guide 2009: The Definitive Annual Review of World Cinema*, ed. by Ian Haydn Smith (London: Wallflower Press, 2009), pp. 250–251

Bibliography

León Frías, Isaac, 'Peru', in *International Film Guide 2010: The Definitive Annual Review of World Cinema*, ed. by Ian Haydn Smith (London: Wallflower Press, 2010), pp. 242-243

León Frías, Isaac, et al., 'Diccionario temático del cine peruano', *La Gran Ilusión*, 6 (1996), 68-82

León Frías, Isaac, 'Peru', in *Variety International Film Guide 2002: The Ultimate Annual Review of World Cinema*, ed. by Peter Cowie (London: Faber and Faber, 2002), pp. 236-237.

López, Ana M., 'Early cinema and modernity in Latin America', in *Theorising National Cinema*, ed. by Valentina Vitali and Paul Willemen (London: British Film Institute, 2006), pp. 209-225

Lury, Karen, *The Child in Film: Tears, Fears and Fairy Tales* (London: I. B. Tauris, 2010)

MacDougall, David, *Transcultural Cinema* (Princeton: Princeton University Press, 1998)

Manrique, Nelson, 'The war for the central sierra', in *Shining and Other Paths: War and Society in Peru, 1980-1995*, ed. by Steve J. Stern (Durham: Duke University Press, 1998), pp. 193-223

Manrique, Nelson, *El tiempo del miedo: la violencia política en el Perú 1980-1996* (Lima: Fondo Editorial del Congreso del Perú, 2002)

Mariátegui, José Carlos, *Seven Interpretative Essays on Peruvian Reality*, trans. by Marjory Urguidi (Austin: University of Texas Press, 1971)

Marsh, Leslie L., 'Memory, youth, and regimes of violence in recent Hispanic and Lusophone cinemas', in *Beyond Tordesillas: Critical Essays in Comparative Luso-Hispanic Studies*, ed. by Richard A. Gordon and Robert Patrick Newcomb (Columbus: Ohio State University Press, 2017), pp. 290-313

Martínez, Gabriela, 'Cinema law in Latin America: Brazil, Peru and Colombia', *Jump Cut: A Review of Contemporary Media*, 50 (2008), www.ejumpcut.org

Maseda, Rebeca, 'Songs of pain: Female active survivors in Claudia Llosa's *The Milk of Sorrow*', *Violence Probing the Boundaries*, conference presentation, Prague, Czech Republic, 9-11 May 2013

Mauceri, Philip, *State under Siege: Development and Policy-Making in Peru* (Colorado: Westview Press, 1996)

McClennen, Sophia A. 'The theory and practice of the Peruvian Grupo Chaski', *Jump Cut: A Review of Contemporary Media*, 50 (2008), www.ejumpcut.org/

Middents, Jeffrey, 'Another Limeño fantasy: Peruvian national cinema and the critical reception of the films of Francisco Lombardi and Federico García', in *Representing the Rural: Space, Place and Identity in Films About the Land*, ed. by Catherine Fowler and Gillian Helfield (Detroit: Wayne State University Press, 2006), pp. 307-322

Bibliography

Middents, Jeffrey, *Writing National Cinema: Film Journals and Film Culture in Peru* (Lebanon: University Press of New England, 2009)

Monaco, James, *How to Read a Film: The Art, Technology, Language, History and Theory of Film and Media*, 3rd edn (Oxford: Oxford University Press, 2000)

Monticelli, Simona, 'Italian post-war cinema and neorealism', in *The Oxford Guide to Film Studies*, ed. by Pamela Church Gibson and John Hill (Oxford: Oxford University Press, 1998), pp. 455–460

Morillo Cano, Nadia, 'Alzando el vuelo: entrevista con Fabrizio Aguilar', *Butaca Sanmarquina*, 18 (2003), 19–20

Moyano, María Elena, '"There have been threats"', in *The Peru Reader: History, Culture, Politics*, ed. by Orin Starn, Carlos Iván Degregori and Robin Kirk (Durham: Duke University Press, 1995), pp. 371–376

Mulvey, Laura, 'Visual pleasure and narrative cinema', in *Film Theory and Criticism: Introductory Readings*, 5th edn, ed. by Leo Braudy and Marshall Cohen (Oxford: Oxford University Press, 1999), pp. 833–844

Muñoz, Hortensia, 'Human rights and social referents: The construction of new sensibilities', in *Shining and Other Paths: War and Society in Peru, 1980–1995*, ed. by Steve J. Stern (Durham: Duke University Press, 1998), pp. 447–469

Núñez Gorritti, Violeta, *Pitas y alambre: la época de oro del cine peruano, 1936–1950* (Lima: Editorial Colmillo Blanco, 1990)

Ojeda, Martha, 'Nicomedes Santa Cruz and the vindication of Afro-Peruvian culture', in *Contemporary Latin American Cultural Studies*, ed. by Stephen Hart and Richard Young (London: Arnold, 2003), pp. 239–252

Orr, John, *Cinema and Modernity* (Edinburgh: Edinburgh University Press, 1993)

Page, Joanna, 'The nation as the *mise-en-scène* of film-making in Argentina', *Journal of Latin American Cultural Studies*, 14:3 (2005), 305–324

Palaversich, Diana, 'Cultural dyslexia and the politics of cross cultural excursion in Claudia Llosa's *Madeinusa*', *Bulletin of Hispanic Studies*, 90:40 (2013), 489–503

Peralta Ruiz, Víctor, *Sendero Luminoso y la prensa, 1980–1994* (Lima: Centro de Estudios Regionales Andinos, Casa de Estudios del Socialismo, 2000)

Pérez Torres, José, 'La década del silencio', *Abre los Ojos*, 2 (2002), 36–38

Perla Anaya, José, *Censura y promoción en el cine* (Lima: Deyco Instituto Peruano de Derecho de las Comunicaciones, 1991)

Perla Anaya, José, *Normas Legales de la Cinematografía Peruuana* (Lima: CONACINE, 1998)

Perla Anaya, José, *Los tres primeros años: memoria, 1996–1998* (Lima: CONACINE, 1998)

Pines, Jim and Paul Willemen, *Questions of Third Cinema* (London: British Film Institute, 1989)

Poe, Edgar Allen, *The Pit and the Pendulum* (London: Travelman Publishing, 1998)

Bibliography

Poole, Deborah and Gerard Rénique, *Peru: Time of Fear* (London: Latin America Bureau, 1992)

Portocarrero, Gonzalo, 'Nuevos modelos de identidad en la sociedad peruana', in *Modelos de identidad y sentidos de pertenencia en Perú y Bolivia*, ed. by Portocarrero and Jorge Komadina (Lima: Instituto de Estudios Peruanos, 2001), pp. 11–88

Portocarrero, Gonzalo, *Razones de sangre: aproximaciones a la violencia política* (Lima: Fondo Editorial de Pontificia Universidad Católica del Perú, 1998)

Radcliffe, 'Ethnicity, Patriarchy, and Incorporation into the Nation', *Environment and Planning D: Society and Space*, 8:4 (1990), p. 379–393.

Ribeyro, Julio Ramón, *Ribeyro: cuentos completos* (Madrid: Alfaguara, 1994)

Rix, Rob, 'Co-productions and common cause', in *Spanish Cinema: Calling the Shots*, ed. by Rob Rix and Roberto Rodríguez-Saona (Leeds: Trinity All Saints, 1999), pp. 113–128

Rojas, Adriana Beatriz, 'From Manchay Tiempo to 'Truth': Cultural Trauma and Resilience in Contemporary Peruvian Narrative', unpublished dissertation (University of Virginia, 2014).

Rojas, Pablo, 'Urpillay: *Paloma de papel*', *Butaca Sanmarquina*, 18 (2003), p. 9

Rosen, Philip, 'History, textuality, nation: Kracauer, Burch and some problems in the study of national cinema', in *Theorising National Cinema*, ed. by Valentina Vitali and Paul Willemen (London: British Film Institute, 2006), pp. 17–28

Rowe, William, 'The limits of readability: El Inca Garcilaso, José María Arguedas and shamanic practices', *Journal of Latin American Cultural Studies*, 15:2 (2006), 215–229

Rowe, William and Schelling, Vivian, *Memory and Modernity: Popular Culture in Latin America* (London: Verso, 1991)

Salomón, Emilio, et al., 'Premios y desencuentros: conversación sobre el estado del cine peruano', *La Gran Ilusión*, 9 (1998), 122–129

Saona, Margarita, 'Cuando la Guerra sigue por dentro: posmemoria y masculinidad entre Yuyanapaq y Días de Santiago', *Inti* 67/68 (2008), 157–172

Schelling, Vivian, *Through the Kaleidoscope: The Experience of Modernity in Latin America* (London: Verso, 2000)

Schlesinger, Philip, 'The sociological scope of "national cinema"', in *Cinema and Nation*, ed. by Mette Hjort and Scott Mackenzie (London: Routledge, 2000), pp. 19–31

Schnitman, Jorge, *Film Industries in Latin America: Dependency and Development* (New Jersey: Ablex Publishing, 1984)

Scott Palmer, David, ed., *Shining Path of Peru* (New York: St Martin's Press, 1992)

Seltzer, Mark, *Serial Killers: Death and Life in America's Wound Culture* (London: Routledge, 1998)

Bibliography

Shaw, Deborah, 'European co-production funds and Latin American cinema: Processes of othering and bourgeois cinephilia in Claudia Llosa's *La teta asustada*', *Diogène: Revue internationale des sciences humaines*, 245 (2014), 1–12

Shohat, Ella and Robert Stam, *Unthinking Eurocentrism: Multiculturalism in the Postmodern Age* (London: Routledge, 1994)

Silva, Enrique, 'Nuevos cines en Lima: crecimiento imparable', *La Gran Ilusión*, 8 (1997), 18

Silverman, Kaja, *Male Subjectivity at the Margins* (London: Routledge, 1994)

Singer, Ben, *Melodrama and Modernity: Early Sensational Cinema and Its Contexts* (New York: Columbia University Press, 2001)

Skidmore, Thomas E. and Peter H. Smith, 'Peru: Soldiers, oligarchs and Indians', in *Modern Latin America*, 6th edn (Oxford: Oxford University Press, 2005), pp. 181–220

Smith, Anthony, 'Memory and modernity: Reflections on Ernest Gellner's theory of nationalism', *Nations and Nationalism*, 3 (1996), 371–388

Snead, James, *White Screens, Black Images: Hollywood from the Dark Side* (London: Routledge, 1994)

Starn, Orin, 'Villager at arms: War and counterrevolution in the Central-South Andes', in *Shining and Other Paths: War and Society in Peru, 1980–1995*, ed. by Steve J. Stern (Durham: Duke University Press, 1998), pp. 224–260

Starn, Orin, Carlos Iván Degregori and Robin Kirk, eds, *The Peru Reader: History, Culture, Politics* (Durham: Duke University Press, 1995)

Stern, Steve J., ed., *Shining and Other Paths: War and Society in Peru, 1980–1995* (Durham: Duke University Press, 1998)

Stock, Ann Marie, 'Migrancy and the Latin American cinemascape: Towards a postnational cinema praxis', in *Transnational Cinema: The Film Reader*, ed. by Elizabeth Ezra and Terry Rowden (London: Routledge, 2006), pp. 157–166

Stone-Miller, Rebecca, *Art of the Andes: from Chavín to Inca* (London: Thames and Hudson, 1995)

Strong, Simon, *Shining Path* (London: Harper Collins, 1992)

Swanson, Philip, *Companion to Latin American Studies* (London: Arnold, 2003)

Thomas, Sarah, '"Yo no soy invisible": Imaginative agency in *Las malas intenciones*', in *Screening Minors in Latin American Cinema*, ed. by Carolina Rocha and Georgia Seminet (Lanham: Rowman and Littlefield, 2014), 53–67

Tompkins, Cynthia, *Experimental Latin American Cinema* (Austin: University of Texas Press, 2013)

Triana Toribio, Nuria, 'Building Latin American cinema in Europe: Cine en Construcción/ Cinéma en construction', in *Transnational Film Financing*, ed. by Stephanie Dennison (Woodbridge: Tamesis, 2013), pp. 89–112

Turner, Graeme, *Film as Social Practice*, 3rd edn (London: Routledge, 2003)

Vich, Víctor, *El caníbal es el otro: violencia y cultura en el Perú contemporáneo* (Lima: Instituto de Estudios Peruanos, 2002)

Vich, Cynthia, 'De desadaptaciones y reiteradas violencias: la distancia entre el film *Magallanes* y la novela *La pasajera*', in *Nuevas aproximaciones a viejas polémicas: cine/literature*, ed. by Giovanna Pollarolo (Lima: Fondo Editorial de la Pontificia Universidad Católica del Perú, forthcoming)

Vitali, Valentina and Paul Willemen, eds, *Theorising National Cinema* (London: British Film Institute, 2006)

Wade, Peter, 'Images of Latin American *mestizaje* and the politics of comparison', *Bulletin of Latin American Research*, 23 (2004), 355–366

Wade, Peter, *Race and Ethnicity in Latin America* (London: Pluto, 1997)

Wayne, Mike, *Political Film: The Dialectics of Third Cinema* (London: Pluto, 2001)

Whittaker, David J., *The Terrorism Reader* (London: Routledge, 2001)

Wiener, Christian, 'Miedos de guerra', *Butaca Sanmarquina*, 12 (2002), 18–20

Wiener, Christian, 'Una Moyano demasiado lejos: *Coraje*', *La Gran Ilusión*, 10 (1999), 105–107

Wiener, Christian, 'El cine peruano en los noventa: la historia sin fin', *La Gran Ilusión*, 5 (1995), 96–104

Wiener, Christian, 'Tan duro de vivir, tan duro de morir: el cine en el Perú de los 1990', in *Changing Reels: Latin American Cinema Against the Odds*, ed. by Rob Rix and Roberto Rodríguez-Saona (Leeds Iberian Papers: University of Leeds, 1997), pp. 17–32

Willemen, Paul, 'The national revisited', in *Theorising National Cinema*, ed. by Valentina Vitali and Paul Willemen (London: British Film Institute, 2006), pp. 29–43

Williamson, Edwin, *The Penguin History of Latin American* (London: Penguin, 1992)

Wilson, Emma, *Personal Histories: French Cinema since 1950* (Durham: Duckworth, 1999)

Wood, David, 'The Peruvian press under recent authoritarian regimes, with special reference to the *Autogolpe* of President Fujimori', *Bulletin of Latin American Research*, 19 (2000), 17–32

Wood, David, *De sabor nacional: el impacto de la cultura popular en el Perú* (Lima: Instituto de Estudios Peruanos, 2005)

Zavaleta, Jorge, 'Cinema and society in contemporary Peru', Conference presentation, PUCP, Lima, 1 December 2016.

Newspaper/Web Sources

'City where sacrificial slaughter was way of life', *Daily Telegraph*, 2 September 2015, p. 3

'*Coraje*', *La República*, 22 November 1998

Bibliography

'Entrevista con Francisco Lombardi', *La República*, 19 December 1988, p. 9

'Entrevista con Marianne Eyde', *La República*, 9 November 1992, p. 11

'Ex-army officer with a dark past tops poll in Peru', *Independent*, 7 April 2006, p. 33

'*Frecuencia Latina*', www.frecuencialatina.com.pe/empresa

'Francisco Lombardi está trabajando en dos nuevos proyectos de película', *El Comercio*, 8 December 1988, p. 7

'Histórico de proyectos', *Programa Ibermedia*, www.programaibermedia.com/esp/htm/home.htm

'Interview with Josué Méndez', *51st Sydney Film Festival*, June–July 2004, www.sydneyfilmfestival.org

'*Los Mojarras*', www.chicama.com/mojarras.htm

'No es tan frágil la paloma', *Diario del Festival*, La Havana Cuba, 10 December 2004, p. 7

'OTI Highlights: Truth Commission', *USAID/OTI Peru Field Report*, June 2002, http://www.usaid.gov/our_work/cross-cutting_programs/transition_initiatives/country/peru/rpt0602.html

'Peru's looming disaster', *New York Times*, 13 May 2006, p. 21

'Peru turns to anti-American "Comandante"', *Sunday Times*, 9 April 2006, p. 35

Programa Ibermedia, www.programaibermedia.com/esp/htm/home.htm

'Truth Commission Report: Summary', Peru Support Group, 2005, www.perusupportgroup.org.uk/key_human.html

'Warrior queen or ritual sacrifice: The amazing secret unearthed in Peru', *Daily Mail*, 18 May 2015, p. 11

Balbi, Mariella, 'Entrevista con Francisco Lombardi', *La República*, 27 November 1988, p. 8

Balbi, Mariella, 'Entrevista con Moyano', *La República*, 22 September 1991, p. 17

Bedoya, Ricardo, '*La vida es una sola*', *Cine*, 8 November 1993, p. 11

Bedoya, Ricardo, 'Un aprendizaje perverso: *Paloma de papel*', *El Dominical*, 5 October 2003, p. 4

Bula, Ricardo, 'Poderoso testimonio social', *Vértigo: Diaro del Festival*, 6 August 2004, p. 1

Cachay A., Raúl, 'Un francotirador en Lima', *El Comercio*, 9 August 2004, p. c8

Cárdenas, Miguel Angel, 'Ser Peruano (I): una ética de la choledad', *El Comercio*, 28 July 2004, p. 16

Castro, Tito and Jorge Paredes, 'La Peruanidad: el mestizaje como emblema. Debate con Norma Fuller, Gonzalo Portocarrero y Carlos Contreras', *El Dominical*, 25 July 2004, pp. 8–10

de Cárdenas, Federico, '*Alias la gringa*', *La República*, 20 September 1991, p. 4

de Cárdenas, Federico, '*La vida es una sola*', *La República*, 15 November 1993, p. 11

de Cárdenas, Federico, '*Paloma de papel*', *Domingo, la revista*, 5 October 2003, pp. 30–31

Bibliography

De Guzmán, Guillermo, 'La boca del lobo: máximo galardón en el festival de La Habana', Lundero, 18 December 1988, p. 8

Díaz Reyes, Miguel, 'Entrevista con Giovanna Pollarolo', La República, 18 December 1988, p. 10

García de Pinilla, Rafaela, 'Anda, corre, vuela ...', La República, 20 October 1995, p. 16

García de Pinilla, Rafaela, 'Coraje', El Comercio, 20 December 1998, p. 17

Hidalgo Vega, David, 'En las butacas del terror', El Comercio, 8 August 2004, p. 32

Koehler, Robert, 'Paper Dove (Paloma de papel)', Variety, 23 February 2004

Leira, Milagros, 'Entrevista con Robles Godoy', El Comercio, 22 November 1998, p. 17

Leira, Milagros, 'Coraje', El Comercio, 30 November 1998, p. 17

León Frías, Isaac, 'La boca del lobo', Caretas, 12 December 1988, p. 17

León Frías, Isaac, 'Alias la gringa', El Peruano, 7 December 1991, p. 15

León Frías, Isaac, 'La vida es una sola', Caretas, 28 October 1993, p. 15

León Frías, Isaac, 'Anda, corre, vuela ...', Caretas, 21 October 1995, p. 3

León Frías, Isaac, 'Coraje', TV+, 21 November 1998, p. 11

Madedo, Fernando and Fanelli, Ana, 'Por un cine humanista', Otrocampo Festivales, 2004, www.otrocampo.com/festivales/mardel04/fabrizioaguilar.html

Núñez del Pozo, Irela, 'Alias la gringa', Revista, El Peruano, 26 September 1991, p. 11.

Robles, Marcelo, 'Coraje', El Comercio, 13 February 1998, p. 16

Seibold, Balthas, 'Peru-Ecuador Peace Agreement: Hemisphere's last armed territorial dispute finally settled', Council on Hemispheric Affairs, 26 October 1998, www.coha.org/Press%20Release%20Archives/1998/98.32_PeruEcuador_Peace_Agreement.htm

Servat, Alberto, 'Entrevista con Francisco Lombardi', TV+, 4 November 1996, p. 11

Servat, Alberto, 'Coraje', Somos, 29 November 1998, p. 15

Servat, Alberto, 'Entre el arte y la realidad', El Comercio, 6 August 2004, p. 3

Vandoorne, Pierre Emile, 'Balance 2015', 12 November 2015, www.latamcinema.com/especiales/balance-2015

Vandoorne, Pierre Emile, 'Incidir en la cultura es incidir en la generación de valores communes', 27 April, 2014, https://redaccion.lamula.pe/2014/04/27/incidir-en-la-cultura-es-incidir-en-la-generacion-de-valores-comunes

Vivas, Fernando, 'La vida es una sola: un filme de una presencia contundente', El Suplemento, 31 October 1993, p. 16

Filmography

All films produced in Peru unless otherwise stated.

A la media noche y media. Marité Ugaz and Mariana Rondón. 2000.
Alerta en la frontera. Kurt Hermann. 1941.
Alias la gringa. Alberto Durant. 1991.
Amigos, Los (episode of *Cuentos inmorales*). Francisco Lombardi. 1978.
Anda, corre, vuela … Augusto Tamayo. 1995.
Asia, el culo del mundo. Juan Carlos Torrico. 1996.
Bajo la piel. Francisco Lombardi. 1996.
Bala perdida. Aldo Salvini. 2001.
Bien esquivo, El. Augusto Tamayo. 2001.
Boca del lobo, La. Francisco Lombardi. 1988.
Caídos del cielo. Francisco Lombardi. 1990.
Camino de la venganza. Luis Ugarte and Narciso Rada. 1922.
Candidato, El. Álvaro Velarde. 2016.
Carnada, La. Marianne Eyde. 1999.
Ciudad de M. Felipe Degregori. 2000.
Ciudad y los perros, La. Francisco Lombardi. 1985.
Coraje. Alberto Durant. 1998.
Cuentos inmorales. José Carlos Huayhuaca, Augusto Tamayo, José Luis Flores, Francisco Lombardi. 1979.
Destino no tiene favoritos, El. Álvaro Velarde. 2003.
Días de Santiago. Josué Méndez. 2004.
Dios tarda, pero no olvida. Palito Ortega Matute. 1997.
Elefante desaparecido, El. Javier Fuentes Leon. 2014.
Fuga del chacal, La. Augusto Tamayo. 1987.
Gregorio. Marita Barea, Fernando Espinoza, Stefan Kaspar, Alejandro Legaspi. Grupo Chaski. 1984.
Hora azul, La. Evelyne Pegot-Ogier. 2014.
Hora final, La. Eduardo Mendoza, 2017.
Huerfanito, El. Flaviano Quispe Chaiña. 2004.
Illary. Nilo Pereira del Mar. 2009.
Jarawi. César Villanueva and Eulogio Nishiyama. 1966.

Filmography

Juliana. Marita Barea, Fernando Espinoza, Stefan Kaspar, Alejandro Legaspi. Grupo Chaski. 1989.
Kukuli. Luis Figueroa. 1961.
Lágrimas de fuego. Mélinton Eusebio. 1996.
Madeinusa. Claudia Llosa. 2006.
Magallanes. Salvador del Solar. 2015.
Malas intenciones, Las. Rosario García-Montero. 2011.
Maldición de las jarjachas. Palito Ortega Matute. 2003.
Maruja en el infierno. Francisco Lombardi. 1983.
Miss Universo en el Perú. Marita Barea, Fernando Espinoza, Stefan Kaspar, Alejandro Legaspi. Grupo Chaski. 1982.
Mudo, El. Diego and Daniel Vega. 2013.
Muerte al amanecer. Francisco Lombardi. 1977.
Muerte de un magnate. Francisco Lombardi. 1980.
Ni con dios ni con el diablo. Nilo Pereira del Mar. 1990.
NN: sin identidad. Héctor Gálvez. 2014.
No se lo digas a nadie. Francisco Lombardi. 1998.
Paloma de papel. Fabrizio Aguilar. 2003.
Pantaleón y las visitadoras. Francisco Lombardi. 1999.
Paraíso. Héctor Gálvez Campos. 2010.
Rincón de los inocentes, El. Palito Ortega Matute. 2005.
Ronderos, Los. Marianne Eyde. 1987.
Sin compasión. Francisco Lombardi. 1994.
Tarata. Fabrizio Aguilar. 2009.
Taxi Driver. Martin Scorsese. 1976. US.
Teta asustada, La. Claudia Llosa. 2009.
Tinta roja. Francisco Lombardi. 2001.
Última tarde, La. Joel Calero. 2016.
Viaje a Timbuctú. Rossana Diaz Costa. 2014.
Vida es una sola, La. Marianne Eyde. 1993.
Vidas paralelas. Rocío Lladó. 2005.
Yo, la peor de todas, María Luisa Bemberg. 1990. Argentina.
Y si te vi, no me acuerdo. Miguel Barreda. 2001.
Yunta brava, La. Federico García. 1999.

Index

References to notes are indicated by n.

Abre los Ojos (journal) 13
Academy Awards 140, 176
African workers 8
aggression 163, 197n.32
agriculture 23, 103
Aguilar, Fabrizio 5, 8, 29, 139, 140–1
   and critics 149, 150, 151
   and exhibition 188
   and human rights 210n.33
   and Lima 177–8
   and memory 153
   and neorealism 146
   see also Paloma de papel
Al pie del acantialdo/At the Foot of the Cliff (Ribeyro) 119
Alcazar, Damien 182
Alegría, Alonso 106
Alerta en la frontera/Alert at the Border (Hermann, 1941) 192n.15
Alias la gringa/AKA 'La gringa' (Durant, 1991) 33, 35, 37, 79–81, 175–6
   and non-violence 188
   and plot 81–2, 83–5, 87–8
   and prison 85–7
   and Shining Path 98
   and society 88–91
alienation 68, 73, 159, 166, 168
Amauta Films 22

Amazon communities 60
Amigos, Los/The Friends (Lombardi, 1978) 194n.4
amnesia 185, 186, 197n.23
Amnesty International 66, 210n.33
Anaya, José Perla 23
Anda, corre, vuela…/Walk, Run, Fly… (Tamayo, 1995) 94–5, 109–10, 121–3, 188
   and plot 111–13, 116–18
   and society 113–14, 115–16, 118–21
Anderson, Benedict 74
Andes, the 60, 175, 177, 185, 205n.60
   and *Anda, corre, vuela…* 117–18
   and *Boca de lobo, La* 36, 39, 44, 48, 52–3, 54–5
   and *Ni con dios ni con el diablo* 62, 64–5, 72–3, 74
   and *Paloma de papel* 143–6, 148–9, 151–3
   and Shining Path 98–9
   and *Vida es una sola, La* 94, 95, 97, 102–4, 106
anti-terrorism 10, 35, 37, 93, 176
   and legislation 97, 115
APRA (Alíanza Popular Revolucionaria Americana) 192n.13
archaeology 4, 189n.4

230

Index

Argentina 27
Arguedas, José María 8, 205n.60
aristocracy 18, 19
armed forces *see* military, the
Asian workers 7, 8
Association of Peruvian Filmmakers (Asociación de Cineastas del Perú) 63
Astengo, Tatiana 149
Ayacucho 64, 179, 209n.16
Azalbert, Nicholas 162–3

Bajo la piel/Under the Skin (Lombardi, 1986) 195n.5
Bardem, Juan 135
Beasley-Murray, Jon 112
Bedoya, Ricardo 12, 18, 19–20, 23, 178
  and *Alias la gringa* 84
  and *Anda, corre, vuela...* 118, 119, 122
  and *Boca del lobo, La* 42, 48, 51, 57–8
  and legislation 24, 25
  and *Ni con dios ni con el diablo* 76
  and *Vida es una sola, La* 104, 107
Bejar Ochante, Edwin 178
Belaúnde, Andrés 8
Belaúnde Terry, Fernando 41, 43, 64, 82
belief systems 14, 72–3, 74, 117–18; *see also* magic
Benavides, General 22
Bidón, Giselle 166
Boca del lobo, La/The Lion's Den (Lombardi, 1998) 8, 9, 30, 33, 142
  and characters 45–52
  and confinement 55–6
  and critics 42–3

and history 41–2
and ideology 37–8
and massacre 187
and the military 34, 35–6, 101
and national identity 52–4, 56–7
and plot 39–40, 41, 43–5
and release 38–9, 58–9, 107, 174–5
and rural life 103
and setting 54–5
and Shining Path 98
and society 188
and the state 184
and success 173
and violence 57–8
Bolívar, Simón 69
boundaries 7, 54, 60, 68, 69
bourgeoisie 19
Bueno, Gustavo 40, 44, 57
Bula, Ricardo 159
Bullitta, Juan M. 12
Buntinx, Fatima 180
Burt, Jo-Marie 129, 131
business 23
Bustamente, Emilio 88
Butaca Sanmartina (journal) 13

Cabrera, Patricia 62
Cáceres, Lucho 183
Cahier du cinema (journal) 12
Caídos del cielo/Fallen from the Sky (Lombardi, 1990) 119
Calderón, Sandro 169
Calero, Joel 5, 174
Callirgos, Antonio 142
camerawork 55, 72
  and *Días de Santiago* 157, 161
  and *Paloma de papel* 145–6, 149–50
  and *Vida es una sola, La* 102–3

Index

Camino de la venganza/The Road to Revenge (Ugarte and Rada, 1922) 20–1
Campos, Enid 29
Candidato, El/The Candidate (Velarde, 2016) 3
Cannes Film Festival 157, 196n.16
capitalism 67
Carbone, Giancarlo 12
Casablanca Films 110
Castillo, Alheli 163
censorship 21, 38, 124–5, 185
Cerro, Luis M. Sánchez 21
Cesti, Eduardo 146
Chakravarty, Sumita 126
Chanan, Michael 15
Channel 4 79
Chaski Group 95, 110–11, 114, 118, 122
  and filmmakers 204n.44
  and music 120
Chavín culture 4
childhood 137, 138, 139, 179, 180–1
  and *Paloma de papel* 140–1, 142, 145, 146
China 7
cholo see urban migration
Ciccia, Giovanni 182
cinema 2, 3, 5–7, 9, 123–4
  and class 187–8
  and exhibition space 10–11
  and national identity 17–18
  and Peru 11–13, 18–31, 94, 173–4, 184–5
Cinema and Audiovisual Law (2017) 189n.2
cinema-goers 10–11, 25–6
Cinema Law
  19327 (1972) 23–6, 30, 34, 63
  26270 (1994) 26–8, 121, 123–4, 138
cinematograph 18
Ciudad y los perros, La/The City and the Dogs (Lombardi, 1985) 195n.4
class 5, 7, 18–19, 56–7
  and *Anda, corre, vuela...* 117
  and cinema 187–8
  and *Días de Santiago* 166–7
  see also inequality
claustrophobia 36, 55–6, 87
close-ups 55, 149, 161
cocaine 154
Coll, Pilar 141
collectivism 109–10, 114
colonialism 8, 19, 34, 60, 69–70, 185
communication 163–4
community 109–10, 114, 129, 130–1, 133–4
  and *Paloma de papel* 145, 147
compassion 80
competitions 26
CONACINE (National Cinema Council) 26, 28, 124, 134, 140, 175
  and *Días de Santiago* 156
confinement 36, 54, 55–6, 84
COPROCI (Commission for Cinema Promotion) 24–5, 26, 37–8, 79, 96, 106
Coraje/Courage (Durant, 1998) 95, 123–4, 134–6, 176
  and Moyano 125–34
Cordero, Isabel 99, 100, 101, 104
counter-insurgency 11, 38, 41, 42, 51–2, 57, 101, 186
  and *Anda, corre, vuela...* 95
  and García 83
Crabtree, John 82, 83, 89

232

Index

criollos see indigenous peoples
Cuba 7, 59, 195n.8
culture 2–3, 8–9, 21, 27
   and diversity 6, 7–8, 30–1, 57
   and *Ni con dios ni con el diablo*
     75–6, 77–8
   and politics 174
   see also belief systems
curfews 26, 178
CVR *see* Truth and Reconciliation Commission

da Gama, Francisca 174
Danós, Carlos 112
de Cárdenas, Federico 12, 98, 140, 146, 147
de Soto, Hernando 113
Debate (magazine) 37
Degregori, Carlos 149
del Carpio, Milagros 97
del Solar, Salvador 29, 135, 174, 182, 207n.110
delinquency 4, 35, 82, 170
   and *Anda, corre, vuela...* 112–13, 115–16
democracy 56, 82
Días de Santiago/Days of Santiago
   (Méndez, 2004) 10, 14, 138, 139–40, 154–6, 158–68, 175, 176
   and masculinity 187
   and release 156–7
   and society 168–9, 170–1, 188
Diaz Costa, Rossana 181–2
Dios tarda, pero no olvida/God Might Be Late but Does Not Forget
   (Ortega Matute, 1997) 178
directors *see* filmmakers
'dirty war' 39, 41, 42, 47, 53–4, 95

and censorship 124–5
and *Ni con dios ni con el diablo* 64–5
and Truth and Reconciliation 138
disappearances 35, 42, 66, 96, 181
diversity 6–8, 30–1, 57
documentaries 18, 19–20, 102, 157–8
D'Onofrio, Katherina 183
drugs trafficking 154, 158
Durant, Alberto 35, 79, 91, 134, 175–6
   and the military 85
   and responsibility 80, 83
   see also Alias la gringa; *Coraje*

economy 22, 33, 65, 76, 82
   and crisis 38, 83
   informal 113
Ecuador 4, 154, 158, 192n.15
   and peace treaty 157, 171, 211n.42
education 21, 23–4, 25, 26, 27
El Frontón 80, 81, 85
elections 76
employment 60–1, 165–6; *see also* unemployment
Escuela de Cine de Cusco (Cusco Film School) 5
ethnic community *see* indigenous peoples; *mestizo* (mixed race) peoples
Europe 19, 21, 74, 122, 135; *see also* Spain
executions 4, 42
exhibition spaces 10–11, 19, 25–6, 187–8, 190n.29
Eyde, Marianne 71, 94, 95–6, 102, 104, 201n.1
   and critics 106–7, 108, 149, 175
   see also Vida es una sola, La
Ezra, Elizabeth 137

233

Index

fear 36, 44, 45, 47, 51, 57
   and *Alias la gringa* 87
   and borders 54
Festival des Trois Continents 156
festivals *see* film festivals
fiction films 9–10, 20–1, 174, 176–7, 184–5
Figueira Film Art 3
film archives 13, 26, 76
film criticism 11–13
film festivals 3, 9, 13, 156–7, 173, 196n.16
   and *Anda, corre, vuela...* 122
   and *Boca del lobo, La* 59
   and funding 29
filmmakers 1–2, 10, 11, 12
   and legislation 23, 24, 25, 29–30, 194n.41
   and politics 185
   and support 28–9
   and violence 4–5
   see also Aguilar, Fabrizio; Durant, Alberto; Eyde, Marianne; Lombardi, Francisco; Méndez, Josué; Pereira del Mar, Nilo; Tamayo, Augusto
flashbacks 145–6, 153, 179
Flores Galindo, Alberto 46, 106, 116, 162
Fraissinnett, Ivonne 62
Frecuencia Latina 115, 134–5
freedom of expression 10, 176, 184, 185, 186
Freiburg Festival 156
Freud, Sigmund 14, 45, 159, 160, 197n.32
friendship 80
Frith, Simon 120
Fromm, Erich 14

Fujimori, Alberto 3, 10, 26, 30
   and *autogolpe* 109, 131, 175, 186
   and control 184, 208n.4
   and corruption 28, 137–8, 141
   and culture 27
   and the military 96
   and neo-liberalism 93
   and protests 210n.32
   and society 122–3
   and victory 34, 90
funding 9, 10, 27–30, 138, 176, 208n.3
   and *Alias la gringa* 79
   and *Anda, corre, vuela...* 121
   and co-production 124, 134–5
   and *Días de Santiago* 156
   and Eyde 107
   and Fujimori 94
   and Ibermedia 193n.39
   and Pereira del Mar 63

Galliani, Sergio 147
Galt, Rosalind 137
Gálvez, Juan 159
Gálvez Campos, Héctor 174, 178, 179–80
García, Alan 33–4, 36–7, 43, 56, 57, 184
   and counter-insurgency 83
   and El Frontón 80
   and repression 66
García, Erick 167
García, Jair 182
García de Pinilla, Rafaela 123
García-Montero, Rosario 29, 174, 180
Gassols, Carlos 115
gender 5, 7, 14, 15, 116–17; *see also* masculinity; women
genre 139, 140

Index

geography 72
Germany 122
Gibbons, Urpi 179
González, Germán 80
Gorriti, Gustavo 85, 86
Gorritti, Violeta Núñez 12
Gran Ilusión, La (journal) 13, 193n.34
Gregorio (Espinoza, 1984) 110–11, 203n.43
gringo/a 200n.93
Grupo Chaski *see* Chaski Group
Guzmán, Abimael 3, 9, 93, 96, 101, 140, 175
and strategy 212n.69
and teachings 103

Hablemos de cine (journal) 12, 13
Havana Film Festival 59, 141, 173
Haya de la Torre, Víctor Raúl 192n.13
Hayward, Susan 6–7, 96, 137, 184, 185
Higson, Andrew 6, 31, 77
history 20
Hjort, Mette 90, 137
Hollywood 30, 107
Hora azul, La/Before Dawn (Pegot-Ogier, 2015) 182
Hora final, La/The Final Hour (Mendoza, 2017) 3
Huayhuaca, José Carlos 43
Hubert Bals Fund 156
Humala, Ollanta 210n.32
human rights 66, 108, 115, 141
and Moyano 127, 132
hyperinflation 26, 33, 83

Ibermedia 29, 94, 140, 193n.39
ICAIC 79, 140
ideology 19–20, 37–8

and Shining Path 66–7, 144–5, 147–9
Illary (Pereira del Mar, 2009) 178, 179
immigrant workers 7, 8, 21
Incan culture 4, 108
indigenista movement 21, 103
indigenous peoples 4, 8, 14, 22, 178–9
and abuses 183
and *Boca del lobo, La* 52–3, 57
and cinema 20–1
and land ownership 99
and Llosa 177
and migration 60–1
and *Ni con dios ni con el diablo* 70–1, 72–4, 76–8
and rights 19
see also Andes, the
industrialisation 20
inequality 7–8, 20, 60–1, 69–70, 71, 141–2
insurgency *see* Shining Path
isolation 46, 55, 144, 145, 162–3, 168
Italy 22

Japan 7
Jarawi (Villneuva and Nishiyama, 1966) 192n.15
Jelin, Elizabeth 14
Jeri, Fabio 179
Johnson, Randal 25
judiciary 115
Juliana (Espinoza, 1989) 110–11, 203n.43
Junín and Ayacucho, battles of 19

Kaspar, Stefan 110, 111, 112–13, 118, 121
Kieslowski, Krzysztof 157

Index

King, John 12, 22, 24
Kukuli (Figueroa, 1961) 192n.15

language 24, 72, 151–2, 183
Larraín, Carlos Rodríguez 12, 20
Latin America 5, 7, 21, 29
  and cinema 12, 13, 17, 25, 174
legislation 10, 12, 13, 21, 107
  and 1972 law 23–6, 30, 34, 63
  and 1994 law 26–8, 121, 123–4, 138
  and 2017 law 189n.2
  and anti-terrorism 97, 115, 176
  and Fujimori 94
Leguía, Augusto 19, 20
León de la Torre, Marino 111
León Frías, Isaac 12, 28–9, 107
Lima 18, 19, 21, 22
  and *Alias la gringa* 87, 89
  and *Anda, corre, vuela...* 109, 111–12, 117, 118–20, 121
  and attacks 33, 38, 65–6, 106, 114–15, 177–8
  and *Boca del lobo, La* 43–4, 48
  and Chaski Group 110
  and cinemas 26, 187, 190n.29
  and *Días de Santiago* 155, 156, 161–2, 168
  and migration 60, 61, 63–4, 78
  and Moyano 125–6, 127, 129
  and national identity 36
  and *Ni con dios ni con el diablo* 67, 72, 73–5
  and violence 185–6
Lima Film Festival 13
Lladó, Rocío 178, 179
Llosa, Claudia 29, 173–4, 177, 188
Lombardi, Francisco 8, 9, 11, 12, 81
  and the Andes 36

  and borders 54
  and classification 39
  and funding 176
  and indigenous peoples 52, 53
  and intentions 37
  and Lima 119
  and location 195n.5
  and massacres 40–1
  and national cinema 173
  and release 58–9
  and symbolism 94
  and violence 194n.4
  see also Boca del lobo, La
López, Ana M. 17
Lucio, Jiménez de 23
Luppi, Federico 182

McClennen, Sophia 110
Madeinusa (Llosa, 2006) 174, 177, 188
Magallanes (del Solar, 2015) 174, 182–3, 188
magic 117–18, 146, 205n.60
Magical Reels (King) 12
Malas intenciones, Las/Bad Intentions (García-Montero, 2011) 174, 180–1
Malatesta, Andrés 27
Maraví, Javier 98
Marcha Nacional (national anthem) 198n.48
Mariátegui, José Carlos 8, 21, 99
Marsh, Leslie 177
Maruja en el Infierno/Maruja in Hell (Lombardi, 1983) 194n.4
masculinity 36, 43, 48, 50–1, 56, 186–7
  and *Alias la gringa* 88
  and *Días de Santiago* 164–5, 167

236

Index

massacres 4, 37, 180, 187
  and Soccos 40-2, 43, 175
  and Uchuraccay 64-5
media 23-4, 38, 64-5, 185
  and censorship 124-5
  and the military 66, 85, 96
Mejía, Ricardo 167
memory 2, 3, 13-14, 30-1, 96, 183, 185-6
  and collective 10
  and *Días de Santiago* 156, 159-60, 168, 170
  and *Paloma de papel* 145-6, 153
Méndez, Josué 29, 139, 156-8, 168; see also *Días de Santiago*
Mendoza, Eduardo 3
mestizaje (miscegenation) 8, 14, 34, 190n.22
mestizo (mixed race) peoples 20-1, 60-1, 68-9, 155, 161
Mexico 19, 22
Middents, Jeffrey 13
middle class 19, 22, 178
migration *see* urban migration
Miguel, Gonzalo de 84
military, the 4, 23-4, 34, 35-6
  and *Boca del lobo, La* 37, 38, 39-42, 43-52, 54, 57-8
  and conscription 211n.43
  and *Coraje* 133
  and counter-insurgency 186
  and *Días de Santiago* 155, 159-61, 169
  and Ecuador 157-8, 171
  and Fujimori 109
  and *Ni con dios ni con el diablo* 69, 70, 71
  and *Paloma de papel* 143-4, 150-1, 152
  and prisoners 85
  and public image 169-70
  and Shining Path 66, 114-15
  and *Vida es una sola, La* 95, 97, 101-2
  and *Vidas paralelas* 179
  and violence 96
mining 23, 65, 72
Ministry of Education 26, 27
mobile cinemas 21-2
Moche culture 4
modernity 17, 18, 20, 68, 72
  and *Vida es una sola, La* 103, 104
Mojarras, Los 120
Mojas, Angel 143
Montesinos, Vladimiro 185
Morfino, Rosa Isabel 111
Movadef 3
Moyano, María Elena 124, 125-34, 136
Muerte al amanecer/Death at Sunrise (Lombardi, 1977) 194n.4
Muerte de un magnate/Death of a Tycoon (Lombardi, 1980) 194n.4
Muñoz, Hortensia 42
music 44, 55
  and *Anda, corre, vuela...* 120
  and *Coraje* 135
  and *Días de Santiago* 157
  and *Ni con dios ni con el diablo* 72, 73
  and *Paloma de papel* 147, 151
  and *Vida es una sola, La* 102
mutilation 57
myths 4

nation-states 5-7, 20
national cinema register 26
National Film Archive (La Filmoteca) 13, 76

Index

national identity 1–2, 3, 6–9, 14–15, 184–5
   and *Alias la gringa* 90, 91
   and *Anda, corre, vuela...* 118–19, 121–2
   and *Boca del lobo, La* 36, 48–9, 52–4, 56–7
   and cinema 17–18, 19–20, 21, 24, 29, 34–5
   and *Días de Santiago* 161, 162, 171
   and fragmentation 31
   and *Ni con dios ni con el diablo* 67–8, 73–4, 77–9
   and non-violence 187
   and *Vida es una sola, La* 95, 96, 104–5, 106, 109
   and violence 4–5
nationalism 7, 20, 77, 96, 185, 199n.87
Native Americans 74
neo-liberalism 10, 26, 93, 167
neorealism 146
newsreels 18
Ni con dios ni con diablo/Neither with God nor the Devil (Pereira del Mar, 1990) 33, 35, 59–62, 177
   and indigenous peoples 72–4
   and inequality 69–70
   and migration 63–4, 67–9, 74–6, 77–9
   and narrative 61–2
   and release 76–7
   and Shining Path 66–7, 70–1
   and violence 64–5
NN: sin identidad/NN: Without Identity (Gálvez, 2014) 174, 181, 187
non-violence 88, 95, 105, 108, 126–30, 187

Ochoa, Juan Manuel 81
oil 23
Ojeda, Martha 8
Olivero, Elsa 81
Olórtegui, Rosa María 99
Ortega Matute, Palito 29, 178–9

Padilla, Anais 143
Pagaza, Berta 46
'Pagina del diario de satan/Pages from Satan's diary' (blog) 12
Palmer, David Scott 78
Paloma de papel/Paper Dove (Aguilar, 2003) 10, 14, 138, 139–42, 146–51, 153–4, 175, 176
   and the Andes 151–3
   and exhibition 188
   and plot 142–6
Paniagua, Valentín 209n.16
Pantaleón y las visitadoras/Pantaleon and the Visitors (Lombardi, 1999) 195n.5
Paraíso/Paradise (Gálvez Campos, 2010) 178, 179–80
Pari, Antonieta 181
Pasajera, La (Cueto) 182
Pastor, Rosana 129, 135
patriarchy 14, 43, 48, 51, 94, 171, 187
   and Shining Path 100
Patriau, Andrea 182
Pegot-Ogier, Evelyne 182
Pereira del Mar, Nilo 59, 62–3, 76, 175, 178, 179
   and politics 66
   see also Ni con dios ni con el diablo
Pérez, César 102
Peru 7–9, 19, 69–70
   and cinema 11–13, 18–31, 184–5

Index

and democracy 82–3
and emigration 88
and Fujimori 93–4
and national anthem 198n.48
and society 112–13, 122–3, 186–7
  see also Andes, the; Lima; national identity; state, the
Peruanidad (Peruvian-ness) 2, 13
Peruvian Film Festival 182
Picho, Aristóteles 101, 143
Piérola, Nicolás de 18
plantations 60
Polar, Antonio Cornejo 8
police, the 115–16, 133
politics 2, 7, 10, 180–1
  and APRA 192n.13
  and cinema 30, 94, 95, 173, 185
  and class 19, 56–7
  and culture 174
  see also state, the
poor, the 23, 65
Portocarrero, Gonzalo 14, 169, 170
Portugal, Guillermo 80
prejudice 138
prison 4, 37
  and *Alias la gringa* 80, 81–2, 84–7, 88, 89
production companies 24, 34, 124
psychoanalysis 13–14
Puicón, Marisela 167

race 5, 7–8, 30, 130–1, 133; see also indigenous peoples; *mestizo* (mixed race) peoples
racism 46–7, 56, 116–17, 138
Radcliffe, Sarah 68, 70
rape 40, 42, 45, 46, 57, 182
repression 66

Ribeyro, Julio Ramón 119
Rincón de los inocentes, El/Where the Innocent People Live (Ortega Matute, 2005) 178–9
riots 85
rituals 73
Robles Godoy, Armando 27, 30, 124, 188
Roca Rey, Ana María 166
Rotterdam Festival 156
rural life 20–1, 22; see also Andes, the

Saba, Adrián 29
Sacha, Orlando 81
Salomón, Emilio 193n.34
Sánchez, Antero 40
Saona, Margarita 160
scriptwriters 24
security forces see military, the
senderistas see sympathisers
Sendero Luminoso see Shining Path
shanty towns 60
Shaw, Deborah 137
Shining Path (Sendero Luminoso) 2, 3, 6, 158, 174
  and *Alias la gringa* 80, 81, 82, 84, 86
  and the Andes 98–9, 141, 152, 175
  and *Boca del lobo, La* 38, 39–40, 41, 42, 44, 45, 55–6, 58
  and childhood 180
  and cinema 9–10, 11, 14–15, 176, 193n.29
  and crackdown 182–3
  and curfews 26
  and *Días de Santiago* 154
  and disappeared 35, 181
  and El Frontón 85
  and emergence 189n.3

239

Index

Shining Path (Sendero Luminoso) (*Cont.*)
  and fragmentation 139–40
  and Fujimori 93
  and García 36–7, 57
  and ideology 96
  and imprisonment 35
  and Lima attacks 33, 65–6, 178
  and the military 114–15
  and Moyano 125–6, 127, 128–9, 130, 131–3, 136
  and *Ni con dios ni con el diablo* 59, 61–2, 64–5, 69, 70–1, 76
  and *Paloma de papel* 142–3, 144, 147–51, 153
  and recruitment 66–7, 73, 108
  and *Teta asustada, La* 177
  and trauma 188
  and *Vida es una sola, La* 97, 102, 103–4, 105
  and violence 4
  and women 99–101, 104
  see also sympathisers
Shohat, Ella 74
Sibille, Pietro 154
sierra *see* Andes, the
silent films 20
Silverman, Kaja 14, 159–60, 163, 169
Smith, Anthony 185, 197n.23
Snead, James 68
Soccos 40–2, 43, 175
social reform 23–4
social responsibility 80
socialism 10
solidarity 109–10, 114, 129
Solier, Magaly 177, 182
soundtrack *see* music
space 72, 74–5

Spain 2, 4, 8, 185
  and funding 107, 135, 176
  see also colonialism
Stam, Robert 74
state, the 2, 4, 5–6, 186
  and *Alias la gringa* 84, 87, 90
  and *Boca del lobo, La* 44, 52, 184
  and *Coraje* 133–4
  and counter-insurgency 42
  and documentaries 19–20
  and funding 9
  and *Ni con dios ni con el diablo* 70, 76
  see also military, the
Stern, Steve 98–9
Stock, Ann Marie 29
symbolism 5, 94, 183
sympathisers (*senderistas*) 42, 47, 50, 57, 83
  and the Andes 95
  and *Vida es una sola, La* 97

Tamayo, Augusto 94, 110; *see also* *Anda, corre, vuela...*
Tarata (Aguilar, 2009) 5, 8, 177–8
Taxi Driver (Scorcese, 1976) 165
technocracy 10
technology 20, 24
Tejado, José 46
Televisión Española (TVE) 38, 79
terrorism 3, 4
  and *Boca del lobo, La* 41
  and *Coraje* 132
  and indigenous peoples 77, 116
  see also anti-terrorism
Teta asustada, La/*Milk of Sorrow* (Llosa, 2009) 174, 177, 180, 188
Third Cinema 7, 58
Toledo, Alejandro 140, 141, 210n.32

Index

Torre, Marino León de la 62
Torres, Gilberto 47
torture 44, 47, 50, 52, 57, 96, 182
transnationalism 137, 138
transport 72
trauma 13–14, 30–1, 42, 168, 188
  and childhood 139
  and memory 137
  and war 159–60
Tren de Sombras (journal) 13
Trujillo, Liliana 143
Truth and Reconciliation Commission 13, 66, 138, 141, 153
  and establishment 209n.16
  and motto 176

Última tarde, La/One Last Afternoon (Calero, 2016) 5, 174, 183, 188
unemployment 65, 76
United States of America (USA) 19, 20, 22, 25, 26; *see also* Hollywood
urban life 20–1; *see also* Lima
urban migration 14, 21, 63–4, 116
  and *Ni con dios ni con el diablo* 59, 60–2, 67–9, 70, 72, 74–5, 76, 77–8
Urbina, Melania 149
USAID 140

Valcarcel, Gisela 178
Vargas Llosa, Mario 34
Vásquez, Jackelyn 179, 182
Vega, Paul 181
Vega, Toño 39
Velarde, Álvaro 3, 29
Velarde, Gisele 8
Velasco Alvarado, General Juan 23, 24, 29
Vergara, Sandra 166

Viaje a Timbuctú/Trip to Timbuktu (Diaz Costa, 2014) 181–2
Vich, Cynthia 183
Vich, Víctor 116, 118, 149–50
Victoria, Enrique 84
Vida es una sola, La/You Only Live Once (Eyde, 1993) 71, 94, 95–7, 108–9, 142
  and community 102–6
  and critics 107–8, 149, 186
  and plot 97–8
  and release 106–7, 175
  and violence 101–2
  and women 99, 100–1
Vidal, Milagros 166
Vidas paralelas/Parallel Lives (Lladó, 2008) 178, 179
violence 2, 3, 4–5, 9–10, 12, 182
  and *Alias la gringa* 82, 86, 89, 90, 91
  and *Anda, corre, vuela...* 113–14, 115–16
  and *Boca del lobo, La* 35–6, 37–8, 40–2, 45, 46–8, 49–52, 56, 57
  and childhood 141
  and cinema 34
  and *Coraje* 132–3
  and *Días de Santiago* 155, 163, 164–5, 167–9, 170–1
  and Lima 185–6
  and national identity 14–15
  and *Ni con dios ni con el diablo* 64–5, 69–70, 71, 78–9
  and *Paloma de papel* 142–3, 144, 148, 149–50
  and racial tension 30
  and *Vida es una sola, La* 95–6, 97–8, 101–2, 103–4
  see also non-violence

Index

Virilio, Paul 7
Vitascope 18
Vivas, Fernando 100, 104, 107

war 7; *see also* 'dirty war'
Westerns 74
Whittaker, David 99
Wiener, Christian 11, 122, 126, 135–6
Wilson, Emma 184
women 70–1, 94, 179
  and *Alias la gringa* 88
  and *Coraje* 95
  and *Días de Santiago* 163–4, 166–7, 171

and sexual violence 189n.5
and Shining Path 99–100
and *Vida es una sola, La* 95, 98, 100–1, 104, 105
see also Moyano, María Elena
Wong Kar-wai 157
Wood, David 63–4
working class 19, 22

Zambrano, Jiliat 97
Zavaleta, Jorge 184
Zúñiga, María Teresa 128
Zweiten Deutschen Fernsehen (ZDF) 122